PRODUCTION AND OPERATIONS MANAGEMENT

Jyotsana Singh

CENTRUM PRESS
NEW DELHI-110002 (INDIA)

CENTRUM PRESS
H.O.: 4360/4, Ansari Road, Daryaganj,
New Delhi-110002 (India)
Tel: 23278000, 23261597, 23255577, 23286875
B.O.: No. 1015, Ist Main Road, BSK IIIrd Stage,
IIIrd Phase, IIIrd Block, Bangalore-560085 (INDIA)
Tel: 080-41723429
Email: centrumpress@gmail.com
Visit us at: www.centrumpress.com

Production and Operations Management

First Edition, 2011

ISBN 978-93-80921-09-9

PRINTED IN INDIA

Printed at Balaji Offset, Delhi.

Contents

Preface *vii*

1. Introduction 1
2. Project Management 28
3. Facility Location and Layout 80
4. Planning 106
5. Production Planning and Control 140
6. Techniques 173
7. Purchasing 190
8. Inventory Management 222
9. Quality Management 244

Index 278

Preface

Production and operations management concerns itself with the conversion of inputs into output, using physical resources, so as to provide the desire utility/utilities-of form, place, possession or state or a combination thereof-to the customer while meeting the other organizational objectives of effectiveness, efficiency and adaptability.

It distinguishes itself from the other functional such as personnel, marketing, etc., by its primary concern for 'conversion by using physical resources'. Of course, there may be and would be a number of situations in either marketing or personnel or other functions which can be classified or sub-classified under production and operations management.

This book on production and operations management addresses the impact of operations decisions on the firm and emphasises cross-functional decision-making. It is a significant characteristic of the recent times has been that the different economies of the world are getting increasingly integrated with each other.

For the emerging economies of the world-that have been of late showing rapid rates of economic growth - such as India, Production and Operations is a vital management discipline. We hope that the discussion made in this book will help the readers to understand and learnt about the different concept of "Production and Operation Management" in a most comprehensive way.

Author

1

Introduction

OPERATIONS MANAGEMENT

Operations management is an area of business concerned with the production of goods and services, and involves the responsibility of ensuring that business operations are efficient in terms of using as little resource as needed, and effective in terms of meeting customer requirements.

It is concerned with managing the process that converts inputs into outputs.Operations traditionally refers to the production of goods and services separately, although the distinction between these two main types of operations is increasingly difficult to make as manufacturers tend to merge product and service offerings.

More generally, Operations Management aims to increase the content of value-added activities in any given process. Fundamentally, these value-adding creative activities should be aligned with market opportunity for optimal enterprise performance.

The U.S. Department of Education, Operations Management, the physical and/or technical functions of a firm or organization, particularly those relating to development, production, and manufacturing.

Instruction in principles of general management, manufacturing and production systems, plant management, equipment maintenance management, production control, industrial labour relations and skilled trades supervision, strategic manufacturing policy, systems analysis, productivity analysis and cost control, and materials planning.

CONCEPT OF PRODUCTION AND OPERATIONS MANAGEMENT

INTRODUCTION

The Subject of Production Management is studied under different Headings-such as Production Planning and control, Production and Inventory control, production and operations control and many more. What ever may be the title of the subject, the contents of the subject are more or less one and the same. Before we discuss about production management, let us discuss about product, production and management. This will give us a rough idea about production Management and with what a production manager has to deal with.

PRODUCT

Though many authors define the product with Consumer orientation, it is better for us to deal with different angles, because it will be helpful for us to understand the subject of production and Operation Management:

- *For a Consumer*: The product is a combination of or optimal mix of potential utilities. This is because every consumer expects some use or uses from the product. Hence he/she always identifies the product in terms of the uses. Say for example-Soap can be identified by complexion, cleanliness of body, freshness, fragrance or health.... etc. Because of this, many producers advertise that they are selling health, or they are selling Cine star Complexion or they are selling freshness and so on.
- *For a Production Manager*: Product is the combination of various surfaces and processes. This is because the production Manager is solely responsible for producing the product. He has to think of the various surfaces by which the product is made of, so that he can plan for processes by which a particular surface can be made and plan for required capacity of the facility by which the surface is produced. While planning he has to see that the required surface is

produced by the best and cheapest method, so as to make the product to face competition in the market.

- *For a Financial Manager*: For him the product is a mix of various cost elements as he is responsible for the profitability of the product.
- *For a Personnel Manager*: For him the product is a mix of various skills, as he is the person who selects and trains the personnel to meet the demand of the skill to produce the product. In general we can define the product as a bundle of tangible and intangible attributes, which along with the service is meant to satisfy the customer wants.

PRODUCTION

Production means application of processes. The raw material to add the use and economic values to arrive at desired product by the best method, with out sacrificing the desired quality.

We have three ways of Production, they are:

- *Production by Disintegration*: By separating the contents of Crude oil or a mixture the desired products are produced. For example the crude oil is disintegrated into various fuel oils. Similarly salt production is also an example for product produced by disintegrated. We can use Mechanical or Chemical or both technologies to get the desired product, so that it will have desired use value.
- *Production by Integration*: In this type of Production various Components of the products are assembled together to get the desired product. In this process, Physical and Chemical Properties of the materials used may change. The examples are: Assembly of Two wheelers, Four wheelers and so on.
- *Production by Service*: Here the Chemical and Mechanical Properties of materials are improved without any physical change. The example for this is Heat Treatment of metals. In real world, a combination of methods is used. In general production is

the use of any process or procedure designed to transform a set of input elements into a set of output elements, which have use value and economic value.

MANAGEMENT

Management can be explained as an art or science, of getting things done by the people, by planning, coordinating, organizing, directing and controlling the activities to meet specified goals, with in the frame work of agreed policies. The explanation put emphasis on getting things done, Planning, Organizing, Coordinating, and controlling and specific objectives and agreed policies. Today's manager needs scientific base as well as personal tactics to manage the people under him to achieve the desired goals. Production and management will help us to understand what exactly the Production Management or Production, and Operations Management.

CRITERIA OF PERFORMANCE

Three aims of performance of the Production and Operations Management system may be identified.

They are,:

- Effectiveness,
- Customer satisfaction,
- Efficiency.

The case of Efficiency is productive utilization of resources is clear. Whether the organization is in 'private sector' or in the 'public sector', is a 'manufacturing or 'non-manufacturing' organization or a 'profit' or a 'non-profit' organization, the optimal utilization of resource inputs is always a desired objective. The effectiveness has more dimensions to it. It involves optimality in the fulfillment of multiple objectives with a possible prioritization within the objectives. Modern production and operations management has to serve the target customers, the people working within, as also the region, country or society at large. Thus Production/Operations Management system, has not only to be profitable and/or efficient, but must necessarily satisfy many more customers.

This effectiveness has to be again viewed in terms of the short and long-term horizons depending upon the operations system.

Optimum, Good, Better operations management can improve:

- Efficiency of operation system to do things right and broader concept.
- Effectiveness of operation system refers to doing right things that is seven rights, they are: Right operation, Right Quantity, Right Quality, Right Supplier or Right Vendor, Right Time, Right Place and Right Price.

Basically, efficiency and effectiveness of the operations system can be measured by four dimensions, they are:

1. Cost,
2. Quality,
3. Dependability and
4. Reliability.

In fact these directly relate to the competitiveness of the organization, both nationally and internationally. Modern developments in better tools and techniques, methods and systems like Automation, Flexible manufacturing, CAD, CAM, CIM at management, CADD, CIMS, Use of Robotics, TQM, OR Techniques etc, are taking place to achieve improvements in Cost, Quality, Dependability, Reliability and Flexibility and thus to help for better management.

DEFINITION OF PRODUCTION MANAGEMENT

It may be defined as:

- The performance of the management activities with regards to selecting, designing, operating, Controlling and updating production system.
- It is the processes of effectively planning, coordinating and controlling the production, that is the operations of that part of an enterprise, it means to say that production and operations Management is responsible for the actual transformation of raw materials into finished products.

- Production management is a function of Management, related to planning, coordinating and controlling the resources required for production to produce specified product by specified methods, by optimal utilization of resources.
- Production management is defined as management function which plans, organizes, coordinates, directs and controls the material supply and Processing activities of an enterprise, so that specified products are produced by specified methods to meet an approved sales programme. These activities are being carried out in such a manner that Labour, Plant and Capital available are used to the best advantage of the organization.

OBJECTIVE OF PRODUCTION MANAGEMENT

The objective of Production Management is to produce the desired product or specified product by specified methods so that the optimal utilization of available resources is met with. Hence the production management is responsible to produce the desired product, which has marketability at the cheapest price by proper planning, the manpower, material and processes. Production management must see that it will deliver right goods of right quantity at right place and at right price. When the objective is achieved, we say that we have effective Production Management system.

SCOPE OF PRODUCTION MANAGEMENT

In fact, we apply Principles of Management; and functions of Management in our day-to-day life. We all know, from morning till night, we plan our activities; we coordinate available resources and control our activities to achieve certain goals. So also any organization must follow the Principles of Management for its survival and growth. The same is applicable to production Management also. Reading and learning Production Management will enable one to be capable of solving the problems of the organization, may be an Educational Institution, Production Shop, Hospital, Departmental shop or even a barber shop. The problems a manager face in various organizations are more or less similar to that of Production department but smaller in magnitude. Hence the knowledge of Production Management will help any professional Manager to tackle the problems of his business easily.

For example: The Production Management consists of Planning, selection of materials, planning of processes, Routing, Scheduling and controlling the activities etc., Take the example of an Educational Institution/University. Here also selection of raw students, Planning of the Course Work, Educating the students and conducting the examination. Therefore this knowledge will enable one to apply the principles of Production Management to any field of life without restriction. Here, we have to remember that this is also applicable to the management of a service organization and the management of a Project.

Here it is better to distinguish between product, Service and Project, so as to help the reader to know on which particular aspect of Production Management to put much emphasis, in managing a service organization or a project.

- *Product*: Manufacturing system often produces standardized products in large volumes. The plant and machinery have a finite capacity. The facilities constitute fixed costs, which are allocated to the products produced. Variable costs, such as, labour cost and materials costs. While manufacturing the product use value and economic values are added to the product. Hence the product is a store of values added during manufacture. Because the input costs and output costs are measurable, the productivity can be measured with certain degree of accuracy. Product can be transported to the markets and stored physically until it is sold.
- *Service*: Service system present more uncertainty with respect to capacity and costs. Services are produced

and consumed in the presence of the customer. We cannot store the service physically. Because of this the service organizations, such as Hotels, Hospitals, Transport Organizations and many other service organizations the capacity must be sufficiently or consciously managed to accommodate a highly variable demand. Sometimes services like legal practice and medical practice involve Professional or intellectual judgments, which cannot be easily standardized. Because of this the calculation of cost and productivity is difficult.

- *Project*: Project system does not produce standardized products. The Plant, Machinery, Men and Materials are often brought to project site and the project is completed. The project is of big size and remains in the site itself after completion. As the costs can be calculated and allocated to the project with considerable accuracy, Productivity can be measured. Once the project is completed, all the resources are removed from site.

BENEFITS DERIVED FROM EFFICIENT PRODUCTION MANAGEMENT

The efficient Production Management will give benefits to the various parts of the society.

They are:

- Consumer benefits from improved industrial Productivity, increased use value in the product. Products are available to him at right place, at right price, at right time, in desired quantity and of desired quality.
- *Investors*: They get increased security for their investments, adequate market returns, and creditability and good image in the society.
- Employee gets adequate Wages, Job security, improved working conditions and increased Personal and Job satisfaction.
- *Suppliers*: Will get confidence in management and their bills can be realised with out any delay.

- *Community*: community enjoys Benefits from economic and social stability.
- The Nation will achieve prospects and security because of increased Productivity and healthy industrial atmosphere.

FUNCTIONS OF PRODUCTION MANAGEMENT DEPARTMENT

The functions of Production Management depend upon the size of the firm. In small firms the production Manager may have to look after production planning and control along with Personnel, Marketing, Finance and Purchase functions. In medium sized firms, there may be separate managers for Personnel, marketing and Finance functions.

But the production planning and control and Purchase and stores may be under the control of Production management department. In large sized firms the activities of Production Management is confined to the management of production activities only.

As such, there are no hard and fast rule or guidelines to specify the function of Production Management, but in the academic interest we can mention some of the functions, which are looked after by the Production Management department.

They are:

- *Materials*: The selection of materials for the product. Production manager must have sound Knowledge of materials and their properties, so that he can select appropriate materials for his product. Research on materials is necessary to find alternatives to satisfy the changing needs of the design in the product and availability of material resumes.
- *Methods*: Finding the best method for the process, to search for the methods to suit the available resources, identifying the sequence of process are some of the activities of Production Management.
- *Machines and Equipment*: Selection of suitable machinery for the process desired, designing the

maintenance policy and design of layout of machines are taken care of by the Production Management department.

- *Estimating*: To fix up the Production targets and delivery dates and to keep the production costs at minimum, production management department does a thorough estimation of Production times and production costs. In competitive situation this will help the management to decide what should be done in arresting the costs at desired level.
- *Loading and Scheduling*: The Production Management department has to draw the time table for various production activities, specifying when to start and when to finish the process required. It also has to draw the timings of materials movement and plan the activities of manpower. The scheduling is to be done keeping in mind the loads on hand and capacities of facilities available.
- *Routing*: This is the most important function of Production Management department. The Routing consists of fixing the flow lines for various raw materials, components etc., from the stores to the packing of finished product, so that all concerned knows what exactly is happening on the shop floor.
- *Despatching*: The Production Management department has to prepare various documents such as Job Cards, Route sheets, Move Cards, Inspection Cards for each and every component of the product. These are prepared in a set of five copies. These documents are to be released from Production Management department to give green signal for starting the production. The activities of the shop floor will follow the instructions given in these documents. Activity of releasing the document is known as dispatching.
- *Expediting or Follow up*: Once the documents are dispatched, the management wants to know whether the activities are being carried out as per the plans or not. Expediting engineers go round the production

floor along with the plans, compare the actual with the plan and feed back the progress of the work to the management. This will help the management to evaluate the plans.

- *Inspection*: Here inspection is generally concerned with the inspection activities during production, but a separate quality control department does the quality inspection, which is not under the control of Production Management. This is true because, if the quality inspection is given to production Management, then there is a chance of qualifying the defective products also. For example Teaching and examining of students is given to the same person, then there is a possibility of passing all the students in the first grade. To avoid this situation an external person does correction of answer scripts, so that the quality of answers are correctly judged.
- *Evaluation*: The Production department must evaluate itself and its contribution in fulfilling the corporate objectives and the departmental objectives. This is necessary for setting up the standards for future. What ever may be the size of the firm; Production management department alone must do Routing, Scheduling, Loading, Dispatching and expediting.

This is because this department knows very well regarding materials, Methods, and available resources etc. If the firms are small, all the functions (i to x) are to be carried out by Production Management Department. In medium sized firms in addition to Routing, Scheduling and Loading, Dispatching and expediting, some more functions like Methods, Machines may be under the control of Production Management Department.

In large firms, there will be Separate departments for Methods, Machines, Materials and others but routing, loading and scheduling are the sole functions of Production Management. All the ten functions are categorized in three stage, that is Preplanning, Planning and control stages as shown in figure.

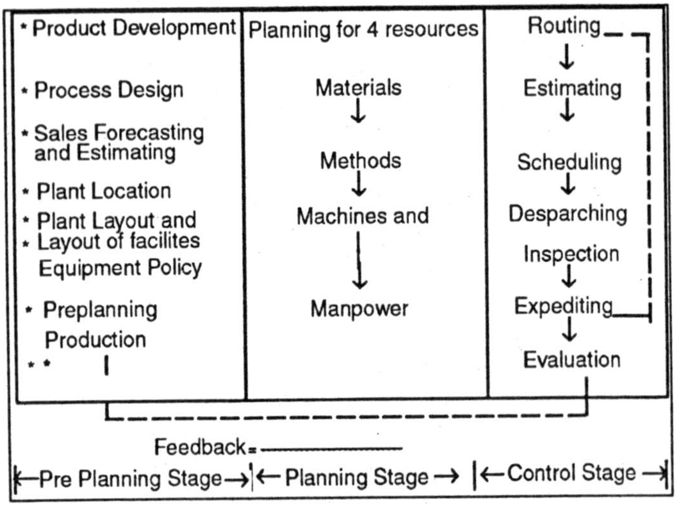

Fig. Production Fuction

PLACE OF PRODUCTION MANAGEMENT DEPARTMENT IN THE ORGANISATION

Production is the centre of all actitivities of an organization. This is to say all the activities of an organization, such as: Finance, Personnel, Marketing...etc., are exists in an organization because of production activity. Hence the position of Production Management in an organization is very important.

Whether it should be a line function or Staff function, more or less depends upon the corporate management policy. In small organization, Production Management is whole and sole of it. In large industries, generally it is advisable to have Production as line function, because, the decision taken by the line manager and the advices given by the Staff personnel will be based on the Production activities.

The Production Manager, directly report to General Manager, who in turn report to the Board. The figure shows a typical organization structure showing the position of Production Management. Figure shows an organization chart for Production and Operations Management department.

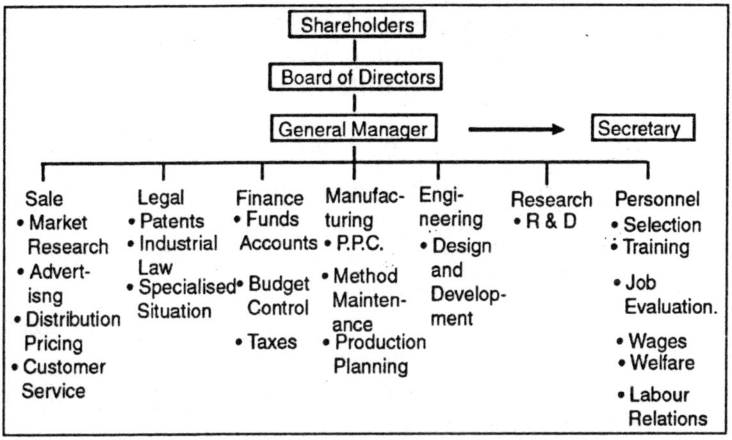

Fig. Typical Organisation Chat for an Organisation

Organisation Chart for P.P.C. Department

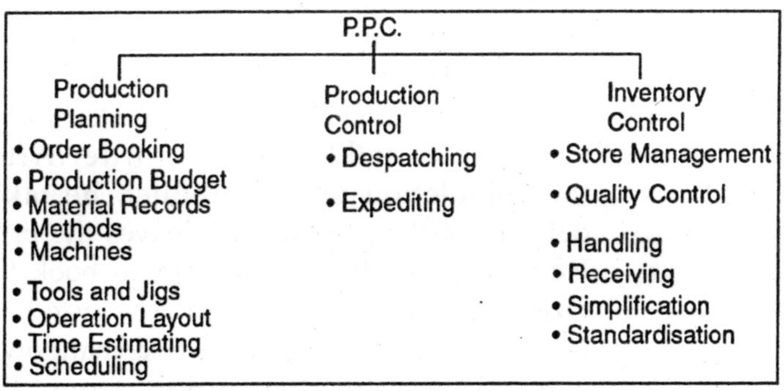

Fig. An Oeganization Chat for Production Management Department

TYPES OF PRODUCTION SYSTEMS

The organization of manufacturing systems, also planning and control of production greatly depends on type of product type of the product line. Basic principles that guide the formation of planning policy and its execution may be the same for all the manufacturing concerns. But emphasis on a particular aspect of production management in fulfilling of specific requirement of the plant and the management approach to the problems of inventory, machine selection, machine setting, tooling, routing, scheduling, loading, follow up and general control will differ depending on the type of production system.

Three main factors generally determine this aspect are:

1. Type of production i.e., quantities of finished products and regularity of manufacture. For example whether Job production or Batch Production or Continuous Production.
2. Size of the Plant i.e., Small Industry, Medium sized Industry or Large Industry.
3. Type of Production: In general there are three classifications in types of Production system..
   - *Job Production*: In this system Products are manufactured to meet the requirements of a specific order. The quality involved is small and the manufacturing of the product will take place as per the specifications given by the customer. This system may be further classified as.
     a. *The Job produced only once*: Here the customer visit the firm and book his order.After the completion of the product, he takes delivery of the product and leaves the firm. He may not visit the firm to book the order for the same product. The firm has to plan for material, process and manpower only after receiving the order from the customer.The firms have no scope for pre-planning the production of the product.
     b. *The job produced at irregular intervals*: Here the customer visits the firm to place orders for the same type of the product at irregular intervals.The firm will not have any idea of customer's visit. Here also planning for materials, process and manpower will start only after taking the order from the Customer. In case the firm maintains

the record of the Jobs Produced by it, it can refer to the previous plans, when the customer arrives at the firm to book the order.

c. *The Jobs Produced periodically at regular intervals*: In this system, the customer arrives at the firm to place orders for the same type of product at regular intervals. Here firm knows very well that the custo-mer visits at regular intervals, it can plan for materials,and process and manpower and have them in a master file. As soon as the customer visits and books the order, the firm can start production. If the volume of the order is considerably large and the number of regularly visiting customers are large in number, the Job Production system slowly transform into Batch Production system.

– Batch Production: Batch Production is the manufacture of number of identical products either to meet the specific order or to satisfy the demand. When the Production of plant and equipment is terminated, the plant and equipment can be used for producing similar products. This system also can be classified under three categories.

a. *A batch produced only once*: Here customer places order with the firm for the product of his specification. The size of the order is greater than that of job production order. The firm has to plan for the resources after taking the order from the customer.

b. *A Batch produced at irregular intervals as per Customer order or when the need arises*: As the frequency is irregular, the firm can maintain a file of its detailed plans and it can refer to its previous files and start production.

c. *A Batch Produced periodically at known*

Intervals: Here the firm either receives order from the customer at regular intervals or it may produce the product to satisfy the demand. It can have well designed file of its plans, material requirement and instructions for the ready reference. It can also purchase materials required in bulk in advance. As the frequency of regular orders goes on increasing the Batch Production system becomes Mass Production System. Here also, incase the demand for a particular product ceases, the plant and machinery can be used for producing other products with slight modification in layout or in machinery and equipment.

– *Continuous Production*: Continuous Production system is the specialized manufacture of identical products on which the machinery and equipment is fully engaged. The continuous production is normally associated with large quantities and with high rate of demand. Hence the advantage of automatic production is taken. This system is classified as

a. *Mass Production*: Here same type of product is produced to meet the demand of an assembly line or the market. This system needs good planning for material, process, maintenance of machines and instruction to operators. Purchases of materials in bulk quantities is advisable.

b. *Flow Production*: The difference between Mass and Flow Production is the type of product and its relation to the plant. In Mass Production identical products are produced in large numbers. If the demand falls or ceases, the machinery and equipment, after slight modification be used for manufacturing products of similar nature. In flow production, the plant and equipment is designed for a specified product. Hence if the demand falls for the product or ceases, the plant cannot be used for manufacturing other products. It is to be scraped. The examples for the production system are:

i. *Job Production Shop*: Tailors shop; cycle and vehicles repair shops, Job typing shops, small Workshops.

ii. *Batch Production Shop*: Tyre Production Shops, Readymade dress companies, Cosmetic manufacturing companies...etc.

iii. *Mass Production Shops*: Components of industrial products,

iv. *Flow Production*: Cement Factory, Sugar factory, Oil refineries...etc.,

Here will give the characteristics of intermittent and continuous Production system.

Table. Characteristics of Intermittent and Continuous Manufacturing System

S. No.	Particulars	Intermittent production system (job and batch production)	Continuous production system.(mass and flow production)
1.	Type of plant layout.	Process layout is most suitable.	Product layout designed according to a process separate line for each product is considered.
2.	Type of machine	As it necessitate frequent changes in the machine set-up required by the specification of each order, general purpose machines are more suitable. Also they have good flexibility. In batch production special	As production flow is permanently in the form of product line, automatic or special purpose machines are used. In flow production specialised machines are used.

		purpose machines Automatic and Semi automatic machines are used.	
3.	Type of labour	The type of production pre-supposes frequent changes in product design and machine setups; which requires highly skilled labour. Repair and maintenance of machines are to be done by these labours.	The manufacturing activity becomes a routine function and as the machines are designed to suit the process required for product and automatic in nature unskillful or semi-skilled labour is required. A specialised team of plant maintenance staff will look after the repair and maintenance of machines.
4.	Number of and product design.	Wide range of products are manufactured in small quantities. The product design changes from lot to lot as per the product specification. Each lot produced in small size.	Few/one standard products products/ productis manufacutred in large quantities. Usually the product line is designed to one or two products of standard specification.
5.	Changes in machine set-up.	As specification of each order changes, the machines are to set according to the requirements of each order, frequent changes in machine setup is a common phenomenon.	In this type of manufacturing, the set up of machines remains unchanged for a longer period. The standard products are manufactured in a continuous flow.
6.	Nature and size of orders.	Generally the size of orders is small and they are not repeated. The	Generally the production is carried on for stock. The production of

		orders are for non-standardised products. The order may involve the production of single product or products in limited lot. Usually the production is done according to first-in-first-out principle. First orders are received and then they are translated into production.	standardised products is the nature of this type of production. Products are produced in anticipation of demand. The size of the order is large. Same type of product is produced in every cycle to satisfy the demand.
7.	Investment on machines and equipment.	As the machines are arranged in process layout and general purpose machines are required for Job production, the investment comparatively less. For batch production as automatic and semi-automatic machines are involved the investment will be higher than job production.	The machines are arranged according to process layout and because of this duplication of machines is fairly high. The machines are fully automatic, the cost is higher than intermittent production.
8.	Investment on inventories	Here the operating cycle takes more time and it is necessary to have standard materials for long period hence inventory cost per product is considerably large.	Bulk purchase of materials is done at periodic intervals. Due to continuous process, less in process inventory exists hence material cost per product is less.
9.	Material	Because of verities of	Mechanisation of

	handling equipments	products, different routes are followed by materials also volume of order is small, mechanisation of material handling is not possible.	material handling is possible. Generally, convenyors, pipe-lines, automatic material handing equipment is used.
10.	Material handling	Material handling per product is costlier because of long distance handling cost (manual) and backtracking.	Due to mechanised material handling, material handling cost per product is less
11.	Plant mainten-ance and service	It is desirable to have a maintenance department to avoid losses due to brake down of machinery.	It is essential to have a good plant maintenance department to avoid stoppage of production due to break down of machines.
12.	Balancing of production capacity	Due to different products and different types of machines with different capacity blocks, possibility of imbalance in plant capacity occurs.	The chances of imbalance in plant capacity is very much less.
13.	Production planning and control	The functions of routing, scheduling and loading becomes relatively complicated due to odd size of order, non-repetitive nature of the order, different delivery dates, etc., production planning and control is complicated.	The function of routing, scheduling and loading are carried on smoothly due to standardised products, rated capacity. Here production planning and control is simpler.

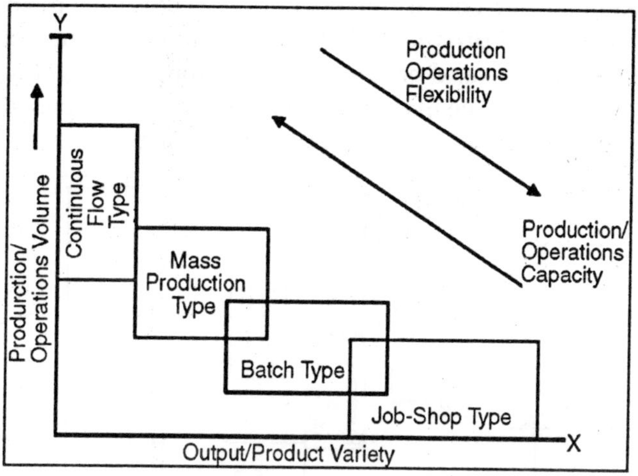

Fig. Production and Operations System

PRODUCTION CYCLE

The production cycle starts from Market Research. Market research reveals consumer preferences and needs. The marketing department will transfer this information to the design department.

The design department basing on the information received from marketing department designs the product to fulfill consumer needs and supplies design specifications and drawings to production department. The production department verifies whether the product can be manufactured with the technology and skill available in the firm. If yes it will give the acceptance. Otherwise the Production Manager, Design engineer and Marketing Manager, discuss together and make alterations in the product without sacrificing the customer needs.

Once this is done the design department conduct the market survey and analyse the demand and submits its sales programme to the top management. The top management after going through the proposals sanctions the budget and gives green signal for production. Production department produces a trial run and sales department release the product in the test markets to get consumer acceptance sells the products. Meanwhile, the production department prepares the detailed production plans and production scheduling. After getting the acceptance from the marketing department, actual production of product starts to meet the marketing programme.

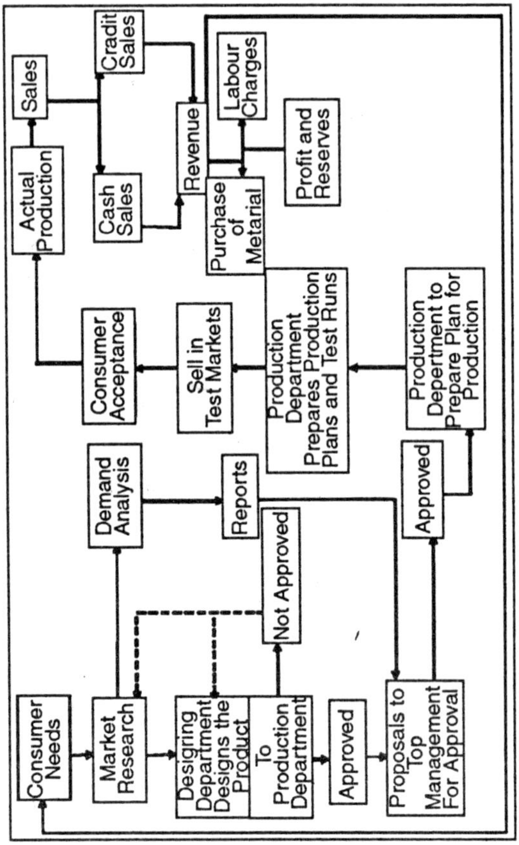

Fig. Production cycle.

PRODUCTION DESIGN

Production design is the creation and organization of the physical world surrounding a film story. The term was coined by producer David O. Selznick to describe the greater-than-normal contribution of designer William Cameron Menzies to

Gone with the Wind, but the exact responsibilities of a production designer inevitably vary from film to film. In some cases, the production designer is almost completely responsible for the overall look of a film; in others, particularly when working with directors with strong visual styles, a designer's contribution tends to be much more limited. Art direction and production design often overlap, although credit for production design is seen as more inclusive. During the studio era, production designers, as opposed to art directors, were the exception.

The production designer's primary, though by no means exclusive, responsibility is the design of the sets. Exact responsibility varies from one film industry to another. In the United States, for example, production design and costume design are usually two separate professions. In other major film industries, the two responsibilities are often held by a single person. Before designing anything, the designer develops a "design concept," an overarching metaphor for the film's appearance that governs individual choices. This "concept" may or may not be established in conjunction with the director. Once settled upon, however, it structures all decisions made, helping the art staff to give an individual film visual distinction.

PRODUCT DEVELOPMENT

Product development is the process of designing, creating, and marketing an idea or product. The product can either be one that is new to the marketplace or one that is new to your particular company, or, an existing product that has been improved. In many instances a product will be labeled new and improved when substantial changes have been made.

PRODUCT DEVELOPMENT PROCESS

All product development goes through a similar planning process. Although the process is a continuous one, it is crucial that companies stand back after each step and evaluate whether the new product is worth the investment to continue. That evaluation should be based on a specific set of objective criteria, not someone's gut feeling. Even if the product is wonderful, if no one buys it the company will not make a profit. Brainstorming and developing a concept is the first step in product development. Once an idea is generated, it is important to determine whether there is a market for the product, what the target market is, and whether the idea will be profitable, as well as whether it is feasible from an engineering and financial standpoint. Once the product is determined to be feasible, the idea or concept is tested on a small sample of customers within the target market to see what their reactions are.

DOCUMENTATION

Simply having an "idea"is worthless--you need to have proof of when you came up with the idea for your invention. Write down everything you can think of that relates to your invention, from what it is and how it works to how you'll make and market it. This is the first step to patenting your idea and keeping it from being stolen. You've probably heard about the "poor man's patent"--writing your idea down and mailing it to yourself in a sealed envelope so you have dated proof of your invention's conception. This is unreliable and unlikely to hold up in court. Write your idea down in an inventor's journal and have it signed by a witness. This journal will become your bible throughout the patent process. An inventor's journal can by any bound notebook whose pages are numbered consecutively and can't be removed or reinserted.

You can find specially designed inventor's journals at bookstores or you can save money and purchase a generic notebook anywhere they're sold, such as the grocery store, office supply store, stationary store, etc.

RESEARCH

You will need to research your idea from a legal and business standpoint.

Before you file a patent, you should:

- *Complete an initial patent search*: Just because you

haven't seen your invention doesn't mean it doesn't already exist. Before you hire a patent attorney or agent. You should also complete a non-patent "prior art"search. If you find any sort of artwork or design related to your idea, you cannot patent it--regardless of whether a prior patent has been filed.

- *Research your market*: Sure, your brother thinks your idea for a new lawn sprinkler is a great idea, but that doesn't mean your neighbour would buy one. More than 95 per cent of all patents never make money for the inventor. Before you invest too much time and money into patenting your invention, do some preliminary research of your target market. Is this something people will actually buy? Once you know there's a market, make sure your product can be manufactured and distributed at a low enough cost so that your retail price is reasonable. You can determine these costs by comparing those of similar products currently on the market. This will also help you size up your competition--which you will have, no matter how unique you think your invention is.

MAKING A PROTOTYPE

A prototype is a model of your invention that puts into practice all of the things you have written in your inventor's journal. This will demonstrate the design of your invention when you present it to potential lenders and licensees. Do not file a patent before you have made a prototype. You will almost always discover a flaw in your original design or think of a new feature you would like to add. If you patent your idea before you work out these kinks, it will be too late to include them in the patent and you will risk losing the patent rights of the new design to someone else.

Here are some general rules of thumb when prototyping your invention:

- *Begin with a drawing*: Before you begin the prototyping phase, sketch out all of your ideas into your inventor's journal.

- Create a concept mockup out of any material that will allow you to create a 3-D model of your design.
- Once you're satisfied with the mockup, create a full-working model of your idea. There are many books and kits that can help you create prototypes. If your invention is something that will cost a lot of money or is unreasonable to prototype, consider using a computer-animated virtual prototype.

FILING A PATENT

Now that you have all of the kinks worked out of your design, it's finally time to file a patent. There are two main patents you will have to choose from: a utility patent or a design patent. You can write the patent and fill out the application yourself, but do not file it yourself until you have had a skilled patent professional look it over first. If the invention is really valuable, someone will infringe on it. If you do not have a strong patent written by a patent attorney or agent, you will be pulling your hair out later when a competitor finds a loophole that allows them to copy your idea. It's best to get the legal help now to avoid any legal problems in the future. When searching for a patent attorney or agent, remember one thing: If you see them advertised on TV, run away!

Once you are far, far away, follow these steps to choosing the best patent professional:

- *Do your homework*: Have your inventor's journal, prototype and notes with you. This will save them time, and you money. This will also help persuade them to work with you.
- *Make sure they are registered with the U.S*: Patent and Trademark Office.
- *Ask them what their technical background is*: If your invention is electronic, find a patent professional who is also an electrical engineer.
- *Discuss fees*: Keep your focus on smaller patent firms. They are less expensive and will work more closely with you. Agree to the estimated total cost before hiring your patent professional.

MARKETING YOUR INVENTION

Now it's time to figure out how you're going to bring your product to market. Create a business plan: How will you get money? Where will you manufacture the product? How will you sell it? Now is a good time to decide if you will manufacture and sell the product yourself, or license it for sale through another company. When you license your product you will probably only receive two per cent to five per cent in royalty fees. This often scares away inventors who feel they deserve more. But consider the upside: You will not have the financial burden associated with maintaining a business. This could end up making you more money in the long run.

Following these five steps will ensure an easy road to patenting your invention. Just remember that an easy road doesn't necessarily mean a short one. From the time you conceive your idea to the time you see your product on the shelf is a very long process. Most inventions take years to come to fruition. Have patience and follow due diligence in your steps to patenting your invention and your years of hard work will finally pay off.

2

Project Management

INTRODUCTION

Project management is the discipline of planning, organizing, and managing resources to bring about the successful completion of specific project goals and objectives. It is sometimes conflated with programme management, however technically a programme is actually a higher level construct: a group of related and somehow interdependent projects. A project is a temporary endeavor, having a defined beginning and end undertaken to meet unique goals and objectives, usually to bring about beneficial change or added value. The temporary nature of projects stands in contrast to business as usual, which are repetitive, permanent or semi-permanent functional work to produce products or services. In practice, the management of these two systems is often found to be quite different, and as such requires the development of distinct technical skills and the adoption of separate management.

The primary challenge of project management is to achieve all of the project goals and objectives while honouring the preconceived project constraints. Typical constraints are scope, time, and budget. The secondary—and more ambitious—challenge is to optimize the allocation and integration of inputs necessary to meet pre-defined objectives.

ESTIMATING TIME ACCURATELY

Accurate time estimation is a skill essential to good project management.

It is important to get time estimates right for two main reasons:

1. Time estimates drive the setting of deadlines for delivery of projects, and hence peoples' assessments of your reliability
2. They often determine the pricing of contracts and hence their profitability.

Usually people vastly underestimate the amount of time needed to implement projects. This is true particularly when they are not familiar with the task to be carried out. They forget to take into account unexpected events or unscheduled high priority work. People also often simply fail to allow for the full complexity involved with a job.

This part discusses how to estimate time on small projects. Time estimates are important inputs into the other techniques used to organize and structure medium and large sized projects. Both of these techniques reduce large projects down into a set of small projects.

HOW TO USE THE TOOL

The first stage in estimating time accurately is to fully understand what you need to achieve. This involves reviewing the task in detail so that there are no unknowns. Inevitably it is the difficult-to-understand, tricky problems that take the greatest amount of time to solve. The best way to review the job is to list all tasks in full detail. Simple techniques such as Drill-Down are useful for this.

Once you have a detailed list of all the tasks that you must achieve, make your best guess at how long each task will take to complete. Ensure that within your estimate you also allow time for project management, detailed project planning, liaison with outside bodies, meetings, quality assurance and any supporting documentation necessary.

Also make sure that you have allowed time for:

- Other high urgency tasks to be carried out which will have priority over this one
- Accidents and emergencies
- Internal meetings
- Holidays and sickness in essential staff

- Contact with other customers, perhaps to arrange the next job
- Breakdowns in equipment
- Missed deliveries by suppliers
- Interruptions
- Quality control rejections

These factors may double the length of time needed to complete a project. If the accuracy of time estimates is critical, you may find it effective to develop a systematic approach to including these factors. If possible, base this on past experience.

KEY POINTS

You can lose a great deal of credibility by underestimating the length of time needed to implement a project. If you underestimate time, not only do you miss deadlines, you also put other project workers under unnecessary stress. Projects will become seriously unprofitable, and other tasks cannot be started.

The first step towards making good time estimates is to fully understand the problem to be solved.You can then prepare a detailed list of tasks that must be achieved. This list should include all the administrative tasks and meetings you need to carry out as well as the work itself. Finally, allow time for all the expected and unexpected disruptions and delays to work that will inevitably happen.

RISK IMPACT/PROBABILITY CHART

Risk management is an important function in organizations today. Companies undertake increasingly complex and ambitious projects, and those projects must be executed successfully, in an uncertain and often risky environment.

As a responsible manager, you need to be aware of these risks. Does this mean that you should try to address each and every risk that your project might face? Probably not - in all but the most critical environments, this can be much too expensive, both in time and resources.

Instead, you need to prioritize risks. If you do this effectively, you can focus the majority of your time and effort on the most important risks. The Risk Impact/Probability Chart provides a useful framework that helps you decide which risks need your attention.

USE THE RISK IMPACT/PROBABILITY CHART

The Risk Impact/Probability Chart is based on the principle that a risk has two primary dimensions:

1. *Probability*: A risk is an event that "may" occur. The probability of it occurring can range anywhere from just above 0% to just below 100%.
2. *Impact*: A risk, by its very nature, always has a negative impact. However, the size of the impact varies in terms of cost and impact on health, human life, or some other critical factor.

The chart allows you to rate potential risks on these two dimensions. The probability that a risk will occur is represented on one axis of the chart - and the impact of the risk, if it occurs, on the other. You use these two measures to plot the risk on the chart. This gives you a quick, clear view of the priority that you need to give to each. You can then decide what resources you will allocate to managing that particular risk. The basic form of the Risk Impact/Probability Chart is shown.

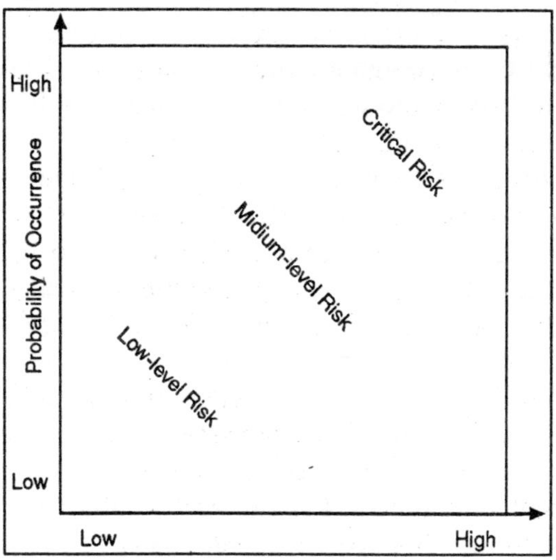

Fig. The Risk Impact/Probability Chart

The corners of the chart have these characteristics:

- *Low impact/Low probability*: Risks in the bottom left corner are low level, and you can often ignore them.
- *Low impact/High probability*: Risks in the top left corner are of moderate importance - if these things happen, you can cope with them and move on. However, you should try to reduce the likelihood that they'll occur.
- *High impact/Low probability*: Risks in the bottom right corner are of high importance if they do occur, but they're very unlikely to happen. For these, however, you should do what you can to reduce the impact they'll have if they do occur, and you should have contingency plans in place just in case they do.
- *High impact/High probability*: Risks towards the top right corner are of critical importance. These are your top priorities, and are risks that you must pay close attention to.

To use the Risk Impact/Probability Chart, print this free worksheet, and then follow these steps:

- List all of the likely risks that your project faces. Make the list as comprehensive as possible.
- Assess the probability of each risk occurring, and assign it a rating. For example, you could use a scale of 1 to 10. Assign a score of 1 when a risk is extremely unlikely to occur, and use a score of 10 when the risk is extremely likely to occur.
- Estimate the impact on the project if the risk occurs. Again, do this for each and every risk on your list. Using your 1-10 scale, assign it a 1 for little impact and a 10 for a huge, catastrophic impact.
- Map out the ratings on the Risk Impact/Probability Chart.
- Develop a response to each risk, according to its position in the chart. Remember, risks in the bottom left corner can often be ignored, while those in the top right corner need a great deal of time and attention. Read Risk Analysis and Risk Management for detailed strategies on developing a risk response plan.

KEY POINTS

To successfully implement a project, you must identify and focus your attention on middle and high-priority risks - otherwise you risk spreading your efforts too thinly, and you'll waste resources on unnecessary risk management. With the Risk Impact/Probability Chart, you map out each risk - and its position determines its priority. High-probability/high-impact risks are the most critical, and you should put a great deal of effort into managing these. The low-probability/high-impact risks and high-probability/low-impact risks are next in priority, though you may want to adopt different strategies for each. Low-probability/low-impact risks can often be ignored.

SCHEDULING SIMPLE PROJECTS

Simple projects involve only one or a few people over a short time. Typically, simple projects will have few tasks dependent on other tasks, and will be relatively simple and easy to coordinate. Examples might be coordinating delivery of resources for a workshop session, implementing a small marketing plan, or delivering a simple software enhancement. With simple projects, tools like Gantt Charts and Critical Path Diagrams may overcomplicate project scheduling and communication. Unless project team members are trained in their use, they can often 'blind people with science', leading to poor communication and muddled projects.

USE

Appropriate Timetables and Action Plans are often sufficient to coordinate and implement simple projects. These should be explained and negotiated with project staff to improve the plans and get staff understanding, input and buy-in. It will often be enough to create a workback schedule, starting from the date by which the project must be completed, and listing all of the tasks in reverse order with due dates for each.Whatever the size of your project, ensure that you have agreed its scope with its sponsor before you start planning. This will help you to resist changes to its scope, which will seriously affect your plans, once you have started working.

KEY POINTS

Simple projects are often best run using simple Timetables and Action Plans. These should be prepared and negotiated with project staff to improve plans and get buy-in. During the project these will contain sufficient control points and deliveries to monitor project progress and take any appropriate remedial action.

GANTT CHARTS

Gantt Charts are useful tools for analyzing and planning more complex projects.

- Help you to plan out the tasks that need to be completed
- Give you a basis for scheduling when these tasks will be carried out
- Allow you to plan the allocation of resources needed to complete the project, and
- Help you to work out the critical path for a project where you must complete it by a particular date.

When a project is under way, Gantt Charts help you to monitor whether the project is on schedule. If it is not, it allows you to pinpoint the remedial action necessary to put it back on schedule.

SEQUENTIAL AND PARALLEL ACTIVITIES

An essential concept behind project planning is that some activities are dependent on other activities being completed first. As a shallow example, it is not a good idea to start building a bridge before you have designed it! These dependent activities need to be completed in a sequence, with each stage being more-or-less completed before the next activity can begin. We can call dependent activities 'sequential' or 'linear'. Other activities are not dependent on completion of any other tasks. These may be done at any time before or after a particular stage is reached. These are nondependent or 'parallel' tasks.

DRAWING A GANTT CHART

To draw up a Gantt diagram, follow these steps:

- *Step 1. List all activities in the plan*: For each task, show the earliest start date, estimated length of time it will take, and whether it is parallel or sequential. If tasks are sequential, show which stages they depend on. You will end up with a task list like the one in figure. This will allow you to compare the results of the two approaches. Figure. Gantt Chart *Example*: Planning a custom-written computer project

Task	Earliest start	Length	Type	Dependent on...
A. High level analysis	Week 0	1 week	Sequential	
B. Selection of hardware platform	Week 1	1 day	Sequential	A
C. Installation and commissioning of hardware	Week 1.2	2 weeks	Parallel	B
D. Detailed analysis of core modules	Week 1	2 weeks	Sequential	A
E. Detailed analysis of supporting modules	Week 3	2 weeks	Sequential	D
F. Programming of core modules	Week 3	2 weeks	Sequential	D
G. Programming of supporting modules	Week 5	3 weeks	Sequential	E
H. Quality assurance of core modules	Week 5	1 week	Sequential	F
I. Quality assurance of supporting modules	Week 8	1 week	Sequential	G
J. Core module training	Week 6	1 day	Parallel	C,H
K. Development and QA of accounting reporting	Week 5	1 week	Parallel	E
L. Development and QA of management reporting	Week 5	1 week	Parallel	E
M. Development of Management Information System	Week 6	1 week	Sequential	L
N. Detailed training	Week 9	1 week	Sequential	I, J, K, M

- Step 2. Head up graph paper with the days or weeks through to task completion
- *Step 3. Plot the tasks onto the graph paper:* Next draw up a rough draft of the Gantt Chart. Plot each task on the graph paper, showing it starting on the earliest possible date. Draw it as a bar, with the length of the bar being the length of the task. The task bars, mark the time taken to complete them. Schedule them in such a way that sequential actions are carried out in the required sequence. Ensure that dependent activities do not start until the activities they depend on have been completed.

This will produce an untidy diagram like the one:

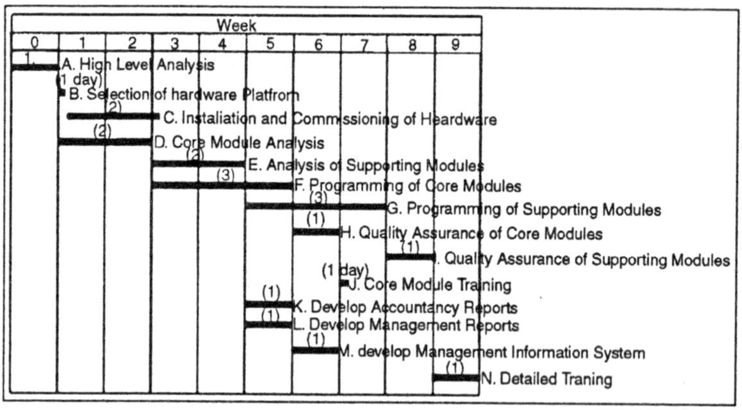

Fig. Draft Gantt Chart: Exampe Computer Project

- *Step 4. Presenting the analysis:* The last stage in this process is to prepare a final version of the Gantt Chart. This shows how the sets sequential activities link together, and the identifies critical path activities. At this stage you also need to check the resourcing of the various activities. While scheduling, ensure that you make best use of the resources you have available, and do not over-commit resource. You can also use color to represent the different resource types that you need to use such as programmers, or analysts.

A redrawn version of the example project is shown:

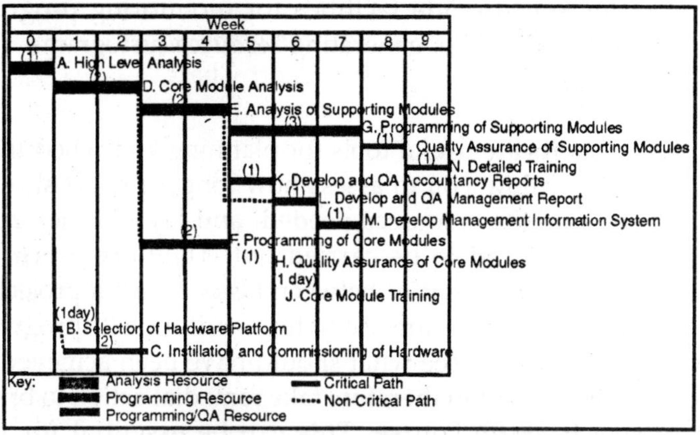

Fig. Critical Path Analysis: Activites Scheduled on a Gantt Chart

By drawing this example Gantt Chart, you can see that:

- If all goes well, the project can be completed in 10 weeks.
- If you want to complete the task as rapidly as possible, you need:
  - 1 analyst for the first 5 weeks.
  - 1 programmer for 5 weeks starting week 4.
  - 1 programmer/QA expert for 3 weeks starting week 6. Note: Activities L and M have been moved back a week. This does not affect the critical path, but it does mean that a single programming/QA resource can carry out all three of activities K, L and M.
- Analysis, development and testing of supporting modules are essential activities that must be completed on time.
- Hardware installation and commissioning is not time-critical as long as it is completed before the Core Module Training starts.

While this part describes how to draw a Gantt Chart manually, in practice project managers use software tools like Microsoft Project to create Gantt Charts. Not only do these ease the drawing of Gantt Charts, they also make modification of plans easier and provide facilities for monitoring progress against plans, as well as generating resource histograms.

KEY POINTS

Gantt charts are useful tools for planning and scheduling projects. They allow you to assess how long a project should take, determine the resources needed, and lay out the order in which tasks need to be carried out. They are useful in managing the dependencies between tasks. When a project is under way, Gantt charts are useful for monitoring its progress. You can immediately see what should have been achieved at a point in time, and can therefore take remedial action to bring the project back on course. This can be essential for the successful and profitable implementation of the project.

CRITICAL PATH ANALYSIS AND PERT CHARTS

Critical Path Analysis and PERT are powerful tools that help you to schedule and manage complex projects. They were developed in the 1950s to control large defence projects, and have been used routinely since then.

As with Gantt Charts, Critical Path Analysis or the Critical Path Method helps you to plan all tasks that must be completed as part of a project. They performance as the basis both for preparation of a schedule, and of resource planning. During management of a project, they allow you to monitor achievement of project goals. They help you to see where remedial action needs to be taken to get a project back on course.

Within a project it is likely that you will display your final project plan as a Gantt Chart.The benefit of using CPA within the planning process is to help you develop and test your plan to ensure that it is robust. Critical Path Analysis formally identifies tasks which must be completed on time for the whole project to be completed on time. It also identifies which tasks can be delayed if resource needs to be reallocated to catch up on missed or overrunning tasks. The disadvantage of CPA, if you use it as the technique by which your project plans are communicated and managed against, is that the relation of tasks to time is not as immediately obvious as with Gantt Charts. This can make them more difficult to understand.

A further benefit of Critical Path Analysis is that it helps you to identify the minimum length of time needed to complete a project. Where you need to run an accelerated project, it helps you to identify which project steps you should accelerate to complete the project within the available time.

HOW TO USE THE TOOL

As with Gantt Charts, the essential concept behind Critical Path Analysis is that you cannot start some activities until others are finished. These activities need to be completed in a sequence, with each stage being more-or-less completed before the next stage can begin.

These are 'sequential' activities. Other activities are not dependent on completion of any other tasks. You can do these at any time before or after a particular stage is reached. These are non-dependent or 'parallel' tasks.

DRAWING A CRITICAL PATH ANALYSIS CHART

Use the following steps to draw a CPA Chart:

- *Step 1. List all activities in the plan:* For each activity, show the earliest start date, estimated length of time it will take, and whether it is parallel or sequential. If tasks are sequential, show which stage they depend on.
- *Step 2. Plot the activities as a circle and arrow diagram:* Critical Path Analyses are presented using circle and arrow diagrams. In these, circles show events within the project, such as the start and finish of tasks. The number shown in the left hand half of the circle allows you to identify each one easily. Circles are sometimes known as nodes. An arrow running between two event circles shows the activity needed to complete that task. A description of the task is

written underneath the arrow. The length of the task is shown it. By convention, all arrows run left to right. Arrows are also sometimes called arcs.

An example of a very simple diagram is shown:

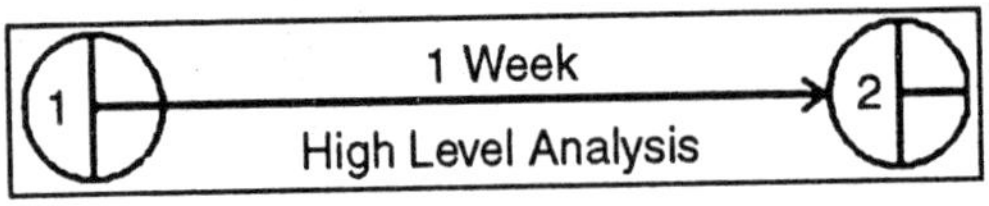

Fig. Simple Circle and Arrow Diagram

This shows the start event and the completion of the 'High Level Analysis' task. The arrow between them shows the activity of carrying out the High Level Analysis. This activity should take 1 week. Where one activity cannot start until another has been completed, we start the arrow for the dependent activity at the completion event circle of the previous activity. An example of this is shown:

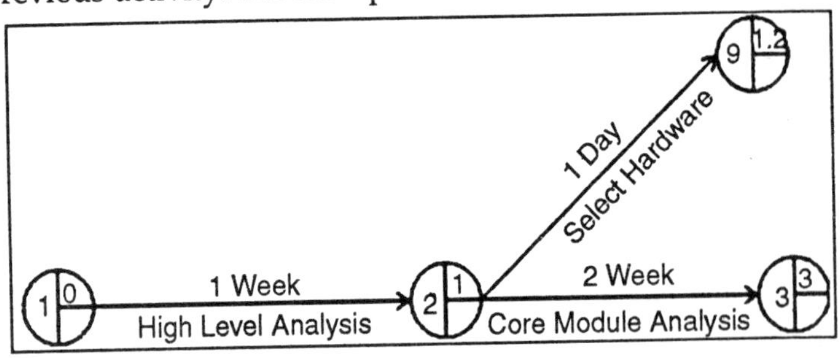

Fig. Circle and Arrow Diagram Showing Two Activities that cannot be Started Unit the First Activity has been Completed

Here the activities of 'Select Hardware' and 'Core Module Analysis' cannot be started until 'High Level Analysis' has been completed.

This diagram also brings out a number of other important points:

- Within Critical Path Analysis, we refer to activities by the numbers in the circles at each end. For example, the task 'Core Module Analysis' would be called activity 2 to 3. 'Select Hardware' would be activity 2 to 9.
- Activities are not drawn to scale. In the diagram,

activities are 1 week long, 2 weeks long, and 1 day long. Arrows in this case are all the same length.

- In the example, you can see a second number in the top, right hand quadrant of each circle. This shows the earliest start time for the following activity. It is conventional to start at 0. Here units are whole weeks.

A different case is shown:

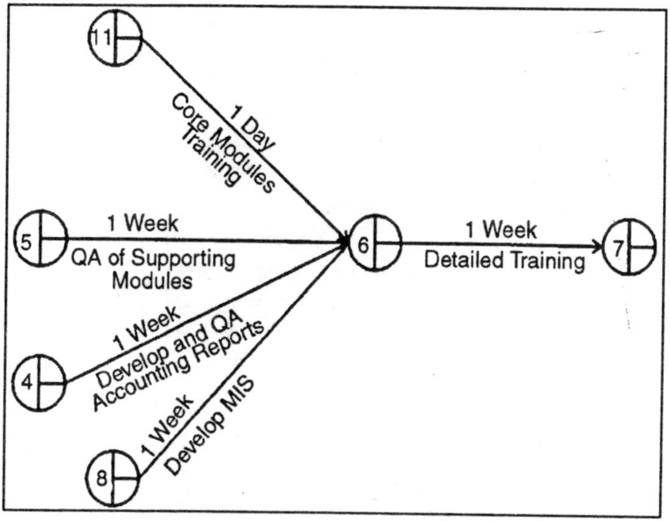

Fig. Circle and Arrow Diagram Showing an Activity (6to7) that cannot start until other Activities have been Completed

Here activity 6 to 7 cannot start until the other four activities have been completed. The full circle and arrow diagram for the computer project we are using as an example. This shows all the activities that will take place as part of the project. Notice that each event circle also has a figure in the bottom, right hand quadrant.

This shows the latest finish time that's permissible for the preceding activity if the project is to be completed in the minimum time possible. You can calculate this by starting at the last event and working backwards. The latest finish time of the preceding event and the earliest start time of the following even will be the same for circles on the critical path.

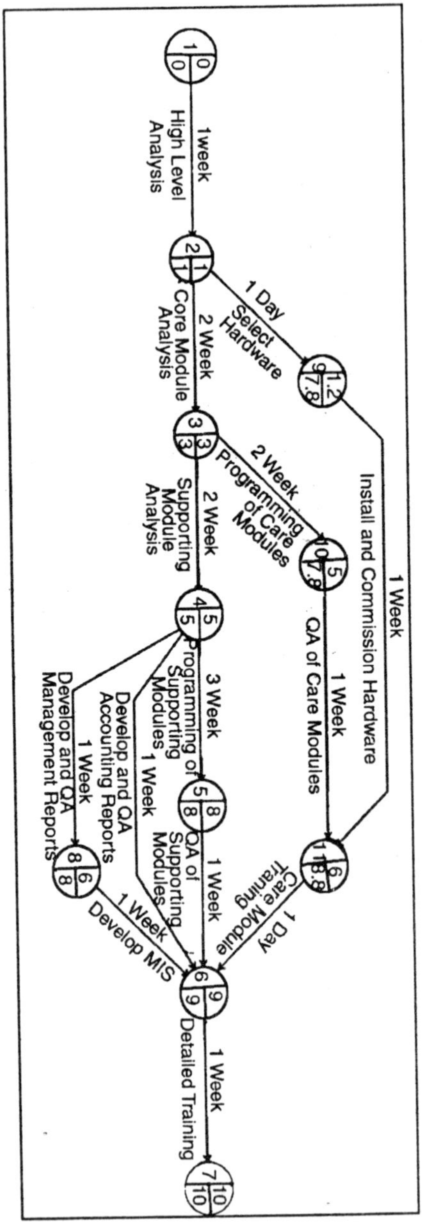

Fig. Critical Path Analysis for Exapmle Computer Project.

You can see that event M can start any time between weeks 6 and 8. The timing of this event is not critical. Events 1 to 2, 2 to 3, 3 to 4, 4 to 5, 5 to 6 and 6 to 7 must be started and completed on time if the project is to be completed in 10 weeks. This is the 'critical path' – these activities must be very closely managed to ensure that activities are completed on time. If jobs on the critical path slip, immediate action should be taken to get the project back on schedule. Otherwise completion of the whole project will slip.

CRASH ACTION

You may find that you need to complete a project earlier than your Critical Path Analysis says is possible. In this case you need to re-plan your project. You have a number of options and would need to assess the impact of each on the project's cost, quality and time required to complete it.

For example, you could increase resource available for each project activity to bring down time spent on each but the impact of some of this would be insignificant and a more efficient way of doing this would be to look only at activities on the critical path. As an example, it may be necessary to complete the computer project in Figure weeks rather than 10 weeks.

In this case you could look at using two analysts in activities 2 to 3 and 3 to 4. This would shorten the project by two weeks, but may raise the project cost – doubling resources at any stage may only improve productivity by, say, 50% as additional time may need to be spent getting the team members up to speed on what is required, coordinating tasks split between them, integrating their contributions etc.

In some situations, shortening the original critical path of a project can lead to a different series of activities becoming the critical path. For example, if activity 4 to 5 were reduced to 1 week, activities 4 to 8 and 8 to 6 would come onto the critical path.

As with Gantt Charts, in practice project managers use software tools like Microsoft Project to create CPA Charts. Not only do these ease make them easier to draw, they also make modification of plans easier and provide facilities for monitoring progress against plans.

PERT

PERT is a variation on Critical Path Analysis that takes a slightly more skeptical view of time estimates made for each project stage. To use it, estimate the shortest possible time each activity will take, the most likely length of time, and the longest time that might be taken if the activity takes longer than expected.

Use the formula to calculate the time to use for each project stage:

$$\frac{\text{shortest time} + 4 \times \text{likely time} + \text{longest time}}{6}$$

This helps to bias time estimates away from the unrealistically short time-scales normally assumed.

KEY POINTS

Critical Path Analysis is an effective and powerful method of assessing:

- What tasks must be carried out.
- Where parallel activity can be performed.
- The shortest time in which you can complete a project.
- Resources needed to execute a project.
- The sequence of activities, scheduling and timings involved.
- Task priorities.
- The most efficient way of shortening time on urgent projects.

An effective Critical Path Analysis can make the difference between success and failure on complex projects. It can be very useful for assessing the importance of problems faced during the implementation of the plan. PERT is a variant of Critical Path Analysis that takes a more skeptical view of the time needed to complete each project stage.

LOGFRAMES, AND THE LOGICAL FRAMEWORK APPROACH

In practice, even the best project managers can find it

difficult to plan major projects without missing important activities, and without failing to spot all significant risks and issues. What's more, once you're immersed in the detail of project planning, it's hard to keep site of the big picture: What are you trying to achieve and why? What are the risks and assumptions? And how you can tell whether the project is a success once it's implemented?

The Logical Framework Approach is a useful technique for helping you do these things, thereby making your projects more robust and coherent – and more successful. The Logical Framework Approach was developed in the 1970s as a tool for strategic planning, using the ideas of Management by Objectives. It's a tool of choice used by development agencies and in the international donor community.

Large aid organizations throughout the world use the LFA for planning, approving, evaluating and monitoring their projects. That said, this is a powerful and useful technique, and is one that richly deserves much wider application than in international development alone.

LOGICAL FRAMEWORK APPROACH AND THE LOGFRAME

The Logical Framework Approach elegantly weaves together top-down and bottom-up approaches to project management. It brings together the classical, top-down, "waterfall approach" for identifying the activities in a project, with a rigorous bottom-up checking process to make sure that these activity lists are comprehensive. It then reinforces this with a rigorous risks and assumptions analysis, which is again thoroughly checked.

And it concludes by identifying the controls needed to monitor and manage the project through to successful conclusion. It does this within the framework of the Logframe Matrix, shown in figure.

This cross-references seven key areas of the project to ensure that the key questions are asked:

- *Goal*: What results do we expect?
- *Purpose*: Why are we doing this?

- *Outputs*: What are the deliverables?
- *Activities*: what will we do to deliver the outputs?
- *Indicators of Achievement*: How will we know we've been successful?
- *Means of Verification*: How will we check our reported results?
- *Risks and Assumptions*: What assumptions underlie the structure of our project and what is the risk they will not prevail?

The answers to these questions are put into a Logical Framework Matrix and become the output of the Logical Framework Analysis exercise. The Logframe is a four by four matrix:

Table. The Logframe Matrix

Project Summary	Indicators of Achievement	Means of Verification Assumptions	Important Risks and
Goal:			
Purpose:			
Outputs:			
Activities:			

The process has significant value for any size of project. It helps identify the big picture and allows you to see how other items cascade down from it. As well, it helps flesh out the core assumptions that are used in the project development process.

USING A LOGFRAME

Carry out the following steps in consultation with your stakeholders, after you've completed a thorough analysis of the situation. By involving stakeholders, you'll end up with a much more robust analysis of the project than you would on your own.

- *Step 1: Identifying Outputs and Activities*: The first step is to brainstorm the outputs and activities required by the project, starting with the project goal. Do this in the Project Summary column of the Logframe. Start by defining the Goal and Purpose of the project and, from these, identify the outputs and the activities required:

- *Goal*: What is the "to be" state of the project? What are you trying to achieve?
- *Purpose*: What good will you do by achieving the goal? Who are the beneficiaries? What is the underlying motivation for starting the project in the first place?
- *Outputs*: What specific things will be delivered as a result of this project? In order for the project to be considered a success, what changes must be made, and what will the result be?
- *Activities*: What will actually be done in order to deliver the intended outputs? The Logframe is not intended as an implementation guide, so this part is typically presented in bullet point form.

- *Step 2*: Verify the Vertical Logic Next, we take a bottom-up approach to checking that this list of activities will deliver the desired results - after all, it's possible that activities have been missed, or that the actual results of these activities may not be the ones wanted. This checking process is an important part of making sure that your project plan is robust. Column one shows a hierarchy of objectives, so it is important to check that actions identified deliver the results wanted. Check the logic in column one by using an if/then test as follows. Starting with your activities, ensure that:
  - *IF you complete the activity, Then the outputs will occur.* You want to make sure your activities and outputs are directly linked.
  - *IF your outputs are achieved, Then the purpose of your project will be satisfied.* Are the planned outputs closely tied to your purpose? Make sure the beneficiaries you identified in your purpose actually receive the beneficial outcome desired.

- *IF your purpose is satisfied, Then the goal of the project is achieved.* Examine your purpose and goal to make sure that the purpose fully incorporates the intent within the goal. If, in this step, you find that activities and outputs are missing or are wrong, add or adjust them appropriately. And bear in mind that if you identify issues with elements higher up in this hierarchy, you'll need to go back to Step 1 and identify appropriate outcomes and activities for those elements.

* *Step 3*: Identify the Risks and Assumptions of your plan We now cross over to the other side of the Logframe to identify risks associated with the project, and possible false assumptions that may undermine it. There are any number of external factors that can throw projects off course. In the planning and design phase, it is prudent to identify the major assumptions you've used and the degree or risk associated with them. For each of the points in the project's structure, identify the assumptions you're making and look at the associated risks. To define your assumptions, ask "What actions or variables must exist for the project to start and proceed as planned?" Start at the bottom and work up.
  - *Activity Assumptions*: What do you need to happen for your activities to be completed successfully? And what conditions and resources are you assuming will be in place?
  - *Output Assumptions*: What factors outside of your control must be present to achieve the outputs you need?
  - *Purpose Assumptions*: To achieve the purpose, what external factors do you need to have in place?
  - *Goal Assumptions*: What are the necessary conditions for long-term viability of the project goal?

- Clarify these assumptions with stakeholders immediately, if you can. If you can't, make sure you have early activities in place within your project plan to confirm that your assumptions are correct.

  Next, repeat this process looking at risks. Make sure you plan in all of the activities needed to manage or eliminate risk, and if risk can neither be managed or eliminated, make sure that it's clearly identified so that it can be evaluated in the next step.

- *Step 4*: Verify the Logic of the Risks andAssumptions
  Once you have identified assumptions and risks, you need to check them to determine:
  - Whether your assumptions will link one level of the project to the next; and
  - Whether risks are too large. First of all, check that your assumptions are logical using an if/and/then analysis. Start at the bottom and work up to ensure:
  - IF the activity is completed successfully, AND the assumptions underlying it are true, THEN the output will be delivered.
  - IF the output is delivered, AND the assumptions underlying it are true, THEN the purpose will be achieved.
  - IF the purpose is achieved, AND the assumptions underlying it are true, THEN the goal will be achieved. Then, check some additional points related to your risk and assumption analysis:
    a. Make sure you have identified as many assumptions and risks as possible. Have you talked to everyone involved? Have you looked at the project from all angles?
    b. Make sure your assumptions are stated specifically and are not too vague. You can't assess risk accurately if you are working with generalities.

c. Do you have plans at each level to manage the risks you have identified?

d. If the risks you're not able to manage are too high, consider redesigning the project or, if you still can't reduce these to sensible levels, reconsider the project's viability. Again, where this process exposes issues with your Logframe, update it appropriately.

- *Step 5*: Determine the Indicators of Achievement and Means of Verification When you are satisfied with the structure of the Logframe so far, and are comfortable that you can manage the risks related to your assumptions, you can move on to think about how you will monitor progress towards success. Performance indicators are the specific measures used to monitor this progress. Here are the criteria for a good indicator of achievement:
  - *Valid*: It must measure the intended result.
  - *Reliable*: The measure must be consistently attained over time.
  - *Sensitive*: The measure should respond to changes, and should sufficiently-quickly identify if things are going wrong.
  - *Simple*: The measure should be easy to collect or perform.
  - *Useful*: It must help with decision making or provide information for future learning.
  - *Affordable*: You need to be able to afford the financial and time costs involved in taking the measurement on a regular basis.

Using these criteria, for each goal, purpose, output and activity, indicate what will be used to determine whether it was successfully achieved. Also note who will be responsible for setting these targets. Then indicate exactly how you will verify that achievement. What sources of data will you use? How will you collect the data? How often? Make sure that appropriate activities are in place within your plan to set up and manage these monitoring systems.

KEY POINTS

The Logical Framework Approach is a great technique for making sure that your project plan is robust and coherent. By using it, you significantly increase the likelihood that your project will be successful. Firstly, it provides a useful framework for working through the design of your project with key stakeholders, making sure that you can take full advantage of their knowledge, insights and experience.

Secondly, it provides a useful process for testing and checking your project plan, making sure that it contains all the necessary activities, is based on sound assumptions, and fairly weighs and manages the risks inherent within the project. Thirdly, it helps you ensure that appropriate control measures are embedded within the project, meaning that you can quickly identify where things are going wrong, and take appropriate corrective action.

PLANNING LARGE PROJECTS AND PROGRAMMES

However, this approach will only scale up to a certain extent – as projects get larger, they can reach a level of complexity where ad hoc approaches to project management become wasteful and inefficient. For these projects, project management becomes a technical discipline in its own right. To run such projects efficiently, project managers use formal project management methodologies such as PMBOK or PRINCE2.

PMBOK, which stands for the "Project Management Body Of Knowledge", was first published in 1996 as a manual called *A Guide to the Project Management Body of Knowledge*. It is now in its fourth edition. It is a standard that represents generally-recognized good practice, and is published by the Project Management Institute. This is a not-for-profit membership association for the project management profession, which administers the associated Project Management Professional qualifications. PMBOK is the dominant project management methodology used in North America.

PRINCE2, which stands for "PRojects IN Controlled Environments", is widely used in the UK and in English-speaking countries outside North America, and was originally devised as a "best practice" standard to be used for managing UK government information systems projects. Since then, it has become increasingly widely used for projects of all kinds, in the private as well as the public sector, and although copyright in it is retained by the Crown and managed by the Office of Government Commerce, its methods are in the public domain and are free for organizations to use.

Various accredited training organizations offer PRINCE2 qualifications at Foundation level, for those who need to be familiar with its terminology, and at Practitioner level, which is aimed at project and programme manages.

PRINCE2 is powerful in that it completely clarifies people's roles in projects, ensures that lines of communication are clear, makes sure that project risk is actively managed, sets up appropriate controls, establishes baseline costs, schedule and scope, and so on. In this, it embodies and codifies much of project management best practice.

KOTTER'S 8-STEP CHANGE MODEL

What was true more than two thousand years ago is just as true today. We live in a world where "business as usual" IS change. New initiatives, project-based working, technology improvements, staying ahead of the competition - these things come together to drive ongoing changes to the way we work.

Whether you're considering a small change to one or two processes, or a systemwide change to an organization, it's common to feel uneasy and intimidated by the scale of the challenge.

You know that the change needs to happen, but you don't really know how to go about doing delivering it. Where do you start? Whom do you involve? How do you see it through to the end?

There are many theories about how to "do" change. Many originate with leadership and change management guru, John Kotter. A professor at Harvard Business School and world-renowned change expert, Kotter introduced his eight-step change process in his 1995.

"We look at his eight steps for leading change":

- *Step One: Create Urgency*: For change to happen, it helps if the whole company really wants it. Develop a sense of urgency around the need for change. This may help you spark the initial motivation to get things moving. This isn't simply a matter of showing people poor sales statistics or talking about increased competition. Open an honest and convincing dialogue about what's happening in the marketplace and with your competition. If many people start talking about the change you propose, the urgency can build and feed on itself.
  What you can do:
  - Identify potential threats, and develop scenarios showing what could happen in the future.
  - Examine opportunities that should be, or could be, exploited.
  - Start honest discussions, and give dynamic and convincing reasons to get people talking and thinking.
  - Request support from customers, outside stakeholders and industry people to strengthen your argument.
- *Step Two: Form a Powerful Coalition*: Convince people that change is necessary. This often takes strong leadership and visible support from key people within your organization. Managing change isn't enough - you have to lead it. You can find effective change leaders throughout your organization - they don't necessarily follow the traditional company hierarchy. To lead change, you need to bring together a coalition, or team, of influential people whose power comes from a variety of sources, including job title, status, expertise, and political importance. Once formed, your "change coalition" needs to work as a team, continuing to build urgency and momentum around the need for change.

What you can do:

- Identify the true leaders in your organization.
- Ask for an emotional commitment from these key people.
- Work on team building within your change coalition.
- Check your team for weak areas, and ensure that you have a good mix of people from different departments and different levels within your company.

• *Step Three: Create a Vision for Change:* When you first start thinking about change, there will probably be many great ideas and solutions floating around. Link these concepts to an overall vision that people can grasp easily and remember. A clear vision can help everyone understand why you're asking them to do something. When people see for themselves what you're trying to achieve, then the directives they're given tend to make more sense.

What you can do:

- Determine the values that are central to the change.
- Develop a short summary that captures what you "see" as the future of your organization.
- Create a strategy to execute that vision.
- Ensure that your change coalition can describe the vision in five minutes or less.
- Practice your "vision speech" often.

• *Step Four: Communicate the Vision:* What you do with your vision after you create it will determine your success. Your message will probably have strong competition from other day-to-day communications within the company, so you need to communicate it frequently and powerfully, and embed it within everything that you do.Don't just call special meetings to communicate your vision. Instead, talk about it every chance you get. Use the vision daily to make decisions and solve problems. When you keep it fresh on everyone's minds, they'll remember it and respond to it. It's also important to "walk the talk." What you do is far more important - and believable - than what you say. Demonstrate the kind of behaviour that you want from others.

What you can do:

- Talk often about your change vision.
- Openly and honestly address peoples' concerns and anxieties.
- Apply your vision to all aspects of operations - from training to performance reviews. Tie everything back to the vision.
- Lead by example.

- *Step Five: Remove Obstacles:* If you follow these steps and reach this point in the change process, you've been talking about your vision and building buy-in from all levels of the organization. Hopefully, your staff wants to get busy and achieve the benefits that you've been promoting. But is anyone resisting the change? And are there processes or structures that are getting in its way? Put in place the structure for change, and continually check for barriers to it. Removing obstacles can empower the people you need to execute your vision, and it can help the change move forward.

  What you can do:

  - Identify, or hire, change leaders whose main roles are to deliver the change.
  - Look at your organizational structure, job descriptions, and performance and compensation systems to ensure they're in line with your vision.
  - Recognize and reward people for making change happen.
  - Identify people who are resisting the change, and help them see what's needed.
  - Take action to quickly remove barriers.

- *Step Six: Create Short-term Wins:* Nothing motivates

more than success. Give your company a taste of victory early in the change process. Within a short time frame, you'll want to have results that your staff can see. Without this, critics and negative thinkers might hurt your progress. Create short-term targets - not just one long-term goal. You want each smaller target to be achievable, with little room for failure. Your change team may have to work very hard to come up with these targets, but each "win" that you produce can further motivate the entire staff.

What you can do:

– Look for sure-fire projects that you can implement without help from any strong critics of the change.
– Don't choose early targets that are expensive. You want to be able to justify the investment in each project.
– Thoroughly analyse the potential pros and cons of your targets. If you don't succeed with an early goal, it can hurt your entire change initiative.
– Reward the people who help you meet the targets.

- *Step Seven: Build on the Change:* Kotter argues that many change projects fail because victory is declared too early. Real change runs deep. Quick wins are only the beginning of what needs to be done to achieve long-term change.Launching one new product using a new system is great. But if you can launch 10 products, that means the new system is working. To reach that 10th success, you need to keep looking for improvements.Each success provides an opportunity to build on what went right and identify what you can improve.

  What you can do:

  – After every win, analyse what went right and what needs improving.
  – Set goals to continue building on the momentum you've achieved.

- Learn about kaizen, the idea of continuous improvement.
- Keep ideas fresh by bringing in new change agents and leaders for your change coalition.

- *Step Eight: Anchor the Changes in Corporate Culture:* Finally, to make any change stick, it should become part of the core of your organization. Your corporate culture often determines what gets done, so the values behind your vision must show in day-to-day work. Make continuous efforts to ensure that the change is seen in every aspect of your organization. This will help give that change a solid place in your organization's culture. It's also important that your company's leaders continue to support the change. This includes existing staff and new leaders who are brought in. If you lose the support of these people, you might end up back where you started.

  What you can do:
  - Talk about progress every chance you get. Tell success stories about the change process, and repeat other stories that you hear.
  - Include the change ideals and values when hiring and training new staff.
  - Publicly recognize key members of your original change coalition, and make sure the rest of the staff - new and old - remembers their contributions.
  - Create plans to replace key leaders of change as they move on. This will help ensure that their legacy is not lost or forgotten.

KEY POINTS

You have to work hard to change an organization successfully. When you plan carefully and build the proper foundation, implementing change can be much easier, and you'll improve the chances of success. If you're too impatient, and if you expect too many results too soon, your plans for change are more likely to fail. Create a sense of urgency, recruit powerful change leaders, build a vision and effectively communicate it, remove obstacles, create quick wins, and build on your momentum. If you do these things, you can help make the change part of your organizational culture. That's when you can declare a true victory. then sit back and enjoy the change that you envisioned so long ago.

STAKEHOLDER ANALYSIS

"Stakeholder management is critical to the success of every project in every organization I have ever worked with. By engaging the right people in the right way in your project, you can make a big difference to its success... and to your career."

– Rachel Thompson, Experienced Project Manager

As you become more successful in your career, the actions you take and the projects you run will affect more and more people. The more people you affect, the more likely it is that your actions will impact people who have power and influence over your projects. These people could be strong supporters of your work – or they could block it.

Stakeholder Management is an important discipline that successful people use to win support from others. It helps them ensure that their projects succeed where others fail.

There are two major elements to Stakeholder Management: Stakeholder Analysis and Stakeholder Planning. Stakeholder Analysis is the technique used to identify the key people who have to be won over. You then use Stakeholder Planning to build the support that helps you succeed.

The benefits of using a stakeholder-based approach are that:

- You can use the opinions of the most powerful stakeholders to shape your projects at an early stage. Not only does this make it more likely that they will support you, their input can also improve the quality of your project.
- Gaining support from powerful stakeholders can help you to win more resources – this makes it more likely that your projects will be successful.
- By communicating with stakeholders early and often, you can ensure that they know what you are doing

and fully understand the benefits of your project – this means they can support you actively when necessary.

- You can anticipate what people's reaction to your project may be, and build into your plan the actions that will win people's support.

HOW TO USE THE TOOL

The first step in Stakeholder Analysis is to identify who your stakeholders are. The next step is to work out their power, influence and interest, so you know who you should focus on. The final step is to develop a good understanding of the most important stakeholders so that you can work out how to win their support. You record this analysis on a stakeholder map.

After you have used this tool and created a stakeholder map, you can use the stakeholder planning tool to plan how you will communicate with each stakeholder.

The steps of Stakeholder Analysis are:

- *Identifying Your Stakeholders*: The first step in your stakeholder analysis is to brainstorm who your stakeholders are. As part of this, think of all the people who are affected by your work, who have influence or power over it, or have an interest in its successful or unsuccessful conclusion. The table shows some of the people who might be stakeholders in your job or in your projects:

Your boss	Shareholders	Government
Senior executives	Alliance partners	Trades associations
Your coworkers	Suppliers	The press
Your team	Lenders	Interest groups
Customers	Analysts	The public
Prospective customers	Future recruits	The community
Your family		

Remember that although stakeholders may be both organizations and people, ultimately you can only communicate with individual people. Make sure that you identify the correct individual stakeholders within a stakeholder organization.

- *Prioritize Your Stakeholders*: You may now have a long list of people and organizations that are affected by your work. Some of these may have the power either to block or advance it. Some may be interested in what you are doing, others may not care. Map out your stakeholders on a Power/Interest Grid on our free template as shown in figure, and classify them by their power over your work and by their interest in your work.

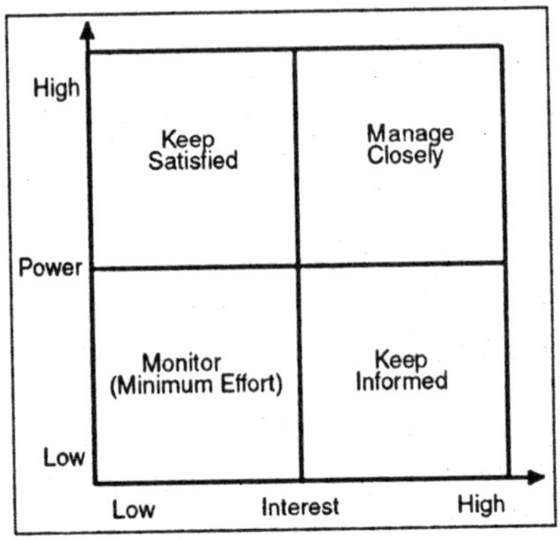

Fig. Power/Interest Grid for Stakeholder Prioritization

For example, your boss is likely to have high power and influence over your projects and high interest. Your family may have high interest, but are unlikely to have power over it.

Someone's position on the grid shows you the actions you have to take with them:

- *High power, interested people*: These are the people you must fully engage with, and make the greatest efforts to satisfy.
- *High power, less interested people*: Put enough work in with these people to keep them satisfied, but not so much that they become bored with your message.
- *Low power, interested people*: Keep these people adequately informed, and talk to them to ensure that no major issues are arising. These people can often be very helpful with the detail of your project.

- *Low power, less interested people*: Again, monitor these people, but do not bore them with excessive communication.
- *Understanding your key stakeholders*: You now need to know more about your key stakeholders. You need to know how they are likely to feel about and react to your project. You also need to know how best to engage them in your project and how best to communicate with them. Key questions that can help you understand your stakeholders are:
  - What financial or emotional interest do they have in the outcome of your work? Is it positive or negative?
  - What motivates them most of all?
  - What information do they want from you?
  - How do they want to receive information from you? What is the best way of communicating your message to them?
  - What is their current opinion of your work? Is it based on good information?
  - Who influences their opinions generally, and who influences their opinion of you? Do some of these influencers therefore become important stakeholders in their own right?
  - If they are not likely to be positive, what will win them around to support your project?
  - If you don't think you will be able to win them around, how will you manage their opposition?
  - Who else might be influenced by their opinions? Do these people become stakeholders in their own right?

A very good way of answering these questions is to talk to your stakeholders directly – people are often quite open about their views, and asking people's opinions is often the first step in building a successful relationship with them.

You can summarize the understanding you have gained on the stakeholder map, so that you can easily see which stakeholders are expected to be blockers or critics, and which stakeholders are likely to be advocates and supporters or your project. A good way of doing this is by color coding: showing advocates and supporters in green, blockers and critics in red, and others who are neutral in orange.

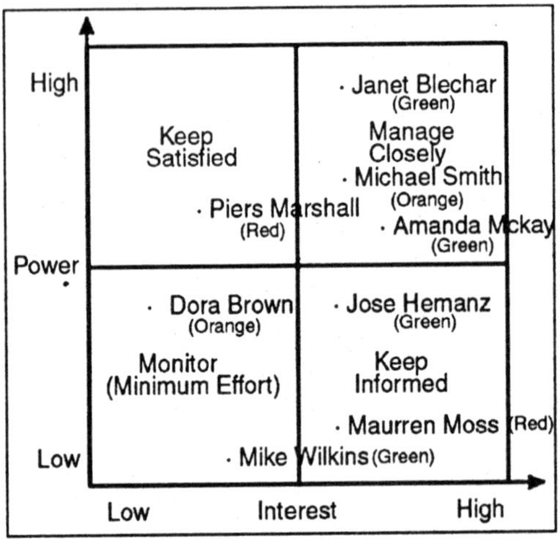

Fig. Example Power/Interest Grid with Stakeholders Marked

Figure shows an example of this - in this example, you can see that a lot of effort needs to be put into persuading Piers and Michael of the benefits of the project – Janet and Amanda also need to managed well as powerful supporters.

INFLUENCE MAPS

Many people can have influence over your projects. Some influencers are obvious and easy to spot. Others are less obvious, but are no less significant. If you fail to recognize and "manage" these influencers, you'll most-likely experience unexpected resistance to your projects, and sometimes bewildering failure. This is increasingly the case as you run large projects, and as the number of people affected by your projects increases.

People within your organization, at least, are supposed to work together openly and willingly. However, even here, your boss, your teammates, your customers, your boss's boss - even the CEO's nephew in the mailroom - can all impact you, given certain sets of circumstances.

However people outside your organization have all sorts of interests and motivations that you can't control. Here, knowing who influences who can be critical if you want to get anything done at all.

INFLUENCE MAPPING

So do you understand who has influence over your projects? Do you know the nature, direction, and strength of these influences? After all, using the normal "chain of command" may not always be the best way to advance your objectives: Knowing who the real influencers are can help you determine where you should put your effort if you really want to succeed.

This is what influence mapping is all about - discovering your project's true stakeholders and the influence relationships between them. This helps you target the key influencers so that you can win the resources and support you need to reach your goal.

ELEMENTS OF AN INFLUENCE MAP

An influence map is a visual model showing the people who influence and make decisions about your project. The map helps you understand how stakeholders relate to one-another, so that you can quickly see the way in which influence flows.

Remember that even the most powerful people rarely performancealone. Top executives and other people in authority rely on advisers. Find out who the advisers are, and understand how they operate. This can be vital to your project's success.

There are three main considerations when you construct an influence map:

1. The importance or weight of a stakeholder's overall influence.
2. The relationships between stakeholders.
3. The amount of influence stakeholders have over others.

Your completed influence map shows the stakeholders with the most influence as individuals with the largest circles.

Lines drawn to other stakeholders indicate the presence and strength of influence.

The resulting influence map looks something like this:

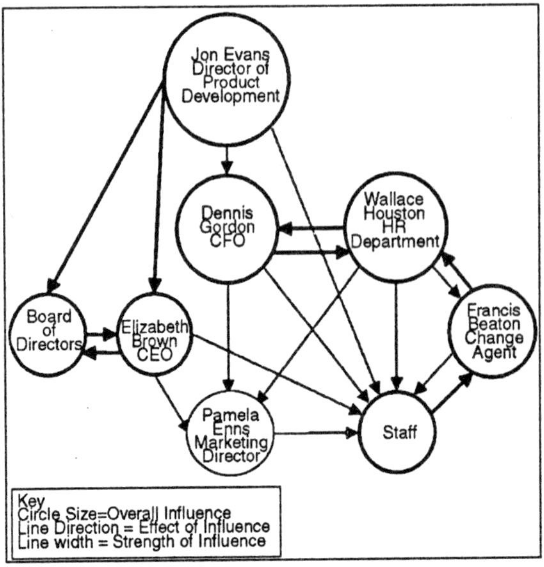

This influence map clearly shows how important Jon Evans is to the success of your restructuring plan. It also indicates that you should spend energy on gaining support from Wallace Houston and Dennis Gordon before moving on to other executives.

Before you thought about stakeholder influences, you might have assumed that the CEO and CFO had the most influence on organization-wide change. But the influence map shows you that this is probably not for the case in this situation.

CREATING AN INFLUENCE MAP

Follow these steps to construct an influence map:

- *Step One: Prepare a stakeholder analysis:* This helps you identify, prioritize, and understand your key stakeholders.
- *Step Two: For each stakeholder, find out the following:*
  - Whom does he or she influence, and who influences him or her?

  - How strong is that influence?
  - What is the history of each relationship? How does this impact overall influence?
  - What role does hierarchy play in the amount of influence?
- *Step Three*: Map the importance of influence using the size and position of the circles. The largest circles belong to stakeholders with the most influence.
- *Step Four*: Map the direction of influence by drawing arrows to link the stakeholders..
- *Step Five*: Map the strength of influence by using thicker lines to indicate stronger influence.
- *Step Six*: Study the map, and identify stakeholders with the most overall influence. Form a stakeholder management plan that will allow you to communicate with, and hopefully influence, these important influencers.
- *Step Seven*: Map these influence relationships on a regular basis. This way, you'll better understand the dynamics of decision making relating to your project.

PROGRAMME EVALUATION AND REVIEW TECHNIQUE

The Programme Evaluation and Review Technique, commonly abbreviated PERT, is a model for project management designed to analyse and represent the tasks involved in completing a given project. It is commonly used in conjunction with the critical path method or CPM.

PERT is a method to analyse the involved tasks in completing a given project, especially the time needed to complete each task, and identifying the minimum time needed to complete the total project.

PERT was developed primarily to simplify the planning and scheduling of large and complex projects. It was developed by Bill Pocock of Booz Allen Hamilton and Gordon Perhson of the U.S. Navy Special Projects Office in 1957 to support the U.S. Navy's Polaris nuclear submarine project. It was able to incorporate uncertainty by making it possible to schedule a project while not knowing precisely the details and durations of all the activities. It is more of an event-oriented technique rather than start- and completion-oriented, and is used more in projects where time, rather than cost, is the major factor. It is applied to very large-scale, one-time, complex, non-routine infrastructure and Research and Development projects.

This project model was the first of its kind, a revival for scientific management, founded by Frederick Taylor and later refined by Henry Ford. DuPont corporation's critical path method was invented at roughly the same time as PERT.

CONVENTIONS

- A PERT chart is a tool that facilitates decision making; The first draft of a PERT chart will number its events sequentially in 10s to allow the later insertion of additional events.
- Two consecutive events in a PERT chart are linked by activities, which are conventionally represented as arrows.
- The events are presented in a logical sequence and no activity can commence until its immediately preceding event is completed.
- The planner decides which milestones should be PERT events and also decides their "proper" sequence.
- A PERT chart may have multiple pages with many sub-tasks.

PERT is valuable to manage where multiple tasks are going simultaneously to reduce the redundancy

TERMINOLOGY

- *PERT event*: A point that marks the start or completion of one or more activities. It consumes no time, and uses no resources. When it marks the completion of one or more tasks, it is not "reached" until all of the activities leading to that event have been completed.
- *Predecessor event*: An event that immediately precedes

some other event without any other events intervening. An event can have multiple predecessor events and can be the predecessor of multiple events.

- *Successor event*: An event that immediately follows some other event without any other intervening events. An event can have multiple successor events and can be the successor of multiple events.
- *PERT activity*: The actual performance of a task which consumes time and requires resources. It can be understood as representing the time, effort, and resources required to move from one event to another. A PERT activity cannot be performed until the predecessor event has occurred.
- *Optimistic time*: The minimum possible time required to accomplish a task, assuming everything proceeds better than is normally expected
- *Pessimistic time*: The maximum possible time required to accomplish a task, assuming everything goes wrong.
- *Most likely time*: The best estimate of the time required to accomplish a task, assuming everything proceeds as normal.
- *Expected time*: The best estimate of the time required to accomplish a task, assuming everything proceeds as normal.

$$T_E = (O + 4M + P) \div 6$$

- Float or Slack is the amount of time that a task in a project network can be delayed without causing a delay - Subsequent tasks –or Project Completion – (total float)
- *Critical Path*: The longest possible continuous pathway taken from the initial event to the terminal event. It determines the total calendar time required for the project; and, therefore, any time delays along the critical path will delay the reaching of the terminal event by at least the same amount.
- *Critical Activity*: An activity that has total float equal to zero. Activity with zero float does not mean it is on the critical path.

- *Lead time*: The time by which a predecessor event must be completed in order to allow sufficient time for the activities that must elapse before a specific PERT event reaches completion.
- *Lag time*: The earliest time by which a successor event can follow a specific PERT event.
- *Slack*: The slack of an event is a measure of the excess time and resources available in achieving this event. Positive slack would indicate ahead of schedule; negative slack would indicate behind schedule; and zero slack would indicate on schedule.
- *Fast tracking*: Performing more critical activities in parallel
- *Crashing critical path*: Shortening duration of critical activities

ADVANTAGES

- PERT chart explicitly defines and makes visible dependencies between the WBS elements
- PERT facilitates identification of the critical path and makes this visible
- PERT facilitates identification of early start, late start, and slack for each activity,
- PERT provides for potentially reduced project duration due to better understanding of dependencies leading to improved overlapping of activities and tasks where feasible.

DISADVANTAGES

- There can be potentially hundreds or thousands of activities and individual dependency relationships
- The network charts tend to be large and unwieldy requiring several pages to print and requiring special size paper
- The lack of a timeframe on most PERT/CPM charts makes it harder to show status although colours can help
- When the PERT/CPM charts become unwieldy, they are no longer used to manage the project.

UNCERTAINTY IN PROJECT SCHEDULING

During project execution, however, a real-life project will never execute exactly as it was planned due to uncertainty. It can be ambiguity resulting from subjective estimates that are prone to human errors or it can be variability arising from unexpected events or risks. And Project Evaluation and Review Technique may provide inaccurate information about the project completion time for main reason uncertainty. This inaccuracy is large enough to render such estimates as not helpful.

One possibility to maximize solution robustness is to include safety in the baseline schedule in order to absorb the anticipated disruptions. This is called proactive scheduling. A pure proactive scheduling is an utopia, incorporating safety in a baseline schedule that allows to cope with every possible disruption would lead to a baseline schedule with a very large make-span. A second approach, reactive scheduling, consists of defining a procedure to react to disruptions that cannot be absorbed by the baseline schedule.

RESOURCE LEVELING

Resource leveling is a project management process used to examine unbalanced use of resources over time, and for resolving over-allocations or conflicts.

When performing project planning activities, the manager will attempt to schedule certain tasks simultaneously. When more resources such as machines or people are needed than are available, or perhaps a specific person is needed in both tasks, the tasks will have to be rescheduled concurrently or even sequentially to manage the constraint. Project planning resource leveling is the process of resolving these conflicts. It can also be used to balance the workload of primary resources over the course of the project[s], usually at the expense of one of the traditional triple constraints.

When using specially designed project software, leveling typically means resolving conflicts or over allocations in the project plan by allowing the software to calculate delays and update tasks automatically. Project management software leveling requires delaying tasks until resources are available. In more complex environments, resources could be allocated across multiple, concurrent projects thus requiring the process of resource leveling to be performed at company level. In either definition, leveling could result in a later project finish date if the tasks affected are in the critical path.

Resource Leveling is also useful in the world of maintenance management. Many organizations have maintenance backlogs. These backlogs consist of work orders. In a "planned state" these work orders have estimates such as 2 electricians for 8 hours. These work orders have other attributes such as report date, priority, asset operational requirements, and safety concerns. These same organizations have a need to create weekly schedules. Resource-leveling can take the "work demand" and balance it against the resource pool availability for the given week. The goal is to create this weekly schedule in advance of performing the work. Without resource-leveling the organization is most likely performing subjective selection. For the most part, when it comes to maintenance scheduling, there are very few logic ties and therefore no need to calculate critical path and total float.

SCHEDULE

In project management, a schedule consists of a list of a project's terminal elements with intended start and finish dates. Terminal elements are the lowest element in a schedule, which is not further subdivided. Those items are often estimated in terms of resource requirements, budget and duration, linked by dependencies and scheduled.

Before a project schedule can be created, a project manager should typically have a work breakdown structure, an effort estimate for each task, and a resource list with availability for each resource. If these are not yet available, it may be possible to create something that looks like a schedule, but it will essentially be a work of fiction. They can be created using a consensus-driven estimation method like Wideband Delphi. The reason for this is that a schedule itself is an estimate: each date in the schedule is estimated, and if those dates do not have the buy-in of the people who are going to do the work, the schedule will be inaccurate. In many industries, such as engineering and construction, the development and maintenance of the project schedule is the responsibility of a full time scheduler or team of schedulers, depending on the size of the project. And though the techniques of scheduling are well developed, they are inconsistently applied throughout industry.

Standardization and promotion of scheduling best practices are being pursued by the Association for the Advancement of Cost Engineering, the Project Management Institute. In some large corporations, scheduling, as well as cost, estimating, and risk management are organized under the department of project controls. Many project scheduling software products exist which can do much of the tedious work of calculating the schedule automatically, and plenty of books and tutorials dedicated to teaching people how to use them. However, before a project manager can use these tools, he or she should understand the concepts behind the WBS, dependencies, resource allocation, critical paths, Gantt charts and earned value. These are the real keys to planning a successful project.

In order for a project schedule to be healthy, the following criteria must be met:

- The schedule must be constantly updated.
- The EAC value must be equal to the baseline value.
- The remaining effort must be appropriately distributed among team members, taking into consideration vacations.

PROCESS MIX

Process is another element of the extended marketing mix, or 7P's.There are a number of perceptions of the concept of process within the business and marketing literature. Some see processes as a means to achieve an outcome, for example - to achieve a 30% market share a company implements a marketing planning process. Another view is that marketing has a number of processes that integrate together to create an overall marketing process, for example - telemarketing and Internet marketing can be integrated. A further view is that marketing processes are used to control the marketing mix, i.e. processes that measure the achievement marketing objectives. All views are understandable, but not particularly customer focused.

For the purposes of the marketing mix, process is an element of service that sees the customer experiencing an organisation's offering. It's best viewed as something that your customer participates in at different points in time. Here are some examples to help your build a picture of marketing process, from the customer's point of view.

Going on a cruise - from the moment that you arrive at the dockside, you are greeted; your baggage is taken to your room. You have two weeks of services from restaurants and evening entertainment, to casinos and shopping. Finally, you arrive at your destination, and your baggage is delivered to you. This is a highly focused marketing process

Booking a flight on the Internet - the process begins with you visiting an airline's website. You enter details of your flights and book them. Your ticket/booking reference arrive by e-mail or post. You catch your flight on time, and arrive refreshed at your destination. This is all part of the marketing process.

At each stage of the process, markets:

- Deliver value through all elements of the marketing mix. Process, physical evidence and people enhance services.
- Feedback can be taken and the mix can be altered.
- Customers are retained, and other serves or products are extended and marked to them.
- The process itself can be tailored to the needs of different individuals, experiencing a similar service at the same time.

Processes essentially have inputs, throughputs and outputs. Marketing adds value to each of the stages. Take a look at the lesson on value chain analysis to consider a series of processes at work.

PRODUCT MIX

Product mix is a combination of products manufactured or traded by the same business house to reinforce their presence in the market, increase market share and increase the turnover for more profitability. Normally the product mix is within the synergy of other products for a medium size organization. However large groups of Industries may have diversified products within core competency. *Larsen and Toubro Ltd, Godrej, Reliance in India are some of the examples.*

One of the realities of business is that most firms deal with multi-products.This helps a firm diffuse its risk across different product groups/Also it enables the firm to appeal to a much larger group of customers or to different needs of the same customer group.So when Videocon chose to diversify into other consumer durables like music systems,washing machines and refrigerators,it sought to satisfy the needs of the middle and upper middle income group of consumers.

Likewise, Bajaj Electricals.a household name in India, has almost ninety products in i8ts portfolio ranging from low value items like bulbs to high priced consumer durables like mixers and luminaires and lighting projects.The number of products carried by a firm at a given point of time is called its product mix. This product mix contains product lines and product items.In other words it's a composite of products offered for sale by a firm.

PRODUCT MIX DECISIONS

Often firms take decisions to change their product mix. These decisions are dictated by the factors and also by the changes occurring in the market place. Like the changing life-styles of Indian consumers led BPL-Sanyo to launch an entire range of white goods like refrigerators, washing machines, and microwave ovens.It also motivate the firm to launch other entertainment electronics.

Rahejas, a well-known builders firm in Bombay, took a major decision to convert one of its theatre buildings in the western suburbs of Bombay into a large garments and accessories store for men,women and children, perhaps the first of its kind in India to have almost all products required by these customer groups Competition from low priced washing powders forced Hindustan Levers to launch different brands of detergent powder at different price levels positioned at different market segments.

Customer preferences for herbs, mainly shikakai motivated Lever to launch black Sunsilk Shampoo,which has shikakai.Also,low purchasing power and cultural bias against shampoo market made Hindustan Lever consider smaller packaging mainly sachets, for single use.So, it is the changes or anticipated changes in the market place that motivates a firm to consider changes in its product mix.

PRODUCT-MIX MANAGEMENT AND RESPONSIBILITIES

It is extremely important for any organization to have a well-managed product mix. Most organizations break down managing the product mix, product line, and actual product into three different levels. Product-mix decisions are concerned with the combination of product lines offered by the company. Management of the companies' product mix is the responsibility of top management.

Some basic product-mix decisions include:

- Reviewing the mix of existing product lines;
- Adding new lines to and deleting existing lines from the product mix;
- Determining the relative emphasis on new versus existing product lines in the mix;
- Determining the appropriate emphasis on internal development versus external acquisition in the product mix;
- Gauging the effects of adding or deleting a product line in relationship to other lines in the product mix; and
- Forecasting the effects of future external change on the company's product mix.

Product-line decisions are concerned with the combination of individual products offered within a given line. The product-line manager supervises several product managers who are responsible for individual products in the line. Decisions about a product line are usually incorporated into a marketing plan at the divisional level. Such a plan specifies changes in the product lines and allocations to products in each line.

Generally, product-line managers have the following responsibilities:

- Considering expansion of a given product line;
- Considering candidates for deletion from the product line;
- Evaluating the effects of product additions and deletions on the profitability of other items in the line; and
- Allocating resources to individual products in the line on the basis of marketing strategies recommended by product managers.

Decisions at the first level of product management involve the marketing mix for an individual brand/product. These decisions are the responsibility of a brand manager. Decisions regarding the marketing mix for a brand are represented in the product's marketing plan. The plan for a new brand would specify price level, advertising expenditures for the coming year, coupons, trade discounts, distribution facilities, and a five-year statement of projected sales and earnings.

The plan for an existing product would focus on any changes in the marketing strategy. Some of these changes might include the product's target market, advertising and promotional expenditures, product characteristics, price level, and recommended distribution strategy.

GENERAL MANAGEMENT WORKFLOW

Top management formulates corporate objectives that become the basis for planning the product line. Product-line managers formulate objectives for their line to guide brand managers in developing the marketing mix for individual brands. Brand strategies are then formulated and incorporated into the product-line plan, which is in turn incorporated into the corporate plan. The corporate plan details changes in the firm's product lines and specifies strategies for growth. Once plans have been formulated, financial allocations flow from top management to product line and then to brand management for implementation.

Implementation of the plan requires tracking performance and providing data from brand to product line to top management for evaluation and control. Evaluation of the current plan then becomes the first step in the next planning cycle, since it provides a basis for examining the company's current offerings and recommending modifications as a result of past performance.

PRODUCT-MIX ANALYSIS

Since top management is ultimately responsible for the product mix and the resulting profits or losses, they often analyse the company product mix. The first assessment involves the area of opportunity in a particular industry or market.

Opportunity is generally defined in terms of current industry growth or potential attractiveness as an investment. The second criterion is the company's ability to exploit opportunity, which is based on its current or potential position in the industry.

The company's position can be measured in terms of market share if it is currently in the market, or in terms of its resources if it is considering entering the market. These two factors—opportunity and the company's ability to exploit it—provide four different options for a company to follow.

- High opportunity and ability to exploit it result in the firm's introducing new products or expanding markets for existing products to ensure future growth.
- Low opportunity but a strong current market position will generally result in the company's attempting to maintain its position to ensure current profitability.
- High opportunity but a lack of ability to exploit it results in either

- Attempting to acquire the necessary resources or
- Deciding not to further pursue opportunity in these markets.

- Low opportunity and a weak market position will result in either
  - Avoiding these markets or
  - Divesting existing products in them.

These options provide a basis for the firm to evaluate new and existing products in an attempt to achieve balance between current and future growth. This analysis may cause the product mix to change, depending on what management decides.

The most widely used approach to product portfolio analysis is the model developed by the Boston Consulting Group. The BCG analysis emphasizes two main criteria in evaluating the firm's product mix: the market growth rate and the product's relative market share.

BCG uses these two criteria because they are closely related to profitability, which is why top management often uses the BCG analysis. Proper analysis and conclusions may lead to significant changes to the company's product mix, product line, and product offerings.

The market growth rate represents the products' category position in the product life cycle. Products in the introductory and growth phases require more investment because of research and development and initial marketing costs for advertising, selling, and distribution.

This category is also regarded as a high-growth area. Relative market share represents the company's competitive strength. Market share is compared to that of the leading competitor.

Once the analysis has been done using the market growth rate and relative market share, products are placed into one of four categories:

1. *Stars*: Products with high growth and market share are know as stars. Because these products have high potential for profitability, they should be given top priority in financing, advertising, product positi-

oning, and distribution. As a result, they need significant amounts of cash to finance rapid growth and frequently show an initial negative cash flow.

2. *Cash cows*: Products with a high relative market share but in a low growth position are cash cows. These are profitable products that generate more cash than is required to produce and market them. Excess cash should be used to finance high-opportunity areas. Strategies for cash cows should be designed to sustain current market share rather than to expand it. An expansion strategy would require additional investment, thus decreasing the existing positive cash flow.
3. *Problem children*: These products have low relative market share but are in a high-growth situation. They are called "problem children" because their eventual direction is not yet clear. The firm should invest heavily in those that sales forecasts indicate might have a reasonable chance to become stars. Otherwise divestment is the best course, since problem children may become dogs and thereby candidates for deletion.
4. *Dogs*: Products in the category are clearly candidates for deletion. Such products have low market shares and unlike problem children, have no real prospect for growth. Eliminating a dog is not always necessary, since there are strategies for dogs that could make them profitable in the short term. These strategies involve "harvesting" these products by eliminating marketing support and selling the product only to intensely loyal consumers who will buy in the absence of advertising. However, over the long term companies will seek to eliminate dogs.

As can be seen from the description of the four BCG alternatives, products are evaluated as producers or users of cash. Products with a positive cash flow will finance high-opportunity products that need cash. The emphasis on cash flow stems from management's belief that it is better to finance new entries and to support existing products with internally produced funds than to increase debt or equity in the company. Based on this belief, companies will normally take money from cash cows and divert it to stars and to some problem children.

The hope is that the stars will turn into cash cows and the problem children will turn into stars. The dogs will continue to receive lower funding and eventually be dropped.

3

Facility Location and Layout

FACILITY MANAGEMENT

Facility management is an interdisciplinary field primarily devoted to the maintenance and care of commercial or institutional buildings, such as hospitals, clinics, hotels, resorts, schools, office complexes, sports arenas or convention centres. Duties may include the care of air conditioning, electric power, plumbing and lighting systems; cleaning; decoration; groundskeeping and security. Some or all of these duties can be assisted by computer programmes.

These duties can be thought of as non-core or support services, because they are not the primary business of the owner organization. It is the role of the facility management function to coordinate and oversee the safe, secure, and environmentally-sound operations and maintenance of these assets in a cost effective manner aimed at long-term preservation of the asset value, and also other janitorial duties such as making sure the environment is properly cleaned and sanitized for its tenants.

In those cases where the operation of the facility directly involves the occupants and/or customers of the owner organization, the satisfactory delivery of facility-related services to these people will be an important consideration too; hence, the term "end-user satisfaction"is often used both as a goal and a measure of performance. The term facility management is similar to property management although not exactly the same. While both manage the day to day operations of a facility the property such as cleaning, maintenance and security, similar to Janitors, one must not confuse it with such a title. The property manager has an expanded role which includes leasing and marketing activities whereas the facility manager role focuses on existing tenants who usually are owner occupants.

An important feature of facility management is that it takes account of human needs of its tenants in the use of buildings and other constructed facilities. These softer factors complement the harder factors associated with the maintenance and care of engineering services installations. Atkin and Brooks, an important concept in the facility management field is that of outsourcing, where the owner enters into an arrangement with external organizations to provide one or more services in preference to their being provided through internal arrangements.

The reasons for this action can vary, including lack of in-house resources, lack of expertise and pressure to reduce costs. Unfortunately, confusion can exist because of the close association that facility management has with outsourcing. The two concepts are not synonymous; rather, outsourcing is one means for providing facility-related services to the owner organization.

Facility management is performed during the operational phase of a building's life cycle, which normally extends over many decades. As such, it will represent a continuous process of service provision to support the owner's core business and one where improvement will be sought on a continuous basis. It is essential that decision-making in the preceding design and construction phases is therefore properly informed about operational requirements if the facility is to provide optimal support to the owner's business.

In this connection, facility management can be seen as an integral part of a coordinated and controlled process of design, engineering, construction and operations. Where a facility is provided on a turnkey basis, for example design-build-finance-operate, the consortium responsible for the delivery of the physical asset and then operating the core service will need to understand implicitly the day-to-day demands in managing that facility. Under such arrangements - typically public-private partnerships- owner-operators must fully integrate operational thinking into early design decision-making. A major challenge facing facility owners is reducing demand for energy for economic reasons, but also because energy consumption goes hand-in-hand with carbon emissions. Reducing energy during the operational phase of a facility's life similarly reduces carbon emissions. When considering that 30-40% of a country's total carbon emissions is attributable to buildings and other constructed facilities, it is clear that operations and, hence, facility management have a significant role to play.

FACILITY LOCATION

The general facility location problem is: given a set of facility locations and a set of customers who are served from the facilities then:

- Which facilities should be used
- Which customers should be served from which facilities so as to minimise the total cost of serving all the customers.

Typically here facilities are regarded as "open" or "closed" and there is a fixed cost which is incurred if a facility is open. Which facilities to have open and which closed is our decision.

We show a graphical representation of the problem.

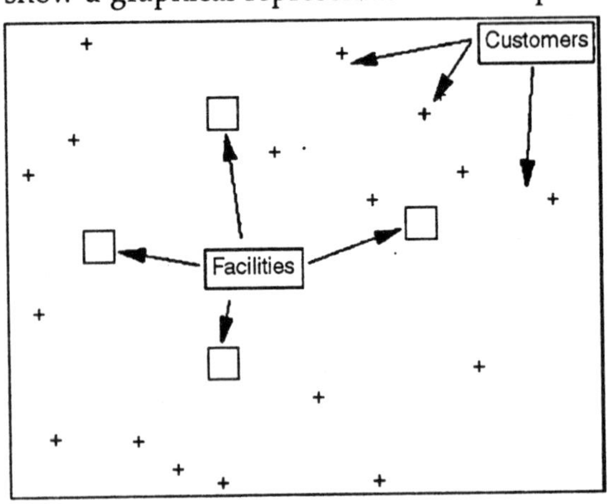

One possible solution is.

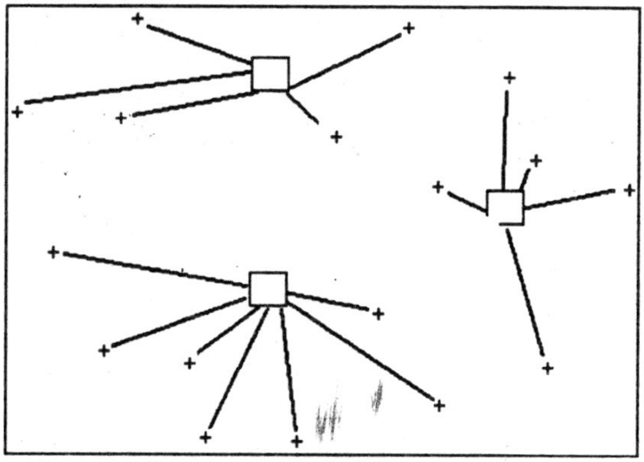

Other factors often encountered here:

- Customers have an associated demand with capacities on the total customer demand that can be served from a facility
- Customers being served by more than one facility.

EXAMPLE

The problems of facility size and facility location are very closely linked and should be considered *simultaneously*. In fact the package used here disregards the problem of facility size and deals only with facility location. We shall illustrate the problem of facility location by means of an example. At Gotham City airport terminal there are 10 arrival gates. A pictorial representation of the terminal is given with the location of the gates being:

Gate	x coordinate	y coordinate
A	0	2
B	2	4
C	5	6
D	5	10
E	7	15
F	10	15
G	12	10
H	12	6
I	15	4
J	20	2

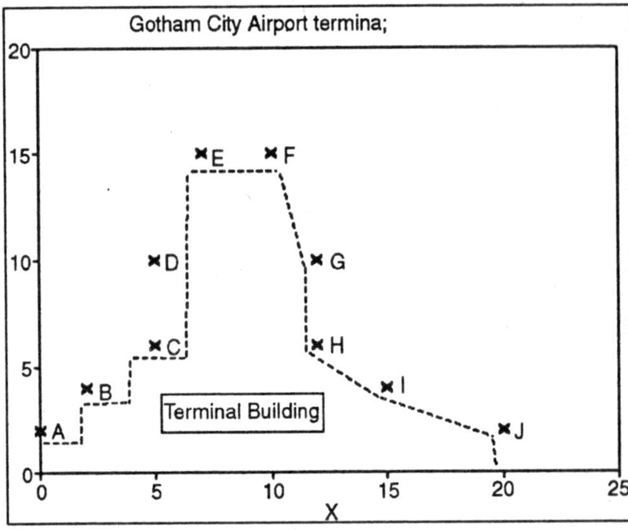

Luggage from arriving flights is unloaded at these gates and moved to a passenger luggage pick-up point. It is estimated that the number of pieces of luggage arriving per day at each gate is: 3600, 2500, 1800, 2200, 1000, 4500, 5600, 1400, 1800 and 3000 respectively. Where should the passenger luggage pick-up point be located in order to minimize movement of luggage?

SOLUTION

In order to logically locate the passenger luggage pick-up point we need to make use of the amount of luggage flowing from the gates to the pick-up point. Logically a gate from which there is a large flow should be nearer to the pick-up point than a gate with a small flow.

Informally therefore we would like to position the pick-up point so as to *minimise* the sum over all gates g. This approach to choosing the location of the pick-up point is precisely the approach used by the facility location module in the package.

Typically in such location problems we are concerned with a *load-distance* score. The initial input to the package for this problem.

Problem Specification

Problem Type
◎ Facility Location
O Functional Layout
O Line Balancing

Objective Criterion
◎ Minimization
O Maximization

Problem Title: Gotham City Terminal

Number of Existing Facilities: 10

Number of Planned New Facilities: 1

Number of Coordinate Dimensions (2/3): 2

ok | Cancel | Help

Note here the package terminology is somewhat peculiar:

- *Existing facilities*: Are points where we know in advance exactly where they are and they are fixed in position
- *New facilities*: Are points where we do not know where they are and their location is what we have to determine

In order to enter the data relating to the gates we can ignore the columns in the package input that are concerned with flows between existing facilities - here all flows are from the existing facilities to the new facility.

Facility Number	Facility Name	To New 1 Flow/Unit Cost	Location X Axis	Location Y Axis
Existing 1	A	3600	0	2
Existing 2	B	2500	2	4
Existing 3	C	1800	5	6
Existing 4	D	2200	5	10
Existing 5	E	1000	7	15
Existing 6	F	4500	10	15
Existing 7	G	5600	12	10
Existing 8	H	1400	12	6
Existing 8	I	1800	15	4
Existing 10	J	3000	20	2
New 1	New			

Note here that in solving the problem we need to specify the appropriate *distance model*. This is because as we do not *yet* know where the new facility is to be we cannot specify the distance between it and the gates *without* a general expression for calculating the distance between two locations.

If (x_i, y_i) and (x_j, y_j) represent the coordinates of two locations i and j then the distance model measures can be:

- *Rectilinear*: Distance between i and j is: $|x_i - x_j| + |y_i - y_j|$
- *Euclidean*: Distance between i and j is: $[(x_i - x_j)^2 + (y_i - y_j)^2]^{0.5}$
- *Squared Euclidean*: Distance between i and j is: $(x_i - x_j)^2 + (y_i - y_j)^2$

The rectilinear distance measure is often used for factories, American cities, etc which are laid out in the form of a rectangular grid.

For this reason it is sometimes called the Manhattan distance measure. The Euclidean distance measure is used where genuine straight line travel is possible. The squared Euclidean distance measure is used where straight line travel is possible but where we wish to discourage excessive distances.

The output from the package for each of the distance measures is:

11-09-2000 14:33:37	Facility Name	X Axis	Y Axis	Flow to All Facilities	Cost to All facilities
1	A	0	2	3600	50400
2	B	2	4	2500	25000
3	C	5	6	1800	9000
4	D	5	10	2200	19800
5	E	7	15	1000	12000
6	F	10	15	4500	40500
7	G	12	10	5600	33600
8	H	12	6	1400	2800
9	I	15	4	1800	12600
10	J	20	2	3000	42000
11	New	10	6	0	0
	Total			27400	247700
	Distance	Measure:	Rectilinear		

Fig. Rectilinear

11-09-2000 14:33:37	Facility Name	X Axis	Y Axis	Flow to All Facilities	Cost to All facilities
1	A	0	2	3600	44,266.76
2	B	2	4	2500	23,819.75
3	C	5	6	1800	10,667.54
4	D	5	10	2200	11,483.13
5	E	7	15	1000	6,776.21
6	F	10	15	4500	27,073.98
7	G	12	10	5600	11,965.45
8	H	12	6	1400	4,938.54
9	I	15	4	1800	12,556.59
10	J	20	2	3000	36,299.11
11	New	9.05	7.67	0	0
	Total			27400	189,847.06
	Distance	Measure:	Euclidean		

Fig. Euclidean

11-09-2000 14:33:37	Facility Name	X Axis	Y Axis	Flow to All Facilities	Cost to All facilities
1	A	0	2	3600	410570
2	B	2	4	2500	157,928.28
3	C	5	6	1800	34,547.77
4	D	5	10	2200	48,070.31
5	E	7	15	1000	57,966.92
6	F	10	15	4500	245,971.59
7	G	12	10	5600	79,154.93
8	H	12	6	1400	16,069.03
9	I	15	4	1800	87,917.11
10	J	20	2	3000	456,010,25
11	New	9.05	7.67	0	0
	Total			27400	1,594,206.25
	Distance	Measure:	Squared	Euclidean	

Fig. Squared Euclidean

From the package output we can see that the location for the luggage pick-up point should be:

Distance measure	x coordinate	y coordinate
Rectilinear	10	6
Euclidean	10.12	8.98
Squared Euclidean	9.05	7.67

The picture shows these three possible locations with respect to the terminal.

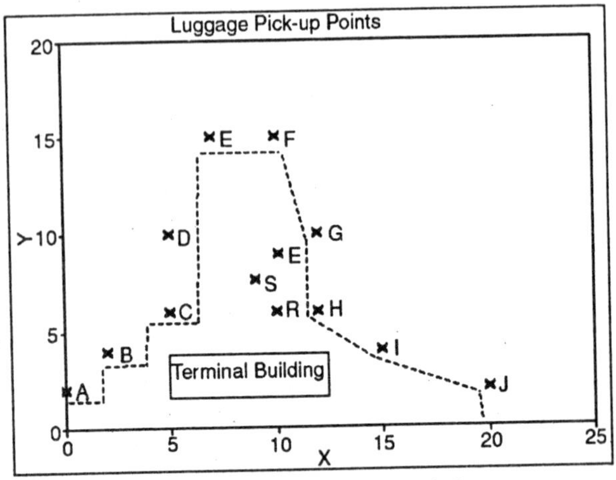

Note here that the initial choice of distance measure is often between rectilinear and Euclidean. If the luggage flows in an Euclidean manner then choosing to use squared Euclidean, rather than Euclidean, penalises excessively long distances.

One point to note about the picture is that we are not really interested in determining positions down to the nearest millimetre. Instead we are using the package to get an *indication* of the approximate region where it would be sensible to site a luggage pick-up point. Note too that the package uses a "centre of gravity" approach to decide where to locate a single pick-up point.

CONCENTRATOR

Suppose now that in the example we just considered the luggage pick-up point for gates C to H is merely acting as a concentrator, concentrating luggage before passing it to the other pick-up point, which collects luggage from gates A,B, I and J directly. In this system all passengers see is a single pick-up point at which they collect their luggage. To locate this concentrator we make use of flows between new facilities. Here the total amount of luggage collected from C to H will flow to the final pick-up point from this intermediate concentrator. This will total 1800+2200+1000+4500+5600+140 =16500 pieces of luggage. Hence the input to the package is:

Facility Number	Facility Name	To New 1 Flow/Unit Cost	To New 2 Flow/Unit Cost	Location X Axis	Location Y Axis
Existing 1	A	0	3600	0	2
Existing 2	B	0	2500	2	4
Existing 3	C	1800		5	6
Existing 4	D	2200		5	10
Existing 5	E	1000		7	15
Existing 6	F	4500		10	15
Existing 7	G	5600		12	10
Existing 8	H	1400		12	6
Existing 9	I	0	1800	15	4
Existing 10	J	0	3000	20	2
New 1	Concentrator		16500		
New 2	Final				

The solutions are:

11-12-2000	New Facility	X Axis	Y Axis
1	Concentrator	10.00	6.12
2	Final	10.00	6.12
Total	Flow to&From	New Location	= 43900
Total	Cost to&From	New Location	= 247,818.11
(by	Rctilinear	Distance)	

Fig. Rectilinear

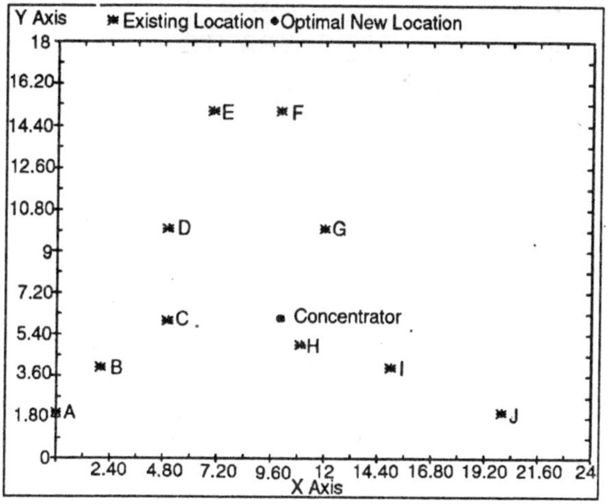

So in this case the final and concentrator locations coincide.

11-12-2000	New Facility	X Axis	Y Axis
1	Concentrator	9.46	6.12
2	Final	8.94	6.12
Total	Flow to&From	New Location	= 43900
Total	Cost to&From	New Location	= 198,276.50
(by	Euclidean	Distance)	

Fig. Euclidean

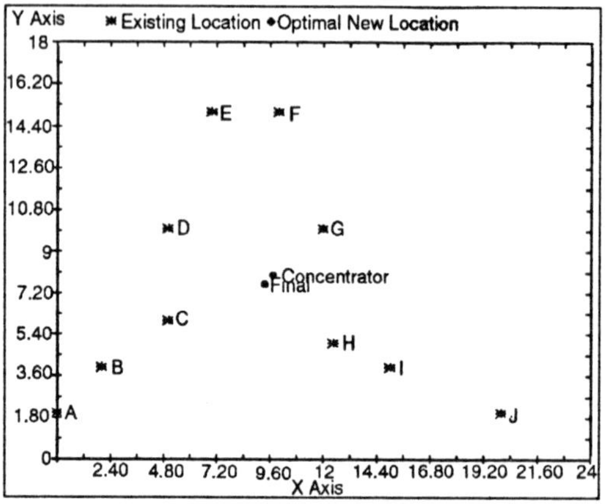

So in this case the final and concentrator locations are near to each other.

11-12-2000	New Facility	X Axis	Y Axis
1	Concentrator	9.17	8.59
2	Final	8.88	6.28
Total	Flow to&From	New Location	= 43900
Total	Cost to&From	New Location	=1,469,664.25
(by	Squared	Euclidean	Distance)

Fig. Squared Euclidean

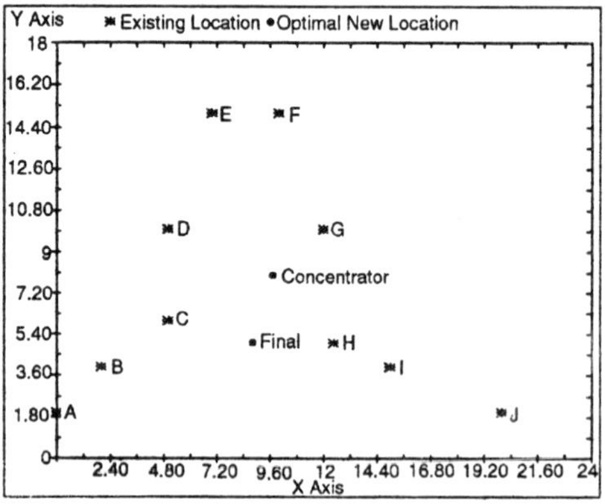

So in this case the final and concentrator locations are not particularly close to each other.

IMPORTANCE OF FACILITY LOCATION

- Location of facility decides the production technology and cost structure. Like location in under developed country will have labour intensive technology.
- Location depends on size and nature of business. A large scale industry needs huge investment and option for extension and can not be shifted in future.
- Location affected the firms ability to serve the customers quickly and efficiently.
- Location affects the competitive advantage.
- Optimum location reduces transporation cost, labour cost, taxes, etc.

FACILITY LAYOUT

A typical manufacturing plant has a number of diverse activities interacting with each other. Thus, raw materials arrive at a shipping dock, they are unpacked and checked in a quality control area, they may then be processed through several processing areas, and finally the finished product again passes through the shipping dock.

In addition to areas specifically related to production, there must be dressing rooms, lunch rooms, and restrooms for employees; offices for supervision, design, and production control; and space for inventory and aisles. In fact, a plant may be viewed as a large number of finite geometric areas arranged on the floor space of the building.

The problem of arranging these areas in an effective manner is the facility layout problem. Clearly, the layout problem has relevance in many areas of facility and equipment design, from the layout of the rooms in a home to the layout of chips on an electronic circuit board.

Although the facility layout problem may arise in many contexts, in this part we assume we are dealing with a plant manufacturing products for sale.

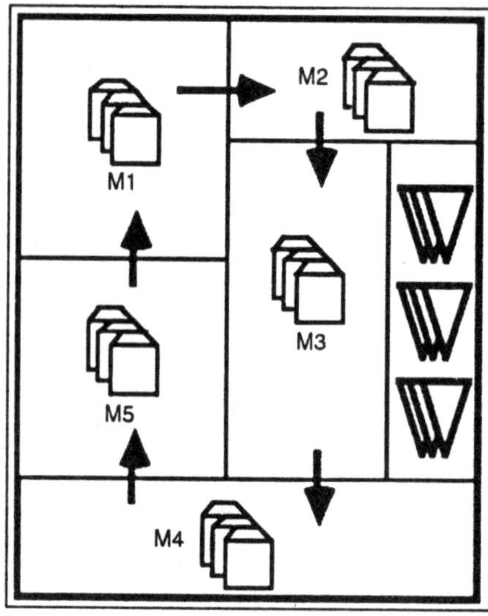

Fig. Facility layout

FACILITY LAYOUT AND DESIGN

Facility layout and design is an important component of a business's overall operations, both in terms of maximizing the effectiveness of production processes and meeting employee needs and/or desires. Writing in *Production and Operations Management,* Howard J. Weiss and Mark E. Gershon defined facility layout as "the physical arrangement of everything needed for the product or service, including machines, personnel, raw materials, and finished goods. The criteria for a good layout necessarily relate to people, materials, machines, and their interactions."

FACTORS IN DETERMINING LAYOUT AND DESIGN

Small business owners need to consider many operational factors when building or renovating a facility for maximum layout effectiveness.

These criteria include the following:

- *Ease of future expansion or change:*Facilities should be designed so that they can be easily expanded or adjusted to meet changing production needs. "Although redesigning a facility is a major, expensive undertaking not to be done lightly, there is always the possibility that a redesign will be necessary," said Weiss and Gershon. "Therefore, any design should be flexible.... Flexible manufacturing systems most often are highly automated facilities having intermediate-volume production of a variety of products. Their goal is to minimize changeover or setup times for producing the different products while still achieving close to assembly line production rates."

- *Flow of movement*: The facility design should reflect a recognition of the importance of smooth process flow. In the case of factory facilities, the editors of *How to Run a Small Business* state that "ideally, the plan will show the raw materials entering your plant at one end and the finished product emerging at the other. The flow need not be a straight line. Parallel flows, U-shaped patterns, or even a zig-zag that ends up with the finished product back at the shipping and receiving bays can be functional. However, backtracking is to be avoided in whatever pattern is chosen. When parts and materials move against or across the overall flow, personnel and paperwork become confused, parts become lost, and the attainment of coordination becomes complicated."
- *Materials handling*: Small business owners should make certain that the facility layout makes it possible to handle materials. In an orderly, efficient—and preferably simple—manner.
- *Output needs*: The facility should be laid out in a way that is conducive to helping the business meet its production needs.
- *Space utilization*: This aspect of facility design includes everything from making sure that traffic lanes are wide enough to making certain that inventory storage warehouses or rooms utilize as much vertical space as possible.

- *Shipping and receiving*: The J.K. Lasser Institute counseled small business owners to leave ample room for this aspect of operations. "While space does tend to fill itself up, receiving and shipping rarely get enough space for the work to be done effectively," it said in *How to Run a Small Business.*
- *Ease of communication and support*: Facilities should be laid out so that communication within various areas of the business and interactions with vendors and customers can be done in an easy and effective manner. Similarly, support areas should be stationed in areas that help them to serve operating areas.
- *Impact on employee morale and job satisfaction*: Since countless studies have indicated that employee morale has a major impact on productivity, Weiss and Gershon counsel owners and managers to heed this factor when pondering facility design alternatives: "Some ways layout design can increase morale are obvious, such as providing for light-colored walls, windows, space. Other ways are less obvious and not directly related to the production process. Some examples are including a cafeteria or even a gymnasium in the facility design. Again, though, there are costs to be traded off. That is, does the increase in morale due to a cafeteria increase productivity to the extent that the increased productivity covers the cost of building and staffing the cafeteria."
- *Promotional value*: If the business commonly receives visitors in the form of customers, vendors, investors, etc., the small business owner may want to make sure that the facility layout is an attractive one that further burnishes the company's reputation. Design factors that can influence the degree of attractiveness of a facility include not only the design of the production area itself, but the impact that it has on, for instance, ease of fulfilling maintenance/cleaning tasks.
- *Safety*: The facility layout should enable the business

to effectively operate in accordance with Occupational Safety and Health Assocation guideliness and other legal restrictions.

"Facility layout must be considered very carefully because we do not want to constantly redesign the facility," summarized Weiss and Gershon. "Some of the goals in designing the facility are to ensure a minimum amount of materials handling, to avoid bottlenecks, to minimize machine interference, to ensure high employee morale and safety, and to ensure flexibility.

Essentially, there are two distinct types of layout. *Product layout* is synonymous with assembly line and is oriented toward the products that are being made. *Process layout* is oriented around the processes that are used to make the products.

Generally, product layout is applicable for high-volume repetitive operations, while process layout is applicable for low-volume custom-made goods."

DIFFERENCES BETWEEN OFFICE AND FACTORY LAYOUTS

Offices and manufacturing facilities are typically designed in much different ways—a reflection of the disparate products that the two entities make. "A factory produces things," wrote Stephan Konz in *Facility Design*.

"These things are moved with conveyors and lift trucks; factory utilities include gas, water, compressed air, waste disposal, and large amounts of power as well as telephones and computer networks. A layout criterion is minimization of transportation cost." Konz pointed out, however, that the mandate of business offices is to produce information, whether disseminated in physical, electronic or oral form. "Office layout criteria, although hard to quantify, are minimization of communication cost and maximization of employee productivity," wrote Konz.

Layout requirements can also differ dramatically by industry. The needs of service-oriented businesses, for instance, are often predicated on whether customers receive their services at the physical location of the business or whether the business goes to the customer's home or place of business to provide the service. In the latter instances, these businesses will likely have facility layouts that emphasize storage space for equipment, chemicals, and paperwork rather than spacious customer waiting areas.

Manufacturers may also have significantly different facility layouts, depending on the unique needs that they have. After all, the production challenges associated with producing jars of varnish or mountaineering equipment are apt to be considerably different than those of making truck chassis or foam beach toys. Retail outlets comprise yet another business sector that have unique facility layout needs. Such establishments typically emphasize sales floor space, inventory logistics, foot traffic issues, and overall store attractiveness when studying facility layout issues.

Konz also observed that differences in factory and office layouts can often be traced to user expectations. "Historically, office workers have been much more concerned with status and aesthetics than factory workers," he noted. "A key consideration in many office layouts is 'Who will get the best window location?'

To show their status, executives expect, in addition to preferred locations, to have larger amounts of space. Rank expects more privacy and more plush physical surroundings." In addition, he stated, "Offices are designed to be 'tasteful' and to 'reflect the organization's approach to business dealings.' " Conversely, in the factory setting, aesthetic elements take a back seat to utility.

Given these emphases, it is not surprising that, as a general rule, office workers will enjoy advantages over their material production brethren in such areas as ventilation, lighting, acoustics, and climate control.

TYPES OF LAYOUTS

There are several alternative layout types that are appropriate for different product mixes and production volumes. Determination of the layout type is a major design decision because it impacts on so many other aspects of the production system. In the Job Shop Layout, machines are grouped according to function into machine centres. Orders for individual products are routed through the various machine centres to obtain the required processing.

This layout may be appropriate when there are many different products, each with a low volume of production. Machines are general purpose, within their general function area, so that a wide variety of products can be handled. Because the expense of automation may be too great to be justified by the low volume, the machines in this arrangement will probably be at a relatively low level of automation. Workers will be highly skilled.

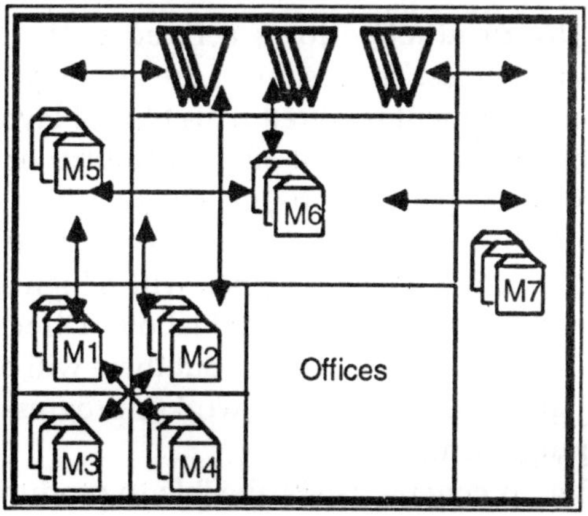

Fig. Job Shop Layout

Production scheduling is difficult with this type of arrangement because the level and type of work is highly variable. This results in large amounts of work-in-process, long product lead times, and high levels of management interaction. Typically there is a high degree of product movement required by the long and variable routes of individual products through the system. The costs for setting up machines to produce the various products will be high because of the variety of different products and small lot sizes. The arrangement can adapt readily to changes in product volume and design because of its inherent flexibility.

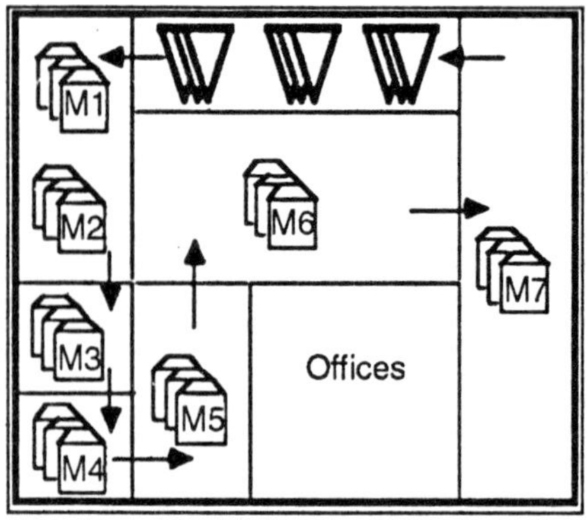

Fig. Assembly Line or Flow Shop Layout

Here the product follows a fixed path through the production resources. The resources are arranged to minimize the material movement required. This type of layout is typical for an assembly line where a single product, or a few very similar products, passes through the line in a continuous fashion. Because of the high volume of production, the machines on the line can be designed with a high level of fixed automation, with very little manual labour. Direct labour will be much less than for the job shop, but there will be high costs for maintenance. Setup costs and work-inprogress will be low for this arrangement.

The line, in general, is not flexible to product or volume changes. It is very sensitive to failures that cause the entire line to shut down. The arrangement is also appropriate for a flow shop that may have a number of products that all pass through the machine centres in the same order. In this case, the machines implementing the system may or may not be automated depending on the product mix and volume, but one would expect a higher level of automation than for the job shop.

The product mix appropriate for this arrangement is similar to that of the job shop. Products are grouped into classes that have some similarity with respect to processing. A manufacturing cell is designed for each group consisting of machines particularly adapted to the processing required. The figure shows the cells as collections of dissimilar machines. Because the range of products manufactured by each cell is less than that for the job shop, the machines and workers can be more specialized.

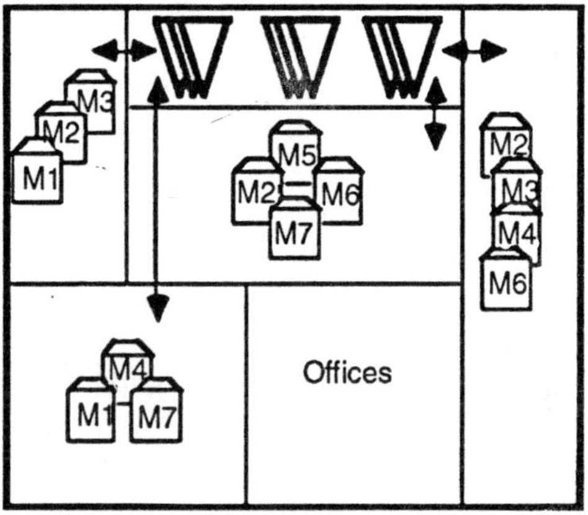

Fig. Group Technology Layout

Typically, the workers in a cell are given more of the responsibility for production scheduling of a product class. This, together with the start-to-finish nature of the processing, results in more interesting jobs for the workers. The group technology arrangement requires less setup time and cost than the job shop because of the greater specialization of function. It is compatible with the just-in-time concept of manufacture, so prevalent today, because of the smaller lot sizes made possible by the low setup costs.

Often the level of automation with group technology is low, indicating the dependence of the concept on the skill of the labour force. Many companies have, however, introduced highly automated flexible manufacturing cells into the system. Because the cell has a smaller range of products than the entire plant, it is easier to design the automation to handle the set of products in a group.

The group technology approach is more sensitive to changes in product mix and volume than the job shop, again because of the specialization introduced because of the manufacturing cell approach. When a product requires processing in more than one cell, problems similar to those of the job shop are introduced.

FIXED LOCATION LAYOUT

For tasks on large objects such as the manufacture of an electrical generator, the construction of a building, or the repair of a large airplane, the machines implementing the operation must come to the product, rather than the product moving to the machines. Here the question is more often the scheduling of operations rather than the layout of machines. For tasks on large objects such as the manufacture of an electrical generator, the construction of a building, or the repair of a large airplane, the machines implementing the operation must come to the product, rather than the product moving to the machines. Here the question is more often the scheduling of operations rather than the layout of machines.

FLEXIBLE MANUFACTURING SYSTEMS

The FMS is a system with automated material handling moving individual units of product between automated processors. Robotic manipulators often handle material. Using computer controlled movement and processing, a wide variety of products can be manufactured. All of this is to be accomplished with very low setup time, great flexibility of function, and very little manual labour. The diversity of possible FMS, and the rapidly changing technologies, makes detailed consideration of the design of FMS beyond the scope of this text. Certainly many of the classical questions associated with facility design are no longer relevant for the FMS. In this text we consider the FMS as just another kind of machine, with perhaps a very broad range of capabilities.

LAYOUT PROBLEM

The layout problem is to arrange the physical spaces required for several departments in a given space provided for the departments. In practice the facility layout problem is often solved by intuition, using the artistic and spatial skills of the human designer; however, when there are quantitative considerations associated with the layout problem, the human is at a disadvantage as compared to the computer. We concentrate on computerized procedures for solving the layout problem. There are a variety of problems regarding layout one might encounter. In this part we explain the problem by specifying the data and describing the decisions.

INPUT DATA

Here we are considering the problem of arranging several departments on a plant with a single floor and fixed dimensions.

Certain data is necessary to describe the layout problem.

- Number of departments, n,
- Physical area of each department, Ai for $i = 1 \ldots n$
- Physical dimensions of the plant in which the departments are to be placed: Length, L, and Width, W.
- Product flow between every pair of departments: f_{ij} for $i = 1 \ldots n$ and $j = 1 \ldots n$.
- Material handling cost between every pair of departments measured in dollars per unit-foot: c_{ij} for $i = 1 \ldots n$ and $j = 1 \ldots n$.

DISTANCE

Our models involve the distance from one department to another. The distance depends on the layout. To illustrate consider a problem with ten departments with each department having an area of 100 square feet. The ten departments are to be placed in an area that is 50 feet long by 20 feet wide. One layout is shown in Figure.

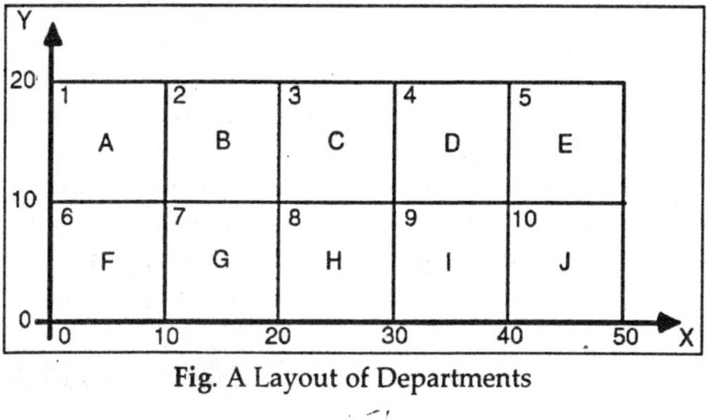

Fig. A Layout of Departments

This is only one of many possible layouts. If we assume that the departments must maintain a square shape, every permutation of the letters A through J is a different layout. There are $n!$ permutations. The matrix as in Fig. describes the flow between the departments. This is called the *From-To* matrix because an element (i, j) contains f_{ij}, the flow from department i to department j.

From \ To	A	B	C	D	E	F	G	H	I	J
A					5				1	9
B				3	4		1			
C				1			9			2
D							6		1	
E						8	3			
F							2	5		
G								6		
H									8	
I										
J										

Fig. From-to Matrix for the Office Example

The criterion for the layout problem involves the distance between departments. First we must prescribe the end points for the distance measurement. Here we assume that distances are measured between the centroids or centres of gravity of departments. Second, we must specify the route of travel. One possibility is that flow will follow a straight-line path. This is the Euclidean measure. More common in layout analysis, is to assume that flow travels via paths that are parallel to the axes of the layout. This is the rectilinear measure.

The centroids are specified in terms of the coordinate system as

$x(i)$ = x-coordinate of the centroid of department i, and

$y(i)$ = y-coordinate of the centroid of department i.

The centroid is the same as the centre of the area when the department is rectangular. For a more general shape, the centroid is the centre of gravity of area. In the example case of Fig. we have the centroids as follows.

Department A: $x(A) = 5$, $y(A) = 15$.
Department B: $x(B) = 15$, $y(B) = 15$.
Department C: $x(C) = 25$, $y(C) = 15$.

The distance between two departments by a rectilinear measure is,

$$d_{ij} = |x(i) - x(j)| + |y(i) - y(j)|.$$

Here the vertical lines indicate absolute value. Fig. shows both the flow and distance between all pairs of departments on the from-to chart. The flow appears the diagonals and the distance appears.

From \ To	A	B	C	D	E	F	G	H	I	J	Sum
A					5 / 40				1 / 40	9 / 50	690
B				3 / 20	4 / 30		1 / 10				190
C				1 / 10			9 / 20			2 / 30	250
D							6 / 30		1 / 10		190
E						8 / 50	3 / 40				520
F							2 / 10	5 / 20			120
G								6 / 10			60
H									8 / 10		80
I											0
J											0

Fig. Computation of the Total Distance Traveled

CRITERION FOR COMPARISON

The flow multiplied by the distance and summed over all cells of the chart. We compute the cost for the flow from i to j as the product of the material handling cost, the flow and the distance between the departments. The cost of the layout is the sum of the flow cost.

$$z = \sum_{i=1}^{n} \sum_{j=1}^{n} c_{ij} f_{ij} d_{ij}$$

The cost associated with each row of the chart is shown at the right of Figure. The cost of the layout is the sum of the row costs. The factors *cij* and *fij* are given as data, but the factor *dij* depends on the layout.

FINDING A LAYOUT WITH THE CRAFT METHOD

The plant layout problem is to find an arrangement of departments that minimizes the total distance traveled. This measure is called the "cost" in the following. The problem is difficult for the human because of the large number of calculations required to evaluate the cost of an alternative. The computer can greatly aid in the layout determination, but the computer also has its weaknesses.

The problem of finding the optimum arrangement is a very difficult one for mathematical optimization. Rather than attempt to obtain the optimum, we use a heuristic approach that tries to better a given solution by switching pairs of departments. At each iteration, every pair of departments is considered for switching locations. The pair that gives the greatest savings in cost will be interchanged and the process will continue by looking for another pair to switch. If no pair results in a positive savings the process stops.

This is commonly called the CRAFT* method. Only the centroids of the two departments are affected. For example, if department A is switched with department H, the centroid of A becomes, while the centroid of H becomes. All other departments remain fixed. The only effect on the cost of the layout is related to the flows entering or leaving the two departments.

The cost of the flow between the other departments is unaffected because the distances between these departments have not changed. This is the logic used by the solution method. The cost savings associated with switching two departments is determined by calculating the effect of interchanging the centroids of the two departments. There are several reasons why the CRAFT method may not yield the optimum solution. First, it may be necessary to switch more than two departments to find a better solution. More complex implementations of the method do allow switching three or more departments, but this increases considerably the computation time.

Problems for which the department areas are not equal cause several new difficulties. If two departments are not of equal area, switching their locations may not be equivalent to switching the centroids. In fact, if two unequally sized departments are not physically adjacent it will not be possible to interchange them.

The method allows departments of different areas to be switched only if they are physically adjacent. Allowing departments with different areas to switch causes another problem. When a small department is interchanged with a larger department there are a number of possible arrangements of the two areas with a corresponding variety of centroids.

It is impossible to enforce a requirement that areas remain rectangular, so often the interchange of such departments causes irregularities in shape that grow worse as the algorithm progresses. Because the change in cost is not exactly represented by the interchange of centroids, the estimate of the cost reduction may not be accurate.

It is possible that the programme will switch two areas and have the total cost increase. To guard against cycling, the method stops if a certain number of successive iterations do not result in an improvement. Since the CRAFT method does not guarantee and optimum solution, it should be run several times with different initial layouts.

4

Planning

CAPACITY PLANNING

Capacity planning is the process of determining the production capacity needed by an organization to meet changing demands for its products. In the context of capacity planning, "capacity" is the maximum amount of work that an organization is capable of completing in a given period of time. The phrase is also used in business computing as a synonym for Capacity Management.

A discrepancy between the capacity of an organization and the demands of its customers results in inefficiency, either in under-utilized resources or unfulfilled customers. The goal of capacity planning is to minimize this discrepancy. Demand for an organization's capacity varies based on changes in production output, such as increasing or decreasing the production quantity of an existing product, or producing new products. Better utilization of existing capacity can be accomplished through improvements in overall equipment effectiveness. Capacity can be increased through introducing new techniques, equipment and materials, increasing the number of workers or machines, increasing the number of shifts, or acquiring additional production facilities.

Capacity is calculated: (number of machines or workers) × (number of shifts) × (utilization) × (efficiency).

The broad classes of capacity planning are lead strategy, lag strategy, and match strategy:

- Lead strategy is adding capacity in anticipation of an increase in demand. Lead strategy is an aggressive strategy with the goal of luring customers away from the company's competitors. The possible disadvantage to this strategy is that it often results in excess inventory, which is costly and often wasteful.

- Lag strategy refers to adding capacity only after the organization is running at full capacity or beyond due to increase in demand. This is a more conservative strategy. It decreases the risk of waste, but it may result in the loss of possible customers.
- Match strategy is adding capacity in small amounts in response to changing demand in the market. This is a more moderate strategy.

In the context of systems engineering, capacity planning is used during system design and system performance monitoring. Capacity planning is long-term decision that establishes a firms' overall level of resources.

It extends over time horizon long enough to obtain resources. Capacity decisions affect the production lead time, customer responsiveness, operating cost and company ability to compete. Inadequate capacity planning can lead to the loss of the customer and business.

Excess capacity can drain the company's resources and prevent investments into more lucrative ventures. The question of when capacity should be increased and by how much are the critical decisions.

LONG-TERM CAPACITY PLANNING

Over the long term, capacity planning relates primarily to strategic issues involving the firm's major production facilities. In addition, long-term capacity issues are interrelated with location decisions. Technology and transferability of the process to other products is also intertwined with long-term capacity planning.

Long-term capacity planning may evolve when short-term changes in capacity are insufficient. For example, if the firm's addition of a third shift to its current two-shift plan still does not produce enough output, and subcontracting arrangements cannot be made, one feasible alternative is to add capital equipment and modify the layout of the plant. It may even be desirable to add additional plant space or to construct a new facility.

SHORT-TERM CAPACITY PLANNING

In the short term, capacity planning concerns issues of scheduling, labour shifts, and balancing resource capacities. The goal of short-term capacity planning is to handle unexpected shifts in demand in an efficient economic manner. The time frame for short-term planning is frequently only a few days but may run as long as six months.

Alternatives for making short-term changes in capacity are fairly numerous and can even include the decision to not meet demand at all. The easiest and most commonly-used method to increase capacity in the short term is working overtime. This is a flexible and inexpensive alternative. While the firm has to pay one and one half times the normal labour rate, it foregoes the expense of hiring, training, and paying additional benefits.

When not used abusively, most workers appreciate the opportunity to earn extra wages. If overtime does not provide enough short-term capacity, other resource-increasing alternatives are available. These include adding shifts, employing casual or part-time workers, the use of floating workers, leasing workers, and facilities subcon-tracting.

Firms may also increase capacity by improving the use of their resources. The most common alternatives in this category are worker cross training and overlapping or staggering shifts. Most manufacturing firms inventory some output ahead of demand so that any need for a capacity change is absorbed by the inventory buffer. From a technical perspective, firms may initiate a process design intended to increase productivity at work stations.

Manufacturers can also shift demand to avoid capacity requirement fluctuation by backlogging, queuing demand, or lengthening the firm's lead times. Service firms accomplish the same results through scheduling appointments and reservations. A more creative approach is to modify the output.

Standardizing the output or offering complimentary services are examples. In services, one might allow customers to do some of the process work themselves. Another alternative—reducing quality—is an undesirable yet viable tactic.

Finally, the firm may attempt to modify demand. Changing the price and promoting the product are common. Another alternative is to partition demand by initiating a yield or revenue management system. Utilities also report success in shifting demand by the use of "off-peak" pricing.

CAPACITY-PLANNING TECHNIQUES

There are four procedures for capacity planning; capacity planning using overall factors, capacity bills, resource profiles, and capacity requirements planning. The first three are rough-cut approaches that can be used with or without manufacturing resource planning systems. CRP is used in conjunction with MRP systems. Capacity using overall factors is a simple, manual approach to capacity planning that is based on the master production schedule and production standards that convert required units of finished goods into historical loads on each work centre.

Bills of capacity is a procedure based on the MPS. Instead of using historical ratios, however, it utilizes the bills of material and routing sheet. Capacity requirements can then be determined by multiplying the number of units required by the MPS by the time needed to produce each. Resource profiles are the same as bills of capacity, except lead times are included so that workloads fall into the correct periods.

Capacity requirements planning is only applicable in firms using MRP or MRP II. CRP uses the information from one of the previous rough-cut methods, plus MRP outputs on existing inventories and lot sizing. The result is a tabular load report for each work centre or a graphical load profile for helping plan-production requirements. This will indicate where capacity is inadequate or idle, allowing for imbalances to be corrected by shifts in personnel or equipment or the use of overtime or added shifts. Finite capacity scheduling is an extension of CRP that simulates job order stopping and starting to produce a detailed schedule that provides a set of start and finish dates for each operation at each work centre.

A failure to understand the critical nature of managing capacity can lead to chaos and serious customer service problems. If there is a mismatch between available and required capacity, adjustments should be made. However, it should be noted that firms cannot have perfectly-balanced material and capacity plans that easily accommodate emergency orders. If flexibility is the firm's competitive priority, excess capacity would be appropriate.

MANUFACTURING PLANNING AND CONTROL

Manufacturing planning and control address decisions on the acquisition, utilization and allocation of production resources to satisfy customer requirements in the most efficient and effective way. Typical decisions include work force level, production lot sizes, assignment of overtime and sequencing of production runs. Optimization models are widely applicable for providing decision support in this context.

We focus on optimization models for production planning for discrete-parts, batch manufacturing environments. We do not cover detailed scheduling or sequencing models, nor do we address production planning for continuous processes. We consider only discrete-time models, and do not include continuous-time models such as developed by Hackman and Leachman.

Our intent is to provide an overview of applicable optimization models; we present the most generic formulations and briefly describe how these models are solved. There is an enormous range of problem contexts and model formulations, as well as solution methods. We make no effort to be exhaustive in the treatment herein.

Rather, we have made choices of what to include based on personal judgment and preferences. We have organized the substance into four major parts. In the first part we present a framework for the decisions, issues and tradeoffs involved in implementing an optimization model for discrete-part production planning. The remaining three parts present and discuss three distinct types of models. In the second part we discuss linear programming models for production planning, in which we have linear costs.

This category is of great practical interest, as many important problem features can be captured with these models and powerful solution methods for linear programmes are readily available. In the third part, we present a production-planning model for a single aggregate product with quadratic costs; this model is of historical significance as it represents one of the earliest applications of optimization to manufacturing planning. In the final part we introduce the multi-item capacitated lot-size problem, which is modeled as a mixed integer linear programme. This is an important model as it introduces economies of scale in production, due to the presence of production setups.

FRAMEWORK

There are a variety of considerations that go into the development and implementation of an optimization model for manufacturing planning and control. In this part we highlight and comment upon a number of key issues and questions that should be addressed. Excellent general references on production planning are Thomas and McClain, Shapiro and Silver et al..

Any planning problem starts with a specification of customer demand that is to be met by the production plan. In most contexts, future demand is at best only partially known, and often is not known at all. Consequently, one relies on a forecast for the future demand. To the extent that any forecast is inevitably inaccurate, one must decide how to account for or react to this demand uncertainty. The optimization models described in this substance treat demand as being known; as such they must be periodically revised and rerun to account for forecast updates. A key choice is what planning decisions to include in the model. By definition, production-planning models include decisions on production and inventory quantities. But in addition, there might be resource acquisition and allocation decision, such as adding to the work force and upgrading the training of the current work force. In many planning contexts, an important construct is to set a planning hierarchy. Namely, one structures the planning process in a hierarchical way by ordering the decisions according to their relative importance.

Hax and Meal introduced the notion of hierarchical production planning and provide a specific framework for this, whereby there is an optimization model with each level of the hierarchy. Each optimization model imposes a constraint on the model at the next level of the hierarchy. Bitran and Tirupati provide a comprehensive survey of hierarchical planning methods and models. The identification of the relevant costs is also an important issue. For production planning, one typically needs to determine the variable production costs, including setuprelated costs, inventory holding costs, and any relevant resource acquisition costs. There might also be costs associated with imperfect customer service, such as when demand is backordered.

A planning problem exists because there are limited production resources that cannot be stored from period to period. Choices must be made as to which resources to include and how to model their capacity and behaviour, and their costs. Also, there may be uncertainty associated with the production function, such as uncertain yields or lead times. One might only include the most critical or limiting resource in the planning problem, e. g., a bottleneck. Alternatively, when there is not a dominant resource, then one must model the resources that could limit production. We describe in this substance two types of production functions.

The first assumes a linear relationship between the production quantity and the resource consumption. The second assumes that there is a required fixed charge or setup to initiate production and then a linear relationship between the production quantity and resource usage. Related to these choices is the selection of the time period and planning horizon. The planning literature distinguishes between "big accomplished, but they do not state 'how' the results are to be achieved. They typically relate to what products will be where in what markets. They are essentially about the match between those "products" and "markets." Objectives for pricing, distribution, advertising and so on are at a lower level, and should not be confused with marketing objectives.

They are part of the marketing strategy needed to achieve marketing objectives. To be most effective, objectives should be capable of measurement and therefore "quantifiable." This measurement may be in terms of sales volume, money value, market share, percentage penetration of distribution outlets and so on. An example of such a measurable marketing objective might be "to enter the market with product Y and capture 10 per cent of the market by value within one year." As it is quantified it can, within limits, be unequivocally monitored, and corrective action taken as necessary.

The marketing objectives must usually be based on the organization's financial objectives; converting these financial measurements into the related marketing measurements.He went on to explain his view of the role of "policies," with which strategy is most often confused: "Policies are rules or guidelines that express the 'limits' within which action should occur."Simplifying somewhat, marketing strategies can be seen as the means, or "game plan," by which marketing objectives will be achieved and, in the framework that we have chosen to use, are generally concerned with the 8 P's.

Examples are:

1. *Price:* The amount of money needed to buy products
2. *Product*: The actual product
3. *Promotion*: Getting the product known
4. *Placement*: Where the product is located
5. *People*: Represent the business
6. *Physical environment:* The ambiance, mood, or tone of the environment
7. *Process* - How do people obtain your product
8. *Packaging*: How the product will be protected

In principle, these strategies describe how the objectives will be achieved. The 7 P's are a useful framework for deciding

This splits the material into three groups:

1. *Review of the marketing environment*: A study of the organization's markets, customers, competitors and the overall economic, political, cultural and technical environment; covering developing trends, as well as the current situation.
2. *Review of the detailed marketing activity*: A study of the company's marketing mix; in terms of the 7 Ps -
3. *Review of the marketing system*: A study of the marketing organization, marketing research systems and the current marketing objectives and strategies. The last of these is too frequently ignored. The marketing system itself needs to be regularly questioned, because the validity of the whole marketing plan is reliant upon the accuracy of the input from this system, and 'garbage in, garbage out' applies with a vengeance.
   - Portfolio planning. In addition, the coordinated planning of the individual products and services can contribute towards the balanced portfolio.
   - 80:20 rule. To achieve the maximum impact, the marketing plan must be clear, concise and simple. It needs to concentrate on the 20 per cent of products or services, and on the 20 per cent of customers, which will account for 80 per cent of the volume and 80 per cent of the profit.
   - 7 P's: Product, Place, Price and Promotion, Physical Environment, People, Process. The 7 P's can sometimes divert attention from the customer, but the framework they offer can be very useful in building the action plans.

It is only at this stage that the active part of the marketing planning process begins. This next stage in marketing planning is indeed the key to the whole marketing process. The "marketing objectives" state just where the company intends to be at some specific time in the future. James Quinn succinctly defined objectives in general as: Goals state what is to be achieved and when results are to be were underpinned by its philosophy of "customer a vision originally promoted by the charismatic ...n dynasty. The emphasis at this stage is on obtaining a complete and accurate picture.

A "traditional" - albeit product-based - format for a "brand reference book" was suggested by Godley more than three decades ago:

1. *Financial data*: Facts for this part will come from management accounting, costing and finance parts.
2. *Product data*: From production, research and development.
3. *Sales and distribution data*: Sales, packaging, distribution parts.
4. *Advertising, sales promotion, merchandising data*: Information from these departments.
5. *Market data and miscellany*: From market research, who would in most cases performanceas a source for this information. His sources of data, however, assume the resources of a very large organization. In most organizations they would be obtained from a much smaller set of people.

It is apparent that a marketing audit can be a complex process, but the aim is simple: "it is only to identify those existing factors which will have a significant impact on the future plans of the company." It is clear that the basic material to be input to the marketing audit should be comprehensive. Accordingly, the best approach is to accumulate this material continuously, as and when it becomes available; since this avoids the otherwise heavy workload involved in collecting it as part of the regular, typically annual, planning process itself - when time is usually at a premium.

Even so, the first task of this annual process should be to check that the material held in the current facts book or facts files actually is comprehensive and accurate, and can form a sound basis for the marketing audit itself. The structure of the facts book will be designed to match the specific needs of the organization, but one simple format - suggested by Malcolm McDonald - may be applicable in many cases.

Marketing Planning Aims and Objectives

Behind the corporate objectives, which in themselve the main context for the marketing plan, will lie the "corpo mission," which in turn provides the context for these corporate objectives. In a sales-oriented organization, the marketing planning function designs incentive pay plans to not only motivate and reward frontline staff fairly but also to align marketing activities with corporate mission. bn

This "corporate mission" can be thought of as a definition of what the organization is, of what it does: "Our business is ...". This definition should not be too narrow, or it will constrict the development of the organization; a too rigorous concentration on the view that "We are in the business of making meat-scales," as IBM was during the early 1900s, might have limited its subsequent development into other areas. On the other hand, it should not be too wide or it will become meaningless; "We want to make a profit" is not too helpful in developing specific plans. Abell suggested that the definition should cover three dimensions: "customer groups" to be served, "customer needs" to be served, and "technologies" to be utilized. Thus, the definition of IBM's "corporate mission" in the 1940s might well have been: "We are in the business of handling accounting information [customer need] for the larger US organizations [customer group] by means of punched cards [technology]."

Perhaps the most important factor in successful marketing is the "corporate vision." Surprisingly, it is largely neglected by marketing textbooks, although not by the popular exponents of corporate strategy - indeed, it was perhaps the main theme of the book by Peters and Waterman, in the form of their "Superordinate Goals." "In Search of Excellence" said: "Nothing drives progress like the imagination. The idea precedes the deed." If the organization in general, and its chief executive in particular, has a strong vision of where its future lies, then there is a good chance that the organization will achieve a strong position in its markets. This will be not least because its strategies will be consistent and will be supported by its staff at all levels. In this context, all of IBM's marketing

...usiness, a financial plan can refer to the three primary activities ...l statements created within a business plan. Financial service," ...st or financial plan can also refer to an annual projection Watso... income and expenses for a company, division or department. A financial plan can also be an estimation of cash needs and a decision on how to raise the cash, such as through borrowing or issuing additional shares in a company. While a financial plan refers to estimating future income, expenses and assets, a financing plan or finance plan usually refers to the means by which cash will be acquired to cover future expenses, for instance through earning, borrowing or using saved cash.

MARKETING PLAN

A marketing plan is a written document that details the necessary actions to achieve one or more marketing objectives. It can be for a product or service, a brand, or a product line. Marketing plans cover between one and five years. A marketing plan may be part of an overall business plan. Solid marketing strategy is the foundation of a well-written marketing plan. While a marketing plan contains a list of actions, a marketing plan without a sound strategic foundation is of little use.

The Marketing Planning Process

Marketing process can be realised by the marketing mix in step 4. The last step in the process is the marketing controlling. In most organizations, "strategic planning" is an annual process, typically covering just the year ahead. Occasionally, a few organizations may look at a practical plan which stretches three or more years ahead.

To be most effective, the plan has to be formalized, usually in written form, as a formal "marketing plan." The essence of the process is that it moves from the general to the specific, from the overall objectives of the organization down to the individual action plan for a part of one marketing programme. It is also an interactive process, so that the draft output of each stage is checked to see what impact it has on the earlier stages, and is amended.

this preparation is what is needed for an event to run smoothly.An event planner needs to be able to manage their time wisely for the event, and the length of preparation needed for each event so it is a success.

Working Conditions

Event planners work is considered either stressful or energizing. This line of work is also considered fast paced and demanding. Planners face deadlines and communicating with multiple people at one time. Planners spend most of their time in offices, but when meeting with clients the work is usually on-site at the location where the event is taking place. Some physical activity is required such as carrying boxes of materials and decorations or supplies needed for the event. Also, long working hours can be a part of the job. The day the event is taking place could start as early as 5:00 a.m. and then work until midnight. Working on weekends is sometimes required, which is when many events take place.

Publications and Resources

Many business-to-business trade publications exist to help event planning and production professionals become educated about the issues and trends in their industry. Many are controlled circulation publications available at no cost to qualified event professionals. Qualification is based on multiple variables like job title, company type, industry segment or geographic region, and is at the publisher's discretion.

FINANCIAL PLAN

In general usage, a financial plan can be a budget, a plan for spending and saving future income. This plan allocates future income to various types of expenses, such as rent or utilities, and also reserves some income for short-term and long-term savings. A financial plan can also be an investment plan, which allocates savings to various assets or projects expected to produce future income, such as a new business or product line, shares in an existing business, or real estate.

ASPECTS OF PLANNING

EVENT PLANNING

Event planning is the process of planning a festival, ceremony, competition, party, or convention. Event planning includes budgeting, establishing dates and alternate dates, selecting and reserving the event site, acquiring permits, and coordinating transportation and parking.

Event planning also includes some or all of the following, depending on the event: developing a theme or motif for the event, arranging for speakers and alternate speakers, coordinating location support, arranging decor, tables, chairs, tents, event support and security, catering, police, fire, portable toilets, parking, signage, emergency plans, health care professionals, and cleanup.

Event Planning is a relatively new career field. There is now training that helps one trying to break into the career field. There must be training for an event planner to handle all the pressure and work efficiently. This career deals with a lot of communication and organization aspects. There are many different names for an event planner such as a conference coordinator, a convention planner, a special event coordinator, and a meeting manager.

Steps to Planning an Event

The first step to planning an event is determining its purpose, whether it is for a wedding, company, birthday, festival, graduation or any other event requiring extensive planning. From this the event planner needs to choose entertainment, location, guest list, speakers, and content. The location for events is endless, but with event planning they would likely be held at hotels, convention centres, reception halls, or outdoors depending on the event. Once the location is set the coordinator/planner needs to prepare the event with staff, set up the entertainment, and keep contact with the client. After all this is set the event planner has all the smaller details to address like set up of the event such as food, drinks, music, guest list, budget, advertising and marketing, decorations, all bucket" and "small bucket" time periods. A time period is a big bucket if multiple items are typically produced within a time period; a small bucket is such that at most one item would be produced in the time period. For big bucket models, one has to worry about how to schedule or sequence the production runs assigned to any time period. The choice of planning horizon is dictated by the lead times to enact production and resource-related decisions, as well as the quality of knowledge about future demand.

Planning is typically done in a rolling horizon fashion. A plan is created for the planning horizon, but only the decisions in the first few periods are implemented before a revised plan is issued. Indeed the plan must be periodically revised due to the uncertainties in the demand forecasts and production. For instance a firm might plan for the next 26 weeks, but then revise this once a month to incorporate new information on demand and production.

Production planning is usually done at an aggregate level, for both products and resources. Distinct but similar products are combined into aggregate product families that can be planned together so as to reduce planning complexity. Similarly production resources, such as distinct machines or labour pools, are aggregated into an aggregate machine or labour resource. Care is required when specifying these aggregates to assure that the resulting aggregate plan can be reasonably disaggregated into feasible production schedules. Finally for complex products, one must decide the level and extent of the product structure to include in the planning process. For instance, in some contexts it is sufficient to just plan the production of end items; the production plan for components and subassemblies is subservient to the master production schedule for end items.

In other contexts, planning just the end items is sub-optimal, as there are critical resource constraints applicable to multiple levels of the product structure. In this instance, a multistage planning model allows for the simultaneous planning of end items and components or subassemblies. Of course, this produces a much larger model.

how the company's resources will be manipulated to achieve the objectives. It should be noted, however, that they are not the only framework, and may divert attention from the real issues. The focus of the strategies must be the objectives to be achieved - not the process of planning itself. Only if it fits the needs of these objectives should you choose, as we have done, to use the framework of the 7 P's.

The strategy statement can take the form of a purely verbal description of the strategic options which have been chosen. Alternatively, and perhaps more positively, it might include a structured list of the major options chosen. One aspect of strategy which is often overlooked is that of "timing."

Exactly when it is the best time for each element of the strategy to be implemented is often critical. Taking the right action at the wrong time can sometimes be almost as bad as taking the wrong action at the right time. Timing is, therefore, an essential part of any plan; and should normally appear as a schedule of planned activities.Having completed this crucial stage of the planning process, you will need to re-check the feasibility of your objectives and strategies in terms of the market share, sales, costs, profits and so on which these demand in practice.

As in the rest of the marketing discipline, you will need to employ judgment, experience, market research or anything else which helps you to look at your conclusions from all possible angles.

Detailed Plans and Programmes

At this stage, you will need to develop your overall marketing strategies into detailed plans and programme. Although these detailed plans may cover each of the 7 P's, the focus will vary, depending upon your organization's specific strategies. A product-oriented company will focus its plans for the 7 P's around each of its products. A market or geographically oriented company will concentrate on each market or geographical area. Each will base its plans upon the detailed needs of its customers, and on the strategies chosen to satisfy these needs.

Again, the most important element is, indeed, that of the detailed plans, which spell out exactly what programmes and individual activities will take place over the period of the plan. Without these specified - and preferably quantified - activities the plan cannot be monitored, even in terms of success in meeting its objectives.It is these programmes and activities which will then constitute the "marketing" of the organization over the period. As a result, these detailed marketing programmes are the most important, practical outcome of the whole planning process.

These plans must therefore be:

- *Clear*: They should be an unambiguous statement of 'exactly' what is to be done.
- *Quantified*: The predicted outcome of each activity should be, as far as possible, quantified, so that its performance can be monitored.
- *Focused*: The temptation to proliferate activities beyond the numbers which can be realistically controlled should be avoided. The 80:20 Rule applies in this context too.
- *Realistic*: They should be achievable.
- *Agreed*: Those who are to implement them should be committed to them, and agree that they are achievable. The resulting plans should become a working document which will guide the campaigns taking place throughout the organization over the period of the plan. If the marketing plan is to work, every exception to it must be questioned; and the lessons learned, to be incorporated in the next year's planning.

Content of the Marketing Plan

A marketing plan for a small business typically includes Small Business Administration Description of competitors, including the level of demand for the product or service and the strengths and weaknesses of competitors

- Description of the product or service, including special features

- Marketing budget, including the advertising and promotional plan
- Description of the business location, including advantages and disadvantages for marketing
- Pricing strategy
- Market Segmentation

Measurement of Progress

The final stage of any marketing planning process is to establish targets so that progress can be monitored. Accordingly, it is important to put both quantities and timescales into the marketing objectives and into the corresponding strategies. Changes in the environment mean that the forecasts often have to be changed. Along with these, the related plans may well also need to be changed. Continuous monitoring of performance, against predetermined targets, represents a most important aspect of this. However, perhaps even more important is the enforced discipline of a regular formal review. Again, as with forecasts, in many cases the best planning cycle will revolve around a quarterly review. Best of all, at least in terms of the quantifiable aspects of the plans, if not the wealth of backing detail, is probably a quarterly rolling review - planning one full year ahead each new quarter. Of course, this does absorb more planning resource; but it also ensures that the plans embody the latest information, and - with attention focused on them so regularly - forces both the plans and their implementation to be realistic. Plans only have validity if they are actually used to control the progress of a company: their success lies in their implementation, not in the writing'.

Performance Analysis

The most important elements of marketing performance, which are normally tracked, are:

Sales Analysis

Most organizations track their sales results; or, in non-profit organizations for example, the number of clients. The more sophisticated track them in terms of 'sales variance' - the deviation from the target figures - which allows a more immediate picture of deviations to become evident.

'Micro-analysis', which is a nicely pseudo-scientific term for the normal management process of investigating detailed problems, then investigates the individual elements which are failing to meet targets.

Market Share Analysis

Few organizations track market share though it is often an important metric. Though absolute sales might grow in an expanding market, a firm's share of the market can decrease which bodes ill for future sales when the market starts to drop.

Where such market share is tracked, there may be a number of aspects which will be followed:

- Overall market share
- Segment share - that in the specific, targeted segment
- Relative share -in relation to the market leaders
- Annual fluctuation rate of market share

Expense Analysis

The key ratio to watch in this area is usually the 'marketing expense to sales ratio'; although this may be broken down into other elements.

Financial Analysis

The "bottom line" of marketing activities should at least in theory, be the net profit.

There are a number of separate performance figures and key ratios which need to be tracked:

- Gross contribution<>net profit
- Gross profit<>return on investment
- Net contribution<>profit on sales

There can be considerable benefit in comparing these figures with those achieved by other organizations; using, for instance, the figures which can be obtained from 'The Centre for Interfirm Comparison'. The most sophisticated use of this approach, however, is typically by those making use of PIMS, initiated by the General Electric Company and then developed by Harvard Business School, but now run by the Strategic Planning Institute.

The performance analyses concentrate on the quantitative measures which are directly related to short-term performance. But there are a number of indirect measures, essentially tracking customer attitudes, which can also indicate the organization's performance in terms of its longer-term marketing strengths and may accordingly be even more important indicators.

Some useful measures are:

- *Market research*: Including customer panels
- *lost business*: The orders which were lost because, for example, the stock was not available or the product did not meet the customer's exact requirements
- *Customer complaints*: How many customers complain about the products or services, or the organization itself, and about what

Use of Marketing Plans

A formal, written marketing plan is essential; in that it provides an unambiguous reference point for activities throughout the planning period. However, perhaps the most important benefit of these plans is the planning process itself. This typically offers a unique opportunity, a forum, for information-rich and productively focused discussions between the various managers involved. The plan, together with the associated discussions, then provides an agreed context for their subsequent management activities, even for those not described in the plan itself.

Budgets as Managerial Tools

The classic quantification of a marketing plan appears in the form of budgets. Because these are so rigorously quantified, they are particularly important. They should, thus, represent an unequivocal projection of actions and expected results. What is more, they should be capable of being monitored accurately; and, indeed, performance against budget is the main management review process. The purpose of a marketing budget is, thus, to pull together all the revenues and costs involved in marketing into one comprehensive document. It is a managerial tool that balances what is needed to be spent against what can be afforded, and helps make choices about priorities. It is then used in monitoring performance in practice.

The marketing budget is usually the most powerful tool by which you think through the relationship between desired results and available means. Its starting point should be the marketing strategies and plans, which have already been formulated in the marketing plan itself; although, in practice, the two will run in parallel and will interact. At the very least, the rigorous, highly quantified, budgets may cause a rethink of some of the more optimistic elements of the plans.

STRATEGIC PLANNING

Strategic planning is an organization's process of defining its strategy, or direction, and making decisions on allocating its resources to pursue this strategy, including its capital and people. Various business analysis techniques can be used in strategic planning, including SWOT analysis, PEST analysis, STEER analysis, and EPISTEL. Strategic planning is the formal consideration of an organization's future course.

All strategic planning deals with at least one of three key questions:

1. "What do we do?"
2. "For whom do we do it?"
3. "How do we excel?"

In business strategic planning, the third question is better phrased "How can we beat or avoid competition?". In many organizations, this is viewed as a process for determining where an organization is going over the next year or more - typically 3 to 5 years, although some extend their vision to 20 years.In order to determine where it is going, the organization needs to know exactly where it stands, then determine where it wants to go and how it will get there. The resulting document is called the "strategic plan." It is also true that strategic planning may be a tool for effectively plotting the direction of a company; however, strategic planning itself cannot foretell exactly how the market will evolve and what issues will surface in the coming days in order to plan your organizational strategy. Therefore, strategic innovation and tinkering with the 'strategic plan' have to be a cornerstone strategy for an organization to survive the turbulent business climate.

Mission, Vision and Values

- *Mission*: Defines the fundamental purpose of an organization or an enterprise, succinctly describing why it exists and what it does to achieve its Vision.
- *Vision*: Defines the desired or intended future state of an organization or enterprise in terms of its fundamental objective and/or strategic direction. Vision is a long term view, sometimes describing how the organization would like the world in which it operates to be. For example a charity working with the poor might have a vision statement which read "A world without poverty" It is sometimes used to set out a 'picture' of the organization in the future. A vision statement provides inspiration, the basis for all the organization's planning. It could answer the question: "Where do we want to go?"
- *Values*: Beliefs that are shared among the stakeholders of an organization. Values drive an organization's culture and priorities.
- *Strategy*: Strategy narrowly defined, means "the art of the general". A combination of the ends for which the firm is striving and the means by which it is seeking to get there.

Mission Statements and Vision Statements

Organizations sometimes summarize goals and objectives into a mission statement and/or a vision statement. Others begin with a vision and mission and use them to formulate goals and objectives. While the existence of a shared mission is extremely useful, many strategy specialists question the requirement for a written mission statement.

However, there are many models of strategic planning that start with mission statements, so it is useful to examine them here:

- A Mission statement tells you the fundamental purpose of the organization. It defines the customer and the critical processes. It informs you of the desired level of performance.
- A Vision statement outlines what the organization wants to be, or how it wants the world in which it operates to be. It concentrates on the future. It is a source of inspiration. It provides clear decision-making criteria.

An advantage of having a statement is that it creates value for those who get exposed to the statement, and those prospects are managers, employees and sometimes even customers. Statements create a sense of direction and opportunity. They both are an essential part of the strategy-making process. Many people mistake vision statement for mission statement, and sometimes one is simply used as a longer term version of the other.

The Vision should describe why it is important to achieve the Mission. A Vision statement defines the purpose or broader goal for being in existence or in the business and can remain the same for decades if crafted well. A Mission statement is more specific to what the enterprise can achieve itself. Vision should describe what will be achieved in the wider sphere if the organization and others are successful in achieving their individual missions.

A mission statement can resemble a vision statement in a few companies, but that can be a grave mistake. It can confuse people. The mission statement can galvanize the people to achieve defined objectives, even if they are stretch objectives, provided it can be elucidated in SMART terms. A mission statement provides a path to realise the vision in line with its values. These statements have a direct bearing on the bottom line and success of the organization. Which comes first? The mission statement or the vision statement? That depends. If you have a new start up business, new programme or plan to re engineer your current services, then the vision will guide the mission statement and the rest of the strategic plan. If you have an established business where the mission is established, then many times, the mission guides the vision statement and the rest of the strategic plan.

Either way, you need to know your fundamental purpose - the mission, your current situation in terms of internal resources and capabilities and external conditions, and where you want to go - the vision for the future. It's important that you keep the end or desired result in sight from the start..

Features of an effective vision statement include:

- Clarity and lack of
- Vivid and clear picture
- Description of a bright future
- Memorable and engaging wording
- Realistic aspirations
- Alignment with organizational values and culture

To become really effective, an organizational vision statement must become assimilated into the organization's culture. Leaders have the responsibility of communicating the vision regularly, creating narratives that illustrate the vision, acting as role-models by embodying the vision, creating short-term objectives compatible with the vision, and encouraging others to craft their own personal vision compatible with the organization's overall vision. In addition, mission statements need to be subjected to an internal assessment and an external assessment.

The internal assessment should focus on how members inside the organization interpret their mission statement. The external assessment — which includes all of the businesses stakeholders — is valuable since it offers a different perspective. These discrepancies between these two assessments can give insight on the organization's mission statement effectiveness.Another approach to defining Vision and Mission is to pose two questions. Firstly, "What aspirations does the organization have for the world in which it operates and has some influence over?", and following on from this, "What can the organization do or contribute to fulfill those aspirations?". The succinct answer to the first question provides the basis of the Vision Statement. The answer to the second question determines the Mission Statement.

Methodologies

There are many approaches to strategic planning but typically a three-step process may be used:

1. *Situation*: Evaluate the current situation and how it came about.
2. *Target*: Define goals and/or objectives
3. *Path*: Map a possible route to the goals/objectives

One alternative approach is called Draw-See-Think:

- *Draw*: What is the ideal image or the desired end state?
- *See*: What is today's situation? What is the gap from ideal and why?
- *Think*: What specific actions must be taken to close the gap between today's situation and the ideal state?
- *Plan*: What resources are required to execute the activities?

An alternative to the Draw-See-Think approach is called See-Think-Draw:

- *See*: What is today's situation?
- *Think*: Define goals/objectives
- *Draw*: Map a route to achieving the goals/objectives

In other terms strategic planning can be as follows:

- *Vision*: Define the vision and set a mission statement with hierarchy of goals and objectives
- *SWOT*: Analysis conducted according to the desired goals
- *Formulate*: Formulate actions and processes to be taken to attain these goals
- *Implement*: Implementation of the agreed upon processes
- *Control*: Monitor and get feedback from implemented processes to fully control the operation

Situational Analysis

When developing strategies, analysis of the organization and its environment as it is at the moment and how it may develop in the future, is important. The analysis has to be executed at an internal level as well as an external level to identify all opportunities and threats of the external environment as well as the strengths and weaknesses of the organizations.

There are several factors to assess in the external situation analysis:

- Markets
- Competition
- Technology
- Supplier markets
- Labour markets
- The economy
- The regulatory environment

It is rare to find all seven of these factors having critical importance. It is also uncommon to find that the first two - markets and competition - are not of critical importance.

Analysis of the external environment normally focuses on the customer. Management should be visionary in formulating customer strategy, and should do so by thinking about market environment shifts, how these could impact customer sets, and whether those customer sets are the ones the company wishes to serve. Analysis of the competitive environment is also performed, many times based on the framework suggested by Michael Porter.

Goals, Objectives and Targets

Strategic planning is a very important business activity. It is also important in the public sector areas such as education. It is practiced widely informally and formally. Strategic planning and decision processes should end with objectives and a roadmap of ways to achieve those objectives.

One of the core goals when drafting a strategic plan is to develop it in a way that is easily translatable into action plans. Most strategic plans address high level initiatives and over-arching goals, but don't get articulated into day-to-day projects and tasks that will be required to achieve the plan. Terminology or word choice, as well as the level a plan is written, are both examples of easy ways to fail at translating your strategic plan in a way that makes sense and is executable to others. Often, plans are filled with conceptual terms which don't tie into day-to-day realities for the staff expected to carry out the plan. The following terms have been used in strategic planning: desired end states, plans, policies, goals, objectives, strategies, tactics and actions.

Definitions vary, overlap and fail to achieve clarity. The most common of these concepts are specific, time bound statements of intended future results and general and continuing statements of intended future results, which most models refer to as either goals or objectives. One model of organizing objectives uses hierarchies.

The items listed may be organized in a hierarchy of means and ends and numbered as follows: Top Rank Objective, Second Rank Objective, Third Rank Objective, etc. From any rank, the objective in a lower rank answers to the question "How?" and the objective in a higher rank answers to the question "Why?" The exception is the Top Rank Objective: there is no answer to the "Why?" question. That is how the TRO is defined.

People typically have several goals at the same time. "Goal congruency" refers to how well the goals combine with each other. Does goal A appear compatible with goal B? Do they fit together to form a unified strategy? "Goal hierarchy" consists of the nesting of one or more goals within other goals. One approach recommends having short-term goals, medium-term goals, and long-term goals. In this model, one can expect to attain short-term goals fairly easily: they stand just slightly one's reach. At the other extreme, long-term goals appear very difficult, almost impossible to attain.

Strategic management jargon sometimes refers to "Big Hairy Audacious Goals" in this context. Using one goal as a stepping-stone to the next involves goal sequencing. A person or group starts by attaining the easy short-term goals, then steps up to the medium-term, then to the long-term goals. Goal sequencing can create a "goal stairway". In an organizational setting, the organization may co-ordinate goals so that they do not conflict with each other. The goals of one part of the organization should mesh compatibly with those of other parts of the organization.

OPERATIONAL PLANNING

An operational planning is a subset of strategic work plan. It describes short-term ways of achieving milestones and explains how, or what portion of, a strategic plan will be put into operation during a given operational period, in the case of commercial application, a fiscal year or another given budgetary term. An operational plan is the basis for, and justification of an annual operating budget request. Therefore, a five-year strategic plan would need five operational plans funded by five operating budgets.

Operational plans should establish the activities and budgets for each part of the organisation for the next 1 - 3 years. They link the strategic plan with the activities the organization will deliver and the resources required to deliver them.

An operational plan draws directly from agency and programme strategic plans to describe agency and programme missions and goals, programme objectives, and programme activities.

Like a strategic plan, an operational plan addresses four questions:

1. Where are we now?
2. Where do we want to be?
3. How do we get there?
4. How do we measure our progress?

The OP is both the first and the last step in preparing an operating budget request. As the first step, the OP provides a plan for resource allocation; as the last step, the OP may be modified to reflect policy decisions or financial changes made during the budget development process.

Operational plans should be prepared by the people who will be involved in implementation. There is often a need for significant cross-departmental dialogue as plans created by one part of the organisation inevitably have implications for other parts.

Operational plans should contain:

- Clear objectives
- Activities to be delivered
- Quality standards
- Desired outcomes
- Staffing and resource requirements
- Implementation timetables
- A process for monitoring progress.

BUSINESS PLAN

A business plan is a formal statement of a set of business goals, the reasons why they are believed attainable, and the plan for reaching those goals. It may also contain background information about the organization or team attempting to reach those goals. The business goals may be defined for for-profit or for non-profit organizations. For-profit business plans typically focus on financial goals, such as profit or creation of wealth. Non-profit and government agency business plans tend to focus on organizational mission which is the basis for their governmental status or their non-profit, tax-exempt status, respectively—although non-profits may also focus on optimizing revenue.

In non-profit organizations, creative tensions may develop in the effort to balance mission with "margin". Business plans may also target changes in perception and branding by the customer, client, tax-payer, or larger community. A business plan having changes in perception and branding as its primary goals is called a marketing plan.

Audience

Business plans may be internally or externally focused. Externally focused plans target goals that are important to external stakeholders, particularly financial stakeholders. They typically have detailed information about the organization or team attempting to reach the goals. With for-profit entities, external stakeholders include investors and customers. External stake-holders of non-profits include donors and the clients of the non-profit's services. For government agencies, external stakeholders include tax-payers, higher-level government agencies, and international lending bodies such as the IMF, the World Bank, various economic agencies of the UN, and development banks. Internally focused business plans target intermediate goals required to reach the external goals. They may cover the development of a new product, a new service, a new IT system, a restructuring of finance, the refurbishing of a factory or a restructuring of the organization.

An internal business plan is often developed in conjunction with a balanced scorecard or a list of critical success factors. This allows success of the plan to be measured using non-financial measures. Business plans that identify and target internal goals, but provide only general guidance on how they will be met are called strategic plans. Operational plans describe the goals of an internal organization, working group or department. Project plans, sometimes known as project frameworks, describe the goals of a particular project. They may also address the project's place within the organization's larger strategic goals.

Presentation Formats

The format of a business plan depends on its presentation context.

It is not uncommon for businesses, especially start-ups to have three or four formats for the same business plan:

1. *An "elevator pitch"*: A three minute summary of the business plan's executive summary. This is often used as a teaser to awaken the interest of potential funders, customers, or strategic partners.
2. *An oral presentation*: A hopefully entertaining slide show and oral narrative that is meant to trigger discussion and interest potential investors in reading the written presentation. The content of the presentation is usually limited to the executive summary and a few key graphs showing financial trends and key decision making benchmarks. If a new product is being proposed and time permits, a demonstration of the product may also be included.

3. *A written presentation for external stakeholders*: A detailed, well written, and pleasingly formatted plan targeted at external stakeholders.
4. *An internal operational plan*: A detailed plan describing planning details that are needed by management but may not be of interest to external stakeholders. Such plans have a somewhat higher degree of candor and informality than the version targeted at external stakeholders.

Typical structure for a business plan for a start up venture:

- Cover page and table of contents
- Executive summary
- Business description
- Business environment analysis
- Industry background
- Competitive analysis
- Market analysis
- Marketing plan
- Operations plan
- Management summary
- Financial plan
- Attachments and milestones

Revisiting the Business Plan

Cost Overruns and Revenue Shortfalls

Cost and revenue estimates are central to any business plan for deciding the viability of the planned venture. But costs are often underestimated and revenues overestimated resulting in later cost overruns, revenue shortfalls, and possibly non-viability. During the dot-com bubble 1997-2001 this was a problem for many technology start-ups.

However, the problem is not limited to technology or the private sector; public works projects also routinely suffer from cost overruns and/or revenue shortfalls. The main causes of cost overruns and revenue shortfalls are optimism bias and strategic misrepresentation. Reference class forecasting has been developed to reduce the risks of cost overruns and revenue shortfalls.

Legal and Liability Issues

Disclosure Requirements

An externally targeted business plan should list all legal concerns and financial liabilities that might negatively affect investors. Depending on the amount of funds being raised and the audience to whom the plan is presented, failure to do this may have severe legal consequences.

Limitations on Content and Audience

Non disclosure agreements with third parties, non-compete agreements, conflicts of interest, privacy concerns, and the protection of one's trade secrets may severely limit the audience to which one might show the business plan. Alternatively, they may require each party receiving the business plan to sign a contract accepting special clauses and conditions.

This situation is complicated by the fact that many venture capitalists will refuse to sign an NDA before looking at a business plan, lest it put them in the untenable position of looking at two independently developed look-alike business plans, both claiming originality. In such situations one may need to develop two versions of the business plan: a stripped down plan that can be used to develop a relationship and a detail plan that is only shown when investors have sufficient interest and trust to sign an NDA.

Open Business Plans

Traditionally business plans have been highly confidential and quite limited in audience. The business plan itself is generally regarded as secret. However the emergence of free software and open source has opened the model and made the notion of an open business plan possible.

An open business plan is a business plan with unlimited audience. The business plan is typically web published and made available to all. In the free software and open source business model, trade secrets, copyright and patents can no longer be used as effective locking mechanisms to provide sustainable advantages to a particular business and therefore a secret business plan is less relevant in those models. While the origin of the open business plan model is in the free software and Libre services arena, the concept is likely applicable to other domains.

Uses

Venture capital:

- *Business plan contests*: Provides a way for venture capitals to find promising projects
- *Venture capital assessment of business plans*: Focus on qualitative factors such as team.

Public offerings:

- In a public offering, potential investors can evaluate perspectives of issuing company

Within Corporations

Fundraising

Fundraising is the primary purpose for many business plans, since they are related to the inherent probable success/ failure of the company risk.

Total Quality Management

Total quality management is a business management strategy aimed at embedding awareness of quality in all organizational processes. TQM has been widely used in manufacturing, education, call centres, government, and service industries, as well as NASA space and science programmes.

Management by Objective

Management by objectives is a process of agreeing upon objectives within an organization so that management and employees agree to the objectives and understand what they are in the organization.

Strategic Planning

Strategic planning is an organization's process of defining its strategy, or direction, and making decisions on allocating its resources to pursue this strategy, including its capital and people. Various business analysis techniques can be used in strategic planning, including SWOT analysis and PEST analysis or STEER analysis involving Socio-cultural, Technological, Economic, Ecological, and Regulatory factors and EPISTELS

Satires

The business plan is the subject of many satires. Satires are used both to express cynicism about business plans and as an educational tool to improve the quality of business plans.

For example:

- Five Criteria for a successful business plan in biotech uses Dilbert comic strips to remind people of what *not* to do when researching and writing a business plan for a biotech start-up. Scott Adams, the author of Dilbert, is an MBA graduate who sees humour as a critical tool that can improve the behaviour of businesses and their managers. He has written numerous critiques of business practices, including business planning. Games has a mission statement generator that satirizes the wording often found in mission statements. His book The Dilbert Principle – A Cubicle's Eye View of Bosses, Meetings, Management Fads and Other Workplace Afflictions discusses the foibles of management and their plans as depicted in the Dilbert comic strips by Scott Adams.
- "South Park's" Investing Lesson, the The Motley Fool columnist "Fool on the Hill" uses the Underpants Gnomes to illustrate the fallacy of focusing on goals without a clear implementation strategy. The Underpants Gnomes episode satirizes the business plans of the Dot-com era.

5

Production Planning and Control

CONCEPT

PLANNING

Planning in organizations and public policy is both the organizational process of creating and maintaining a plan; and the psychological process of thinking about the activities required to create a desired goal on some scale. As such, it is a fundamental property of intelligent behaviour.

This thought process is essential to the creation and refinement of a plan, or integration of it with other plans, that is, it combines forecasting of developments with the preparation of scenarios of how to react to them. An important, albeit often ignored aspect of planning, is the relationship it holds with forecasting. Forecasting can be described as predicting what the future will look like, whereas planning predicts what the future should look like.

The term is also used to describe the formal procedures used in such an endeavor, such as the creation of documents, diagrams, or meetings to discuss the important issues to be addressed, the objectives to be met, and the strategy to be followed. Beyond this, planning has a different meaning depending on the political or economic context in which it is used. Two attitudes to planning need to be held in tension: on the one hand we need to be prepared for what may lie ahead, which may mean contingencies and flexible processes. On the other hand, our future is shaped by consequences of our own planning and actions.

An Overview

Planning is a process for accomplishing purpose. It is a blue print of business growth and a road map of development. It helps in deciding objectives both in quantitative and qualitative terms. It is setting of goals on the basis of objectives and keeping in view the resources.

What should a Plan be?

A plan should be a realistic view of the expectations. Depending upon the activities, a plan can be long range, intermediate range or short range. It is the framework within which it must operate. For management seeking external support, the plan is the most important document and key to growth. Preparation of a comprehensive plan will not guarantee success, but lack of a sound plan will almost certainly ensure failure.

Purpose of a Plan

Just as no two organizations are alike, so also their plans. It is therefore important to prepare a plan keeping in view the necessities of the enterprise. A plan is an important aspect of business.

It serves the following three critical functions:

1. Helps management to clarify, focus, and research their business's or project's development and prospects.
2. Provides a considered and logical framework within which a business can develop and pursue business strategies over the next three to five years.
3. Offers a benchmark against which actual performance can be measured and reviewed.

Importance of the Planning Process

A plan can play a vital role in helping to avoid mistakes or recognize hidden opportunities. Preparing a satisfactory plan of the organization is essential. The planning know the business and that they have thought through its development in terms of products, management, finances, and most importantly, markets and competition. Planning helps in forecasting the future, makes the future visible to some extent. It bridges between where we are and where we want to go. Planning is looking ahead.

Types of Plans or Planning

- Architectural planning
- Business plan
- Comprehensive planning
- Enterprise Architecture Planning
- Event Planning and Production
- Family planning
- Financial planning
- Infrastructure planning
- Land use planning
- Life planning
- Marketing plan
- Network resource planning
- Strategic planning
- Urban planning
- Operational planning

Objectives and Policies

Objectives

The objectives are general parts of the planning process. They are the end-results towards which all business activities are directed. They are needed in every aspect where performance and result directly and vitally affect the survival and success of the firm. In other words, the objective of the firm justifies its existence. Robert C. Appley, "Objectives are goals; they are aims which management and administration wish the organization to achieve." In other words, goals, aims and purposes are also used to signify objectives. Newman and Summer stated, "For managerial purposes, it is useful to think of objectives as the results we want to achieve. Objective covers firm's long-range plans specific departmental goals and short-term individual assignment also."

Policies

George R. Ferry, "Policy is a verbal, written or implied overall guide setting up boundaries that supply the general units and directions in which managerial action will take place." Policies are specific guidelines and constraints for managerial thinking on decision-making and action. Policies provide the framework within which decision-makers are expected to operate while making organizational decisions. They are the basic guides to be consistent in decision-making.

Planning Basics

Essentials of Planning

Planning is not done off hand. It is prepared after careful and extensive research.

For a comprehensive business plan, management has to:

- Clearly define the target/goal in writing.
  - It should be set by a person having authority.
  - The goal should be realistic.
  - It should be specific.
  - Acceptability
  - Easily measurable
- Identify all the main issues which need to be addressed.
- Review past performance.
- Decide budgetary requirement.
- Focus on matters of strategic importance.
- What are requirements and how will they be met?
- What will be the likely length of the plan and its structure?
- Identify shortcomings in the concept and gaps.
- Strategies for implementation.
- Review periodically.

Applications

In Organizations

Planning is also a management process, concerned with defining goals for future organizational performance and deciding on the tasks and resources to be used in order to attain those goals. To meet the goals, managers may develop plans such as a business plan or a marketing plan. Planning always has a purpose.

The purpose may be achievement of certain goals or targets. The planning helps to achieve these goals or target by using the available time and resources. To minimize the timing and resources also require proper planning. The concept of planning is to identify what the organization wants to do by using the four questions which are "where are we today in terms of our business or strategy planning? Where are we going? Where do we want to go? How are we going to get there?..."

In Public Policy

Planning refers to the practice and the profession associated with the idea of planning an idea yourself. In many countries, the operation of a town and country planning system is often referred to as "planning" and the professionals which operate the system are known as "planners".

It is a conscious as well as sub-conscious activity. It is "an anticipatory decision making process" that helps in coping with complexities. It is deciding future course of action from amongst alternatives. It is a process that involves making and evaluating each set of interrelated decisions.

It is selection of missions, objectives and "translation of knowledge into action." A planned performance brings better results compared to an unplanned one. A manager's job is planning, monitoring and controlling. Planning and goal setting are important traits of an organization. It is done at all levels of the organization.

Planning includes the plan, the thought process, action, and implementation.Planning gives more power over the future. Planning is deciding in advance what to do, how to do it, when to do it, and who should do it. It bridges the gap from where the organization is to where it wants to be. The planning function involves establishing goals and arranging them in logical order.

CONTROL

Control is one of the managerial functions like planning, organizing, staffing and directing. It is an important function because it helps to check the errors and to take the corrective action so that deviation from standards are minimized and stated goals of the organization are achieved in desired manner.

Modern concepts, control is a foreseeing action whereas earlier concept of control was used only when errors were detected. Control in management means setting standards, measuring actual performance and taking corrective action. Thus, control comprises these three main activities.

Characteristics of Control

- Control is a continuous process
- Control is a management process
- Control is embedded in each level of organizational hierarchy
- Control is forward looking
- Control is closely linked with planning
- Control is a tool for achieving organizational activities

Elements of Control

The four basic elements in a control system:

1. The characteristic or condition to be controlled,
2. The sensor,
3. The comparator, and
4. *The activator*: Occur in the same sequence and maintain a consistent relationship to each other in every system.

The first element is the characteristic or condition of the operating system which is to be measured. We select a specific characteristic because a correlation exists between it and how the system is performing. The characteristic may be the output of the system during any stage of processing or it may be a condition that has resulted from the output of the system. For example, it may be the heat energy produced by the furnace or the temperature in the room which has changed because of the heat generated by the furnace. In an elementary school system, the hours a teacher works or the gain in knowledge demonstrated by the students on a national examination are examples of characteristics that may be selected for measurement, or control. The second element of control, the sensor, is a means for measuring the characteristic or condition. The control subsystem must be designed to include a sensory device or method of measurement. In a home heating system this device would be the thermostat, and in a quality-control system this measurement might be performed by a visual inspection of the product.

The third element of control, the comparator, determines the need for correction by comparing what is occurring with what has been planned. Some deviation from plan is usual and expected, but when variations are beyond those considered acceptable, corrective action is required. It is often possible to identify trends in performance and to take action before an unacceptable variation from the norm occurs. This sort of preventative action indicates that good control is being achieved.

The fourth element of control, the activator, is the corrective action taken to return the system to expected output. The actual person, device, or method used to direct corrective inputs into the operating system may take a variety of forms. It may be a hydraulic controller positioned by a solenoid or electric motor in response to an electronic error signal, an employee directed to rework the parts that failed to pass quality inspection, or a school principal who decides to buy additional books to provide for an increased number of students. As long as a plan is performed within allowable limits, corrective action is not necessary; this seldom occurs in practice, however. Information is the medium of control, because the flow of sensory data and later the flow of corrective information allow a characteristic or condition of the system to be controlled. To illustrate how information flow facilitates control, let us review the elements of control in the context of information.

Relationship between the Elements of Control and Information

Controlled Characteristic or. Condition The primary requirement of a control system is that it maintain the level and kind of output necessary to achieve the system's objectives. It is usually impractical to control every feature and condition associated with the system's output. Therefore, the choice of the controlled item is extremely important. There should be a direct correlation between the controlled item and the system's operation. In other words, control of the selected characteristic should have a direct relationship to the goal or objective of the system.

Sensor

After the characteristic is sensed, or measured, information pertinent to control is fed back. Exactly what information needs to be transmitted and also the language that will best facilitate the communication process and reduce the possibility of distortion in transmission must be carefully considered. Information that is to be compared with the standard, or plan, should be expressed in the same terms or language as in the original plan to facilitate decision making. Using machine methods may require extensive translation of the information.

Since optimal languages for computation and for human review are not always the same, the relative ease of translation may be a significant factor in selecting the units of measurement or the language unit in the sensing element. In many instances, the measurement may be sampled rather than providing a complete and continuous feedback of information about the operation. A sampling procedure suggests measuring some segment or portion of the operation that will represent the total.

Comparison with Standard

In a social system, the norms of acceptable behaviour become the standard against which so-called deviant behaviour may be judged. Regulations and laws provide a more formal collection of information for society. Social norms change, but very slowly. In contrast, the standards outlined by a formal law can be changed from one day to the next through revision, discontinuation, or replacement by another. Information about deviant behaviour becomes the basis for controlling social activity. Output information is compared with the standard or norm and significant deviations are noted. In an industrial example, frequency distribution may be used to show the average quality, the spread, and the comparison of output with a standard.

If there is a significant and uncorrectable difference between output and plan, the system is "out of control." This means that the objectives of the system are not feasible in relation to the capabilities of the present design. Either the objectives must be reevaluated or the system redesigned to add new capacity or capability. For example, the traffic in drugs has been increasing in some cities at an alarming rate. The citizens must decide whether to revise the police system so as to regain control, or whether to modify the law to reflect a different norm of acceptable behaviour.

Implimentor

The activator unit responds to the information received from the comparator and initiates corrective action. If the system is a machine-to-machine system, the corrective inputs are designed into the network.

When the control relates to a man-to-machine or man-to-man system, however, the individual(s) in charge must evaluate:

- The accuracy of the feedback information,
- The significance of the variation, and
- What corrective inputs will restore the system to a reasonable degree of stability. Once the decision has been made to direct new inputs into the system, the actual process may be relatively easy. A small amount of energy can change the operation of jet airplanes, automatic steel mills, and hydroelectric power plants. The pilot presses a button, and the landing gear of the airplane goes up or down; the

operator of a steel mill pushes a lever, and a ribbon of white-hot steel races through the plant; a worker at a control board directs the flow of electrical energy throughout a regional network of stations and substations. It takes but a small amount of control energy to release or stop large quantities of input.

The comparator may be located far from the operating system, although at least some of the elements must be in close proximity to operations. For example, the measurement is usually at the point of operations. The measurement information can be transmitted to a distant point for comparison with the standard and when deviations occur, the correcting input can be released from the distant point. However, the input will be located at the operating system. This ability to control from afar means that aircraft can be flown by remote control, dangerous manufacturing processes can be operated from a safe distance, and national organizations can be directed from centralized headquarters.

Process of Controlling

- Setting performance standards.
- Measurement of actual performance.
- Comparing actual performance with standards.
- Analysing deviations.
- Correcting deviations.

Kinds of Control

Control may be grouped according to three general classifications:

1. The nature of the information flow designed into the system,
2. The kind of components included in the design, and
3. The relationship of control to the decision process.

Open- and Closed-Loop Control

A street-lighting system controlled by a timing device is an example of an open-loop system. At a certain time each evening, a mechanical device closes the circuit and energy flows through the electric lines to light the lamps. Note, however, that the timing mechanism is an independent unit and is not measuring the objective function of the lighting system. If the lights should be needed on a dark, stormy day the timing device would not recognize this need and therefore would not activate energy inputs. Corrective properties may sometimes be built into the controller but this would not close the loop. In another instance, the sensing, comparison, or adjustment may be made through action taken by an individual who is not part of the system. For example, the lights may be turned on by someone who happens to pass by and recognizes the need for additional light. If control is exercised as a result of the operation rather than because of outside or predetermined arrangements, it is a closed-loop system. The home thermostat is the classic example of a control device in a closed-loop system. When the room temperature drops below the desired point, the control mechanism closes the circuit to start the furnace and the temperature rises. The furnace-activating circuit is turned off as the temperature reaches the preselected level. The significant difference between this type of system and an open-loop system is that the control device is an element of the system it serves and measures the performance of the system. In other words, all four control elements are integral to the specific system.

An essential part of a closed-loop system is feedback; that is, the output of the system is measured continually through the item controlled, and the input is modified to reduce any difference or error toward zero. Many of the patterns of information flow in organizations are found to have the nature of closed loops, which use feedback. The reason for such a condition is apparent when one recognizes that any system, if it is to achieve a predetermined goal, must have available to it at all times an indication of its degree of attainment. In general, every goal-seeking system employs feedback.

Man and Machine Control

The elements of control are easy to identify in machine systems. For example, the characteristic to be controlled might be some variable like speed or temperature, and the sensing device could be a speedometer or a thermometer. An expectation of precision exists because the characteristic is quantifiable and the standard and the normal variation to be expected can be described in exact terms. In automatic machine systems, inputs of information are used in a process of continual adjustment to achieve output specifications. When even a small variation from the standard occurs, the correction process begins. The automatic system is highly structured, designed to accept certain kinds of input and produce specific output, and programmed to regulate the transformation of inputs within a narrow range of variation.

For an illustration of mechanical control, as the load on a steam engine increases and the engine starts to slow down, the regulator reacts by opening a valve that releases additional inputs of steam energy. This new input returns the engine to the desired number of revolutions per minute. This type of mechanical control is crude in comparison to the more sophisticated electronic control systems in everyday use. Consider the complex missile-guidance systems that measure the actual course according to predetermined mathematical calculations and make almost instantaneous corrections to direct the missile to its target.

Machine systems can be complex because of the sophisticated technology, whereas control of people is complex because the elements of control are difficult to determine. In human control systems, the relationship between objectives and associated characteristics is often vague; the measurement of the characteristic may be extremely subjective; the expected standard is difficult to define; and the amount of new inputs required is impossible to quantify. To illustrate, let us refer once more to a formalized social system in which deviant behaviour is controlled through a process of observed violation of the existing law, court hearings and trials, incarceration when the accused is found guilty and release from custody after rehabilitation of the prisoner has occurred. The speed limit established for freeway driving is one standard of performance that is quantifiable, but even in this instance, the degree of permissible variation and the amount of the actual variation are often a subject of disagreement between the patrolman and the suspected violator. The complexity of our society is reflected in many of our laws and regulations, which establish the general standards for economic, political, and social operations. A citizen may not know or understand the law and consequently would not know whether or not he was guilty of a violation.

Most organized systems are some combination of man and machine; some elements of control may be performed by machine whereas others are accomplished by man. In addition, some standards may be precisely structured whereas others may be little more than general guidelines with wide variations expected in output. Man must performanceas the controller when measurement is subjective and judgment is required. Machines such as computers are incapable of making exceptions from the specified control criteria regardless of how much a particular case might warrant special consideration. A pilot acts in conjunction with computers and automatic pilots to fly large jets. In the event of unexpected weather changes, or possible collision with another plane, he must intercede and assume direct control.

Organizational and Operational Control

The concept of organizational control is implicit in the bureaucratic theory of Max Weber. Associated with this theory are such concepts as "span of control", "closeness of supervision", and "hierarchical authority". Weber's view tends to include all levels or types of organizational control as being the same. More recently, writers have tended to differentiate the control process between that which emphasizes the nature of the organizational or systems design and that which deals with daily operations.

To illustrate the difference, we "evaluate" the performance of a system to see how effective and efficient the design proved to be or to discover why it failed. In contrast, we operate and "control" the system with respect to the daily inputs of material, information, and energy. In both instances, the f feedback are present, but organizational control tends to review and evaluate the nature and arrangement of components in the system, whereas operational control tends to adjust the daily inputs. The direction for organizational control comes from the goals and strategic plans of the organization. General plans are translated into specific performance measures such as share of the market, earnings, return on investment, and budgets.

The process of organizational control is to review and evaluate the performance of the system against these established norms. Rewards for meeting or exceeding standards may range from special recognition to salary increases or promotions. On the other hand, a failure to meet expectations may signal the need to reorganize or redesign. In organizational control, the approach used in the programme of review and evaluation depends on the reason for the evaluation — that is, is it because the system is not effective (accomplishing its objectives)? Is the system failing to achieve an expected standard of efficiency? Is the evaluation being conducted because of a breakdown or failure in operations? Is it merely a periodic audit-and-review process?

When a system has failed or is in great difficulty, special diagnostic techniques may be required to isolate the trouble areas and to identify the causes of the difficulty. It is appropriate to investigate areas that have been troublesome before or areas where some measure of performance can be quickly identified. For example, if an organization's output backlog builds rapidly, it is logical to check first to see if the problem is due to such readily obtainable measures as increased demand or to a drop in available man hours. When a more detailed analysis is necessary, a systematic procedure should be followed.

In contrast to organizational control, operational control serves to regulate the day-to-day output relative to schedules, specifications, and costs. Is the output of product or service the proper quality and is it available as scheduled? Are inventories of raw materials, goods-in-process, and finished products being purchased and produced in the desired quantities? Are the costs associated with the transformation process in line with cost estimates? Is the information needed in the transformation process available in the right form and at the right time? Is the energy resource being utilized efficiently?

The most difficult task of management concerns monitoring the behaviour of individuals, comparing performance to some standard, and providing rewards or punishment as indicated. Sometimes this control over people relates entirely to their output. For example, a manager might not be concerned with the behaviour of a salesman as long as sales were as high as expected. In other instances, close supervision of the salesman might be appropriate if achieving customer satisfaction were one of the sales organization's main objectives.

The larger the unit, the more likely that the control characteristic will be related to some output goal. It also follows that if it is difficult or impossible to identify the actual output of individuals, it is better to measure the performance of the entire group. This means that individuals' levels of motivation and the measurement of their performance become subjective judgments made by the supervisor. Controlling output also suggests the difficulty of controlling individuals' performance and relating this to the total system's objectives.

Problems of Control

The perfect plan could be outlined if every possible variation of input could be anticipated and if the system would operate as predicted. This kind of planning is neither realistic, economical, nor feasible for most business systems. If it were feasible, planning requirements would be so complex that the system would be out of date before it could be operated. Therefore, we design control into systems.

This requires more thought in the systems design but allows more flexibility of operations and makes it possible to operate a system using unpredictable components and undetermined input. Still, the design and effective operation of control are not without problems. The objective of the system is to perform some specified function. The purpose of organizational control is to see that the specified function is achieved; the objective of operational control is to ensure that variations in daily output are maintained within prescribed limits. It is one thing to design a system that contains all of the elements of control, and quite another to make it operate true to the best objectives of design.

Operating "in control" or "with plan" does not guarantee optimum performance. For example, the plan may not make the best use of the inputs of materials, energy, or information — in other words, the system may not be designed to operate efficiently. Some of the more typical problems relating to control include the difficulty of measurement, the problem of timing information flow, and the setting of proper standards.

Measurement of Output

When objectives are not limited to quantitative output, the measurement of system effectiveness is difficult to make and subsequently perplexing to evaluate. Many of the characteristics pertaining to output do not lend themselves to quantitative measurement. This is true particularly when inputs of human energy cannot be related directly to output. The same situation applies to machines and other equipment associated with human involvement, when output is not in specific units.

In evaluating man-machine or human-oriented systems, psychological and sociological factors obviously do not easily translate into quantifiable terms. For example, how does mental fatigue affect the quality or quantity of output? And, if it does, is mental fatigue a function of the lack of a challenging assignment or the fear of a potential injury? Subjective inputs may be transferred into numerical data, but there is always the danger of an incorrect appraisal and transfer, and the danger that the analyst may assume undue confidence in such data after they have been quantified. Let us suppose, for example, that the decisions made by an executive are rated from 1 to 10, 10 being the perfect decision. After determining the ranking for each decision, adding these, and dividing by the total number of decisions made, the average ranking would indicate a particular executive's score in his decision-making role. On the basis of this score, judgments — which could be quite erroneous — might be made about his decision-making effectiveness. One executive with a ranking of 6.75 might be considered more effective than another who had a ranking of 6.25, and yet the two managers may have made decisions under different circumstances and conditions. External factors over which neither executive had any control may have influenced the difference in "effectiveness".

Quantifying human behaviour, despite its extreme difficulty, subjectivity, and imprecision in relation to measuring physical characteristics is the most prevalent and important measurement made in large systems. The behaviour of individuals ultimately dictates the success or failure of every man-made system.

Information Flow

Another problem of control relates to the improper timing of information introduced into the feedback channel. Improper timing can occur in both computerized and human control systems, either by mistakes in measurement or in judgment. The more rapid the system's response to an error signal, the more likely it is that the system could overadjust; yet the need for prompt action is important because any delay in providing corrective input could also be crucial. A system generating feedback inconsistent with current need will tend to fluctuate and will not adjust in the desired manner.

The most serious problem in information flow arises when the delay in feedback is exactly one-half cycle, for then the corrective action is superimposed on a variation from norm which, at that moment, is in the same direction as that of the correction. This causes the system to overcorrect, and then if the reverse adjustment is made out of cycle, to correct too much in the other direction, and so on until the system fluctuates out of control. If, at Point A, the trend below standard is recognized and new inputs are added, but not until Point B, the system will overreact and go beyond the allowable limits. Again, if this is recognized at Point C, but inputs are not withdrawn until Point D, it will cause the system to drop below the lower limit of allowable variation.

One solution to this problem rests in anticipation, which involves measuring not only the change but also the rate of change. The correction is outlined as a factor of the type and rate of the error. The difficulty also might be overcome by reducing the time lag between the measurement of the output and the adjustment to input.

If a trend can be indicated, a time lead can be introduced to compensate for the time lag, bringing about consistency between the need for correction and the type and magnitude of the indicated action. It is usually more effective for an organization to maintain continuous measurement of its performance and to make small adjustments in operations constantly. Information feedback, consequently, should be timely and correct to be effective. That is, the information should provide an accurate indication of the status of the system.

Setting Standards

Setting the proper standards or control limits is a problem in many systems. Parents are confronted with this dilemma in expressing what they expect of their children, and business managers face the same issue in establishing standards that will be acceptable to employees. Some theorists have proposed that workers be allowed to set their own standards, on the assumption that when people establish their own goals, they are more apt to accept and achieve them.

Standards should be as precise as possible and communicated to all persons concerned. Moreover, communication alone is not sufficient; understanding is necessary. In human systems, standards tend to be poorly defined and the allowable range of deviation from standard also indefinite. For example, how many hours each day should a professor be expected to be available for student consultation? Or, what kind of behaviour should be expected by students in the classroom? Discretion and personal judgment play a large part in such systems, to determine whether corrective action should be taken. Perhaps the most difficult problem in human systems is the unresponsiveness of individuals to indicated correction. This may take the form of opposition and subversion to control, or it may be related to the lack of defined responsibility or authority to take action. Leadership and positive motivation then become vital ingredients in achieving the proper response to input requirements.

Most control problems relate to design; thus the solution to these problems must start at that point. Automatic control systems, provided that human intervention is possible to handle exceptions, offer the greatest promise. There is a danger, however, that we may measure characteristics that do not represent effective performance or that improper information may be communicated.

OBJECTIVES

- *Effectiveness*: Goods to fulfill customers' needs
- *Maximising output*: Maximum output with minimum input
- *Quality control*: Product/service quality meets planned quality specifications
- *Minimise throughput time*: Conversion of RM to FG in minimum time
- *Capacity*: full utilisation of men and machines
- Minimise cost: minimum cost of production
- *Maintaining inventory*: Optimal inventory
- *Flexibility*: Flexibility in production operations
- *Coordination*: Between men and machines
- *Capacity*: Plan for current and future needs
- *Reduce bottlenecks*: Solve production problems early
- *Maximise profit*: Minimise cost
- *Production schedules*: As per plan
- *Routes and schedules*: To optimise use of men, material and machinery
- *Maintain performance*: Maintain standards

FUNCTIONS OF PRODUCTION PLANNING

- Product selection and design
- Process selection and planning
- Facility location
- Facility layout and materials handling
- Capacity planning
- Systems and procedures
- Estimating quantity/costs of production, men
- Routing operation sequence
- Job scheduling and loading

FUNCTIONS OF PRODUCTION CONTROL

- Inventory control: MRP; JIT
- Time management
- Quality control
- Maintenance and Replacement
- Cost reduction and cost control
- Dispatch
- Expediting/Follow-up/Progressing

SCOPE OF PRODUCTION PLANNING AND CONTROL

- *Material*: RM, components, spares; right quantity; right time
- Methods
- Machines and equipments
- Manpower
- Routing
- Estimating
- Loading and sceduling
- Dispatching
- Expediting
- Inspection
- Evaluating
- Cost control

PHASES IN PRODUCTION PLANNING AND CONTROL SYSTEM

- *Planning*:
  - Pre-planning
  - Product planning and development;
  - Demand forecasting;
  - Resource planning;
  - Facilities planning;
  - Plant location and layout
- Active planning
  - Quantity planning;
  - Product mix;
  - Routing;
  - Scheduling;
  - Material planning;
  - Process planning;
  - Capacity planning;
  - Tool planning

BENEFITS OF PRODUCTION PLANNING AND CONTROL

- Higher quality
- Better resource utilization
- Reduced inventory
- Reduced manufacturing cycle time
- Faster delivery
- Better customer services
- Lower production costs
- Lower capital investment
- Higher customer service
- Improved sales turnover
- Improved market share
- Improved profitability
- Competitive advantage
- Flexibility
- Dependability
- Lower prices

LIMITATIONS OF PRODUCTION PLANNING AND CONTROL

- Based on assumptions
- Resistance to change
- Time consuming
- Difficult due to rapid environment changes

MEASURING EFFECTIVENESS OF PRODUCTION PLANNING AND CONTROL

- Delivery
- Inventory levels
- Production/Operations Management

REQUIREMENTS FOR EFFECTIVE PRODUCTION PLANNING AND CONTROL

- Sound organisational structure
- Delegation of authority
- Reliable, up-to-date feedback
- Standardisation
- Trained people
- Flexibility to adapt
- Appropriate management policies
- Accurate assessment of manufacturing/procurement lead times
- Adequate plant capacity

TECHNIQUES

- Planning and Control of Reserves;
  - Deterministic/non-deterministic systems
- Network analysis:
- PERT
  - Project Evaluation
  - Review Technique
- CPM
  - Critical Path Method
- Reliability Theory:
  - Probability
    - a. Series structure
    - b. Parallel structure

WORK STUDY

Work Study is the systemeatic examination of the methods of carrying out activities such as to improve the effective use of resources and to set up standards of performance for the activities carried out.

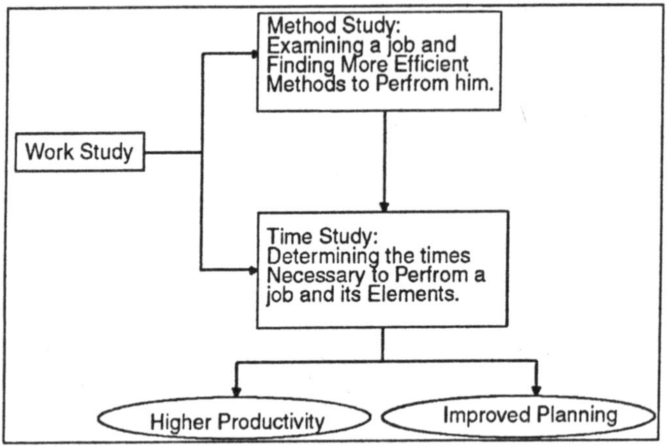

Fig. Components of Work Study

Another definition of Work Study could be: A generic term for those techniques, particularly method study and work measurement, which are used in the examination of human work in all its contexts, and which lead systematically to to the investigation of all the factors which affect the efficiency and economy of the situation being reviewed, in order to effect improvement'. This has to do with Productivity Improvement, but also improvement of Quality and Safety.

PRODUCTIVITY

In this post we're going to take a deep look into the concept of productivity.

Here's our personal definition of productivity:

Productivity = Value/Time

By this definition there are two primary ways of increasing productivity:

1. Increase the value created
2. Decrease the time required to create that value

You can complicate this definition by including other factors like energy and resources, but we prefer the simplicity of time because in most cases factors like energy and resources are reducible to time anyway. Time also makes it very easy to compare different levels of productivity, such as output per hour or per day. Apparently you can make some significant gains on the time side. There are many personal productivity optimizations which, especially if you introduce them in your youth, will produce a massive net savings of time over the course of your life. Consider your typing speed, for instance. If you invest the time to get your speed up to 90 words per minute or faster, it will be well worth the initial time investment if you happen to do a lot of typing over your lifetime, compared to allowing your speed to linger at 50 wpm or slower year after year.

The extra hours of practice will be nothing compared to the time you save typing emails, letters, or blog entries over the next few decades. Other time-based optimizations include improving your sleeping habits, minimizing commute time, or dropping time-wasting habits like smoking. The main limit of time-based optimizations is that the optimization process requires an input of time itself. It takes time to save time. So the more time you invest in optimizing time usage, the greater your initial time investment, and the greater your need for a long-term payoff to justify that investment. This limit creates an upper bound for any time-based optimizations you attempt, in accordance with the law of diminishing returns. The more time you invest in any optimization attempt, the lower your net return, all else being equal. This law of diminishing returns points us back to the value side. While we might be stuck with diminshing returns by trying to optimize the time side alone, we may notice that working to optimize the value side is less limiting and more open-ended.

WHAT IS THE "VALUE" IN OUR PRODUCTIVITY EQUATION?

Value is a quality you must define for yourself. Hence, any definition of productity is relative to the definition of value. In circles where people can agree on a common definition of value, they can also agree on a common definition of productivity. However, in terms of your own personal productivity, you aren't obligated to define value the same way anyone else would. You are free to adopt your own definition, such that your pursuit of greater productivity becomes a personal quest that produces the value that matters most to you.

Too often we adopt a socially conditioned definition of value, which tends to be very limiting. Perhaps we define value in terms of work output within our career, number of tasks completed, number and quality of important projects finished, etc. You may not be able to verbalize it clearly, but perhaps you have a working definition of value that feels comfortable to you. You can tell when you've had a productive day and when you haven't based on how much value you created, in accordance with your own sense of what value means.

But how much conscious thought did you put into your personal definition of value? I'm going to challenge you to put a bit more thought into your definition, which will consequently redefine your sense of productivity.

IMPACT

First, according to your definition of value, to what extent is the value provided? Who receives the value? Yourself, your boss, your coworkers, your friends, your family, your company, your customers, your team, certain investors, your community, your country, the world, your family, God, all conscious beings, etc? What degree of value is ultimately received by each person or group? Are you providing value to one person, 10 people, 100 people, 1000 people, millions of people, the whole planet? How much do you feel the value you provide ripples outward beyond those you provide it to directly? How quickly do those ripples dissipate? What's your sense of the basic level of impact of your value? Is it limited or expansive? For example, if you're the CEO of a Fortune 500 corporation or the leader of a country, you'll have a far greater ability to provide value to large numbers of people vs. if you work as a janitor. The more people you can influence, the greater your potential value. Greater leverage means greater potential impact.

ENDURANCE

Secondly, how long does the value you create endure? An hour, a day, a week, a month, a year, a decade, a lifetime, 100 years, 1000 years, 10,000 years, until the end of time? To what extent does your value carry forward in time? Is it quickly consumed and forgotten? Or does it continue to regenerate itself year after year? Does your value create ripples through time?

The Mona Lisa *is still providing value hundreds of years after its creation. But other works of art do not provide any enduring value beyond the lifetime of the artist. They are quickly abandoned and eventually replaced.*

ESSENCE

Thirdly, what is the essence of the value you produce? Do you help people survive? Entertain them? Enlighten them? How much do others value what you produce? What price would they be willing to pay for it? Do they consider your value essential, optional, or undesirable? How unique is your value? Are you the only one who can provide it, or are there plenty of equivalent choices?

The essence of value provided by a janitor is low because it is easy to find people to do such work for little pay. The essence of value of a physicist is potentially enormous because a new theoretical concept could yield a more accurate understanding of the universe.

VOLUME

Lastly, what is the volume of value you create? How much of it are you putting out in a given period of time? What is the quantity in which you produce that value? For example, Picasso was a prolific artist who created hundreds of different works over his lifetime. Other artists had a far lower volume of output.

So now we have this little formula:

Value = Impact x Endurance x Essence x Volume

And therefore:

Productivity = Impact x Endurance x Essence x Volume/Time

Now what's interesting here is that most of the productivity literature I've read focuses almost exclusively on volume and time. But those are the most limiting parts of this equation.

PRODUCTIVITY CONCEPTUAL MODEL

The Productivity Conceptual Model, takes the form of a 'productivity tree'. The roots denote the inputs to the system, the trunk the conversion process and the foliage and fruits the systems outputs.

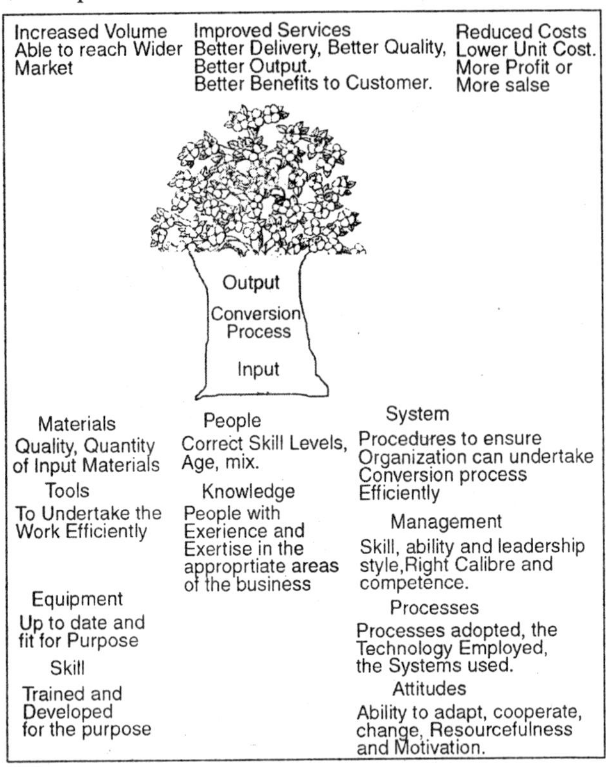

Fig. Productivity Conceptual Model

The successful management of this process, is ultimately the key to survival of any organization. It should be the concern of and a development goal for all organizational members, irrespective of their position.

METHOD STUDY

Method study is the process of subjecting work to systematic, critical scrutiny in order to make it more effective and/or more efficient.

It was originally designed for the analysis and improvement of repetitive, manual work, but it can be used for all types of activity at all levels of an organisation.

The process is often seen as a linear, described by its main steps of:

- Select;
- Record;
- Examine;
- Develop;
- Install;
- Maintain.

Although this linear representation shows the underlying simplicity of method study, in practice the process is much more one of iteration around the steps with each dominating at a different stage of the investigation. The cyclic process often starts with a quick, rough pass in which preliminary data are collected and examined, before subsequent passes provide and handle more comprehensive and more detailed data to obtain and analyse a more complete picture.

Work is selected for method study on the basis of it being an identified problem area or an identified opportunity and usually because it meets certain conditions of urgency and/or priority.Before any method study investigation is begun, it is necessary to establish clear terms of reference which define the aims, scale, scope and constraints of the investigation.

This should also include an identification of who "owns" the problem or situation and ways in which such "ownership" is shared. This may lead to a debate on the aims of the project, on reporting mechanisms and frequencies, and on the measures of success. This process is sometimes introduced as a separate and distinct phase of method study, as the "define" stage. It leads to a plan for the investigation which identifies appropriate techniques, personnel, and timescale.

The Record stage of method study is to provide sufficient data to performanceas the basis of evaluation and examination. A wide range of techniques are available for recording; the choice depends on the nature of the investigation and the work being studied, and on the level of detail required. Many of the techniques are simple charts and diagrams, but these may be supplemented by photographic and video recording, and by computer based techniques.

Especially with "hard" problems, method study often involves the construction and analysis of models, from simple charts and diagrams used to record and represent the situation to full, computerised simulations. Manipulation of and experimentation on the models leads to ideas for development.

The recorded data are subjected to examination and analysis; formalised versions of this process are critical examination and systems analysis. The aim is to identify, often through a structured, questioning process, those points of the overall system of work that require improvements or offer opportunity for beneficial change.

The Examine stage merges into the Develop stage of the investigation as more thorough analysis leads automatically to identified areas of change. The aim here is to identify possible actions for improvement and to subject these to evaluation in order to develop a preferred solution.

Sometimes it is necessary to identify short-term and long-term solutions so that improvements can be made immediately, while longer-term changes are implemented and come to fruition.

The success of any method study project is realised when actual change is made 'on the ground' - change that meets the originally specified terms of reference for the project. Thus, the Install phase is very important. Making theoretical change is easy; making real change demands careful planning - and handling of the people involved in the situation under review. They may need reassuring, retraining and supporting through the acquisition of new skills. Install, in some cases,will require a parallel running of old and new systems, in others, it may need the build-up of buffer stocks, and in others..... what matters is that the introduction of new working methods is successful. There is often only one chance to make change!

Some time after the introduction of new working methods, it is necessary to check that the new method is working, that it is being adhered to, and that it has brought about the desired results. This is the Maintain phase. Method drift is common - when people start to either revert to old ways of working, or introduce new changes. Some of these may be helpful; others may be inefficient or unsafe. A methods audit can be used to formally compare practice with the defined method and identify such 'irregularities'.

WORK MEASUREMENT

Work measurement is the process of establishing the time that a given task would take when performed by a qualified worker working at a defined level of performance.

There are various ways in which work may be measured and a variety of techniques have been established.

The basic procedure, irrespective of the particular measurement technique being used, consists of three stages:

1. An analysis phase in which the job is divided into convenient, discrete components, commonly known as elements;
2. A measurement phase in which the specific measurement technique is used to establish the time required to complete each element of work;
3. A synthesis phase in which the various elemental times are added, together with appropriate allowances to construct the standard time for the complete job.

The techniques used to measure work can be classified into those that rely on direct observation of the work, and those that do not. For example, some techniques, such as predetermined motion-time systems and the use of synthetic or standard data can provide times from simulation or even visualisation of the work. However, the data on which such techniques are based were almost certainly based on earlier observation of actual work.

RATING

Direct observation techniques include a process for converting observed times to times for the "qualified worker working at a defined level of performance." The commonest of these processes is known as rating.

This involves the observer making an assessment of the worker's rate of working relative to the observer's concept of the rate corresponding to standard rating. This assessment is based on the factors involved in the work - such as effort, dexterity, speed of movement, and consistency. The assessment is made on a rating scale, of which there are three or four in common usage. Thus on the 0-100 scale, the observer makes a judgement of the worker's rate of working as a percentage of the standard rate of working.

The rating is then used to convert the observed time to the basic time using the simple formula:

Basic time = observed time x observed rating/standard rating

Rating is regarded by many as a controversial area of measurement since it is a subjective assessment. Where different observers rate differently, the resulting basic times are not comparable. However, practised rating practitioners are remarkably consistent. It is important that those undertaking the rating are properly trained, and that this training is regularly updated through rating 'clinics'.

ALLOWANCES

When carrying out work over a complete shift or working day, workers obviously suffer from the fatigue imposed both by the work undertaken and the conditions under which they are working. The normal practice is to make an addition to the basic time to allow the worker to recover from this fatigue and to attend to personal needs. The amount of the allowance depends on the nature of the work and the working environment, and is often assessed using an agreed set of guidelines and scales. It is usual to allow some of the recovery period inherent in these allowances to be taken away from the workplace. Thus, work design should include the design of an effective work-rest regime. The addition of allowances should never be used to compensate for an unsafe or unhealthy working environment.

One minority school of thought suggests that relaxation allowances are unnecessary. With work which involves, say, the carrying of heavy weights, this school suggests that the observer automatically adjusts the concept of standard rating to allow for the weight. Thus, if the standard rate of performance for walking on level ground carrying no weight is equivalent to four miles per hour, then an observer rating a worker walking while carrying a weight will not expect the equivalent rate.

Thus, it is argued that the weight has been allowed for in the adjustment of standard rating and any relaxation allowance is simply a duplication of this adjustment. In many jobs there are small amounts of work that may occur irregularly and inconsistently. It is often not economic to measure such infrequent work and an additional allowance is added to cover such work and similar irregular delays. This allowance is known as a contingency allowance and is assessed either by observation, by analysis of historical records or by experience. The end result is a standard time which includes the time the work "should" take plus additional allocations in the form of allowances, where appropriate, to cover relaxation time, contingency time and, perhaps, unoccupied time which increases the overall work cycle.

CHOOSING A MEASUREMENT TECHNIQUE

The choice of a suitable measurement technique depends on a number of factors including:

- The purpose of the measurement;
- The level of detail required;
- The time available for the measurement;
- The existence of available predetermined data;
- And the cost of measurement.

To some extent there is a trade off between some of these factors. For example, techniques which derive times quickly may provide less detail and be less suitable for some purposes, such as the establishment of individual performance levels on short-cycle work.

The advantage of structured and systematic work measurement is that it gives a common currency for the evaluation and comparison of all types of work. The results obtained from work measurement are commonly used as the basis of the planning and scheduling of work, manpower planning, work balancing in team working, costing, labour performance measurement, and financial incentives. They are less commonly used as the basis of product design, methods comparison, work sequencing, and workplace design.

6

Techniques

JUST IN TIME

Just in time is a 'pull' system of production, so actual orders provide a signal for when a product should be manufactured. Demand-pull enables a firm to produce only what is required, in the correct quantity and at the correct time. This means that stock levels of raw materials, components, work in progress and finished goods can be kept to a minimum. This requires a carefully planned scheduling and flow of resources through the production process.

Modern manufacturing firms use sophisticated production scheduling software to plan production for each period of time, which includes ordering the correct stock. Information is exchanged with suppliers and customers through EDI to help ensure that every detail is correct. Supplies are delivered right to the production line only when they are needed. For example, a car manufacturing plant might receive exactly the right number and type of tyres for one day's production, and the supplier would be expected to deliver them to the correct loading bay on the production line within a very narrow time slot.

ADVANTAGES OF JIT

- Lower stock holding means a reduction in storage space which saves rent and insurance costs
- As stock is only obtained when it is needed, less working capital is tied up in stock
- There is less likelihood of stock perishing, becoming obsolete or out of date

- Avoids the build-up of unsold finished product that can occur with sudden changes in demand
- Less time is spent on checking and re-working the product of others as the emphasis is on getting the work right first time

DISADVANTAGES OF JIT

- There is little room for mistakes as minimal stock is kept for re-working faulty product
- Production is very reliant on suppliers and if stock is not delivered on time, the whole production schedule can be delayed
- There is no spare finished product available to meet unexpected orders, because all product is made to meet actual orders – however, JIT is a very responsive method of production.

KANBAN SYSTEM

A Kanban system is a means to achieve Just-in-time production. It works on the basis that each process on a production line pulls just the number and type of components the process requires, at just the right time. The mechanism used is a Kanban card. This is usually a physical card but other devices can be used. Two kinds of Kanban cards are mainly used: A Withdrawal Kanban - specifies the kind and quantity of product which a manufacturing process should withdraw from a preceding process.

The withdrawal Kanban illustrated shows that the preceding process which makes this part is forging, and the person carrying this Kanban from the subsequent process must go to position B-2 of the forging department to withdraw drive pinions. Each box of drive pinions contains 20 units and the shape of the box is 'B'. This Kanban is the 4th of 8 issued. The item back number is an abbreviation of the item.

A Production-ordering Kanban - specifies the kind and quantity of product which the preceding process must produce. The one illustrated shows that the machining process SB-8 must produce the crankshaft for the car type SX50BC-

150. The crankshaft produced should be placed at store F26-18. The production-ordering Kanban is often called an in-process Kanban or simply a production Kanban.

USING KANBANS ON A PRODUCTION LINE

Each process on the production line has two Kanban 'post-boxes', one for withdrawal and one for production-ordering Kanbans. At regular intervals a worker takes withdrawal Kanbans that have accumulated in his process post-box, and any empty pallets, to the location where finished parts from the preceding process are stored. Each full pallet has attached to it one or more production-ordering Kanbans which he removes and puts in the appropriate post-box belonging to the process that produced the parts.

The worker now attaches a withdrawal Kanban to the pallet and takes it back to his own process area. When this new pallet begins to be used, its withdrawal Kanban is put back into the withdrawal post-box. At each process on the line, production-ordering Kanbans are periodically removed from their post-box and used to define what parts and quantities to produce next.

WHEN AND HOW KANBANS ARE EFFECTIVE

Kanbans help simplify planning and to fine-tune production to meet changing customer demand of up to + or - 10%. The system requires planned monthly and weekly production schedules. Kanbans simplify day to day flexibility, and changes to the production schedule need only to be given to the final assembly process and will then automatically work their way back up the line.

Kanban systems can be tightened by removing cards or by reducing the number of parts on a pallet. The effect will be to speed the flow through the process and hence reduce lead times. However it also makes the system more vulnerable to breakdowns and other causes of dislocation. By identifying the areas within the line that are causing disruption, efforts can be made to improve them. Thus the overall efficiency of the line is raised by tackling the key points. Other types of Kanban also used are Supplier Kanbans - to withdraw goods from external suppliers, and two types of Signal Kanban, which are inserted near the bottom of a stack of items. These automatically initiate production of batch produced items when the stock reaches a pre-set re-order level.

SINGLE CARD KANBAN SYSTEMS

In a single-card Kanban system, parts are produced and bought according to a daily schedule, and deliveries to the user are controlled by a 'conveyancing' Kanban. In effect, the single-card system is a push system for production coupled with a pull system for delivery to the point of use. Single-card Kanban controls deliveries very tightly, so that the using work centre never has more than a container or two of parts and the stock point serving the work centre is eliminated. Single-card systems work well in companies in which it is relatively easy to associate the required quantity and timing of component parts with the schedule of end products. These are usually companies with a relatively small range of end products, or products which are not subject to rapid, unexpected changes in demand levels.

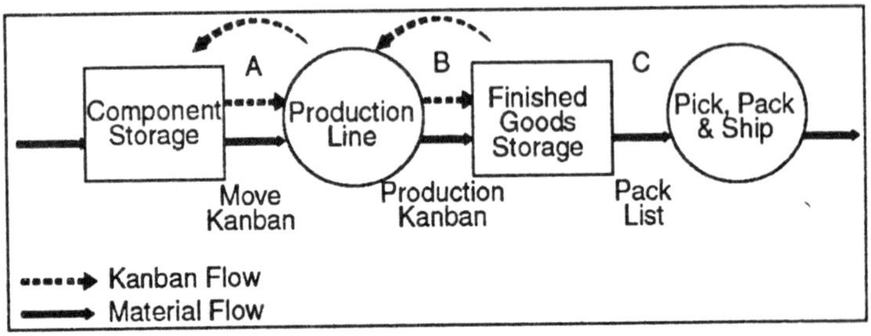

Fig. Kanban System

ADVANTAGES O F KANBAN PROCESSING

Provides a simple and understandable process. Provides quick and precise information. There are low costs associated with the transfer of information. Provides quick response to changes. There is a strict limit of over-capacity in processes.

Avoids overproduction. Minimizes waste. Full control can be maintained. Delegates responsibility to line workers

SIX SIGMA

Six Sigma is a business management strategy originally developed by Motorola, USA in 1981. As of 2010[update], it enjoys widespread application in many sectors of industry, although its application is not without controversy.

Six Sigma seeks to improve the quality of process outputs by identifying and removing the causes of defects and minimizing variability in manufacturing and business processes. It uses a set of quality management methods, including statistical methods, and creates a special infrastructure of people within the organization who are experts in these methods. Each Six Sigma project carried out within an organization follows a defined sequence of steps and has quantified targets. These targets can be financial or whatever is critical to the customer of that process.

The term *six sigma* originated from terminology associated with manufacturing, specifically terms associated with statistical modelling of manufacturing processes. The maturity of a manufacturing process can be described by a *sigma* rating indicating its yield, or the percentage of defect-free products it creates. A six-sigma process is one in which 99.99966% of the products manufactured are free of defects, compared to a one-sigma process in which only 31% are free of defects. Motorola set a goal of "six sigmas" for all of its manufacturing operations and this goal became a byword for the management and engineering practices used to achieve it.

Six Sigma originated as a set of practices designed to improve manufacturing processes and eliminate defects, but its application was subsequently extended to other types of business processes as well. In Six Sigma, a defect is defined as any process output that does not meet customer specifications, or that could lead to creating an output that does not meet customer specifications. Bill Smith first formulated the particulars of the methodology at Motorola in 1986. Six Sigma was heavily inspired by six preceding decades of quality improvement methodologies such as quality control, TQM, and Zero Defects, based on the work of pioneers such as Shewhart, Deming, Juran, Ishikawa, Taguchi and others.

Like its predecessors, Six Sigma doctrine asserts that:

- Continuous efforts to achieve stable and predictable process results are of vital importance to business success.
- Manufacturing and business processes have characteristics that can be measured, analysed, improved and controlled.
- Achieving sustained quality improvement requires commitment from the entire organization, particularly from top-level management.

Features that set Six Sigma apart from previous quality improvement initiatives include:

- A clear focus on achieving measurable and quantifiable financial returns from any Six Sigma project.
- An increased emphasis on strong and passionate management leadership and support.
- A special infrastructure of "Champions," "Master Black Belts," "Black Belts," "Yellow Belts", etc. to lead and implement the Six Sigma approach.
- A clear commitment to making decisions on the basis of verifiable data, rather than assumptions and guesswork.

The term "Six Sigma" comes from a field of statistics known as process capability studies. Originally, it referred to the ability of manufacturing processes to produce a very high proportion of output within specification. Processes that operate with "six sigma quality" over the short term are assumed to produce long-term defect levels below 3.4 defects per million opportunities. Six Sigma's implicit goal is to improve all processes to that level of quality or better.

Six Sigma is a registered service mark and trademark of Motorola Inc. As of 2006[update] Motorola reported over US$17 billion in savings from Six Sigma. Other early adopters of Six Sigma who achieved well-publicized success include

Honeywell and General Electric, where Jack Welch introduced the method. By the late 1990s, about two-thirds of the Fortune 500 organizations had begun Six Sigma initiatives with the aim of reducing costs and improving quality.

In recent years[update], some practitioners have combined Six Sigma ideas with lean manufacturing to yield a methodology named Lean Six Sigma.

METHODS

Six Sigma projects follow two project methodologies inspired by Deming's Plan-Do-Check-Act Cycle. These methodologies, composed of five phases each, bear the acronyms DMAIC and DMADV.

- DMAIC is used for projects aimed at improving an existing business process. DMAIC is pronounced as "duh-may-ick".
- DMADV is used for projects aimed at creating new product or process designs. DMADV is pronounced as "duh-mad-vee".

DMAIC

The DMAIC project methodology has five phases:

1. *Define* the problem, the voice of the customer, and the project goals, specifically.
2. *Measure* key aspects of the current process and collect relevant data.
3. *Analyse* the data to investigate and verify cause-and-effect relationships. Determine what the relationships are, and attempt to ensure that all factors have been considered. Seek out root cause of the defect under investigation.
4. *Improve* or optimize the current process based upon data analysis using techniques such as design of experiments, poka yoke or mistake proofing, and standard work to create a new, future state process. Set up pilot runs to establish process capability.
5. *Control* the future state process to ensure that any deviations from target are corrected before they result

in defects. Control systems are implemented such as statistical process control, production boards, and visual workplaces and the process is continuously monitored.

DMADV

The DMADV project methodology, also known as DFSS, features five phases:

1. *Define* design goals that are consistent with customer demands and the enterprise strategy.
2. *Measure* and identify CTQs, product capabilities, production process capability, and risks.
3. *Analyse* to develop and design alternatives, create a high-level design and evaluate design capability to select the best design.
4. *Design* details, optimize the design, and plan for design verification. This phase may require simulations.
5. *Verify* the design, set up pilot runs, implement the production process and hand it over to the process owner.

Quality Management Tools and Methods used in Six Sigma

Within the individual phases of a DMAIC or DMADV project, Six Sigma utilizes many established quality-management tools that are also used outside of Six Sigma.

- 5 Whys
- Analysis of variance
- ANOVA Gauge RandR
- Axiomatic design
- Business Process Mapping
- Catapult exercise on variability
- Cause and effects diagram
- Chi-square test of independence and fits
- Control chart
- Correlation
- Cost-benefit analysis

- CTQ tree
- Design of experiments
- Failure mode and effects analysis
- General linear model
- Histograms
- Homoscedasticity
- Quality Function Deployment
- Pareto chart
- Pick chart
- Process capability
- Quantitative marketing research through use of Enterprise Feedback Management systems
- Regression analysis
- Root cause analysis
- Run charts
- SIPOC analysis
- Stratification
- Taguchi methods
- Taguchi Loss Function
- TRIZ

IMPLEMENTATION ROLES

One key innovation of Six Sigma involves the "professionalizing" of quality management functions. Prior to Six Sigma, quality management in practice was largely relegated to the production floor and to statisticians in a separate quality department. Formal Six Sigma programmes borrow martial arts ranking terminology to define a hierarchy that cuts across all business functions.

Six Sigma identifies several key roles for its successful implementation:

1. *Executive Leadership:* Includes the CEO and other members of top management. They are responsible for setting up a vision for Six Sigma implementation. They also empower the other role holders with the freedom and resources to explore new ideas for breakthrough improvements.
2. *Champions:* Take responsibility for Six Sigma

implementation across the organization in an integrated manner. The Executive Leadership draws them from upper management. Champions also performanceas mentors to Black Belts.

3. *Master Black Belts:* Identified by champions, performanceas in-house coaches on Six Sigma. They devote 100% of their time to Six Sigma. They assist champions and guide Black Belts and Green Belts. Apart from statistical tasks, they spend their time on ensuring consistent application of Six Sigma across various functions and departments.
4. *Black Belts:* Operate under Master Black Belts to apply Six Sigma methodology to specific projects. They devote 100% of their time to Six Sigma. They primarily focus on Six Sigma project execution, whereas Champions and Master Black Belts focus on identifying projects/functions for Six Sigma.
5. *Green Belts*: The employees who take up Six Sigma implementation along with their other job responsibilities, operate under the guidance of Black Belts.
6. *Yellow Belts*: Trained in the basic application of Six Sigma management tools, work with the Black Belt throughout the project stages and are often the closest to the work.

Certification

In the United States. Six Sigma certification for both green and black belts is offered by the Institute of Industrial Engineers and by the American Society for Quality.

ORIGIN AND MEANING OF THE TERM "SIX SIGMA PROCESS"

The term "six sigma process" comes from the notion that if one has six standard deviations between the process mean and the nearest specification limit, as shown in the graph, practically no items will fail to meet specifications. This is based on the calculation method employed in process capability studies. Capability studies measure the number of standard deviations between the process mean and the nearest specification limit in sigma units. As process standard deviation goes up, or the mean of the process moves away from the centre of the tolerance, fewer standard deviations will fit between the mean and the nearest specification limit, decreasing the sigma number and increasing the likelihood of items outside specification.

Role of the 1.5 Sigma Shift

Experience has shown that processes usually do not perform as well in the long term as they do in the short term. As a result, the number of sigmas that will fit between the process mean and the nearest specification limit may well drop over time, compared to an initial short-term study.

To account for this real-life increase in process variation over time, an empirically-based 1.5 sigma shift is introduced into the calculation. A process that fits six sigmas between the process mean and the nearest specification limit in a short-term study will in the long term only fit 4.5 sigmas – either because the process mean will move over time, or because the long-term standard deviation of the process will be greater than that observed in the short term, or both.

Hence the widely accepted definition of a six sigma process as one that produces 3.4 defective parts per million opportunities. This is based on the fact that a process that is normally distributed will have 3.4 parts per million beyond a point that is 4.5 standard deviations above or below the mean. So the 3.4 DPMO of a "Six Sigma" process in fact corresponds to 4.5 sigmas, namely 6 sigmas minus the 1.5 sigma shift introduced to account for long-term variation. This takes account of special causes that may cause a deterioration in process performance over time and is designed to prevent underestimation of the defect levels likely to be encountered in real-life operation.

Sigma Levels

The table gives long-term DPMO values corresponding to various short-term sigma levels.

Note that these figures assume that the process mean will shift by 1.5 sigma toward the side with the critical specification limit. In other words, they assume that after the initial study determining the short-term sigma level, the long-term C_{pk} value will turn out to be 0.5 less than the short-term C_{pk} value. So, for example, the DPMO figure given for 1 sigma assumes that the long-term process mean will be 0.5 sigma *beyond* the specification limit (C_{pk} = –0.17), rather than 1 sigma *within* it, as it was in the short-term study (C_{pk} = 0.33). Note that the defect percentages only indicate defects exceeding the specification limit to which the process mean is nearest. Defects beyond the far specification limit are not included in the percentages.

Sigma level	DPMO	Percent defective	Percentage yield	Short-term C_{pk}	Long-term C_{pk}
1	691,462	69%	31%	0.33	–0.17
2	308,538	31%	69%	0.67	0.17
3	66,807	6.7%	93.3%	1.00	0.5
4	6,210	0.62%	99.38%	1.33	0.83
5	233	0.023%	99.977%	1.67	1.17
6	3.4	0.00034%	99.99966%	2.00	1.5
7	0.019	0.0000019%	99.9999981%	2.33	1.83

CRITICISM

Lack of Originality

Noted quality expert Joseph M. Juran has described Six Sigma as "a basic version of quality improvement", stating that "here is nothing new there. It includes what we used to call facilitators. They've adopted more flamboyant terms, like belts with different colors. We think that concept has merit to set apart, to create specialists who can be very helpful. Again, that's not a new idea. The American Society for Quality long ago established certificates, such as for reliability engineers."

Role of Consultants

The use of "Black Belts" as itinerant change agents has fostered a cottage industry of training and certification. Critics argue there is overselling of Six Sigma by too great a number of consulting firms, many of which claim expertise in Six Sigma when they only have a rudimentary understanding of the tools and techniques involved.

Potential Negative Effects

A *Fortune* substance stated that "of 58 large companies that have announced Six Sigma programmes, 91 per cent have trailed the SandP 500 since". The statement is attributed to "an analysis by Charles Holland of consulting firm Qualpro." The summary of the substance is that Six Sigma is effective at what it is intended to do, but that it is "narrowly designed to fix an existing process" and does not help in "coming up with new products or disruptive technologies." Advocates of Six Sigma have argued that many of these claims are in error or ill-informed. A *BusinessWeek,* that James McNerney's introduction of Six Sigma at 3M may have had the effect of stifling creativity. It cites two Wharton School professors who say that Six Sigma leads to incremental innovation at the expense of blue-sky work. *Going Lean,* which describes a related approach known as lean dynamics and provides data to show that Ford's "6 Sigma" programme did little to change its fortunes.

Based on Arbitrary Standards

While 3.4 defects per million opportunities might work well for certain products/processes, it might not operate optimally or cost effectively for others. A pacemaker process might need higher standards, for example, whereas a direct mail advertising campaign might need lower standards. The basis and justification for choosing 6 as the number of standard deviations is not clearly explained. In addition, the Six Sigma model assumes that the process data always conform to the normal distribution. The calculation of defect rates for situations where the normal distribution model does not apply is not properly addressed in the current Six Sigma literature.

Criticism of the 1.5 Sigma Shift

The statistician Donald J. Wheeler has dismissed the 1.5

sigma shift as "goofy" because of its arbitrary nature. Its universal applicability is seen as doubtful. The 1.5 sigma shift has also become contentious because it results in stated "sigma levels" that reflect short-term rather than long-term performance: a process that has long-term defect levels corresponding to 4.5 sigma performance is, by Six Sigma convention, described as a "6 sigma process." The accepted Six Sigma scoring system thus cannot be equated to actual normal distribution probabilities for the stated number of standard deviations, and this has been a key bone of contention about how Six Sigma measures are defined. The fact that it is rarely explained that a "6 sigma" process will have long-term defect rates corresponding to 4.5 sigma performance rather than actual 6 sigma performance has led several commentators to express the opinion that Six Sigma is a confidence trick.

DESIGN FOR SIX SIGMA

Design for Six Sigma is a separate and emerging business-process management methodology related to traditional Six Sigma. While the tools and order used in Six Sigma require a process to be in place and functioning, DFSS has the objective of determining the needs of customers and the business, and driving those needs into the product solution so created. DFSS is relevant to the complex system/product synthesis phase, especially in the context of unprecedented system development. It is process *generation* in contrast with process *improvement*.

DMADV, Define – Measure – Analyse – Design – Verify, is sometimes synonymously referred to as DFSS. The traditional DMAIC Six Sigma process, as it is usually practiced, which is focused on evolutionary and continuous improvement manufacturing or service process development, usually occurs after initial system or product design and development have been largely completed. DMAIC Six Sigma as practiced is usually consumed with solving existing manufacturing or service process problems and removal of the defects and variation associated with defects. On the other hand, DFSS strives to generate a new process where none existed, or where an existing process is deemed to be inadequate and in need of replacement. DFSS aims to create a process with the end in mind of optimally building the efficiencies of Six Sigma methodology into the process *before* implementation; traditional Six Sigma seeks for continuous improvement *after* a process already exists.

DFSS as an Approach to Design

DFSS seeks to avoid manufacturing/service process problems by using advanced Voice of the Customer techniques and proper systems engineering techniques to avoid process problems at the outset. When combined, these methods obtain the proper needs of the customer, and derive engineering system parameter requirements that increase product and service effectiveness in the eyes of the customer. This yields products and services that provide greater customer satisfaction and increased market share.These techniques also include tools and processes to predict, model and simulate the product delivery system as well as the analysis of the developing system life cycle itself to ensure customer satisfaction with the proposed system design solution.

In this way, DFSS is closely related to systems engineering, operations research, systems architecture and concurrent engineering. DFSS is largely a design activity requiring specialized tools including: quality function deployment, axiomatic design, TRIZ, Design for X, design of experiments, Taguchi methods, tolerance design, Robustification and response surface methodology. While these tools are sometimes used in the classic DMAIC Six Sigma process, they are uniquely used by DFSS to analyse new and unprecedented systems/products. A graphical flowchart of common DFSS tools can be seen at DFSS Roadmap.

Arguments over the Separation of DFSS from Six Sigma

Proponents of DMAIC techniques might claim that DFSS falls under the general rubric of Six Sigma. It is often seen that the tools used for DFSS techniques vary widely from those used for DMAIC Six Sigma. In particular, DMAIC practitioners often use new or existing mechanical drawings and manufacturing process instructions as the originating information to perform their analysis, while DFSS practitioners often use system simulations and parametric system design/ analysis tools to predict both cost and performance of candidate system architectures.

While it can be claimed that two processes are similar, in practice the working medium differs enough so that DFSS requires different tool sets in order to perform its system design tasks. DMAIC Six Sigma may still be used during depth-first plunges into the system architecture analysis and for "back end" Six Sigma processes; DFSS provides system design processes used in front-end complex system designs.

Similarities with other Methods

Arguments about what makes DFSS different from Six Sigma demonstrate the similarities between DFSS and other established engineering practices such as Probabilistic design and design for quality. In general Six Sigma with its DMAIC roadmap focuses on improvement of an existing process or processes.

DFSS focuses on the creation of new value with inputs from customers, suppliers and business needs. While traditional Six Sigma may also use those inputs, the focus is again on improvement and not design of some new product or system. It also shows the engineering background of DFSS. However, like other methods developed in engineering, there is no theoretical reason why DFSS can't be used in areas outside of engineering. It has been used to design processes for example.

DFSS, Applied to Software Engineering

Historically, Design for Six Sigma was created in part because Six Sigma organisations found that they could not optimise products past three or four Sigma without fundamentally redesigning the product. This means that 'Six Sigma' levels of performance have to be 'built-in' or 'by design'. The DFSS for Software Engineering is essentially a non superficial modification of "classical DFSS" since the character and nature of software is different from other fields of engineering.

The methodology describes the detailed process for successfully applying DFSS methods and tools throughout the Software Product Design, covering the overall Software Development life cycle: Requirements, Architecture, Design, Implementation, Integration, Verification and Validation. The methodology explains how to build predictive statistical models for software reliability and robustness and shows how simulation and analysis techniques can be combined with structural design and architecture methods to effectively produce software and information systems at Six Sigma levels.

DFSS in Software Engineering acts as a glue to blend the classical modelling techniques of software engineering such as OOD or ERD with statistical, predictive models and simulation techniques. The methodology provides Software Engineers with practical tools for measuring and predicting the quality attributes of the software product and also enables them to include software in system reliability models. It introduces techniques and measurements from different stages of the life cycle: Requirements, Design, Implementation, Verification and Validation.

7

Purchasing

DEFINITION OF PURCHASING

Purchasing refers to a business or organization attempting to acquire goods or services to accomplish the goals of the enterprise. Though there are several organizations that attempt to set standards in the purchasing process, processes can vary greatly between organizations. Typically the word "purchasing" is not used interchangeably with the word "procurement", since procurement typically includes Expediting, Supplier Quality, and Traffic and Logistics in addition to Purchasing.

Purchasing managers/directors, and procurement managers/directors guide the organization's acquisition procedures and standards. Most organizations use a three-way check as the foundation of their purchasing programmes. This involves three departments in the organization completing separate parts of the acquisition process.

The three departments do not all report to the same senior manager to prevent unethical practices and lend credibility to the process. These departments can be purchasing, receiving; and accounts payable or engineering, purchasing and accounts payable; or a plant manager, purchasing and accounts payable. Combinations can vary significantly, but a purchasing department and accounts payable are usually two of the three departments involved.

When the receiving department is not involved, it's typically called a two-way check or two-way purchase order. In this situation, the purchasing department issues the purchase order receipt not required. When an invoice arrives against the order, the accounts payable department will then go directly to the requestor of the purchase order to verify that the goods or services were received. This is typically what is done for goods and services that will bypass the receiving department. A few examples are software delivered electronically, NRE work consulting hours, etc...

Historically, the purchasing department issued Purchase Orders for supplies, services, equipment, and raw materials. Then, in an effort to decrease the administrative costs associated with the repetitive ordering of basic consumable items, "Blanket" or "Master" Agreements were put into place. These types of agreements typically have a longer duration and increased scope to maximize the Quantities of Scale concept. When additional supplies are required, a simple release would be issued to the supplier to provide the goods or services.

Another method of decreasing administrative costs associated with repetitive contracts for common material, is the use of company credit cards, also known as "Purchasing Cards" or simply "P-Cards". P-card programmes vary, but all of them have internal checks and audits to ensure appropriate use. Purchasing managers realised once contracts for the low dollar value consumables are in place, procurement can take a smaller role in the operation and use of the contracts. There is still oversight in the forms of audits and monthly statement reviews, but most of their time is now available to negotiate major purchases and setting up of other long term contracts. These contracts are typically renewable annually.

This trend away from the daily procurement function resulted in several changes in the industry. The first was the reduction of personnel. Purchasing departments were now smaller. There was no need for the army of clerks processing orders for individual parts as in the past. Another change was the focus on negotiating contracts and procurement of large capital equipment. Both of these functions permitted purchasing departments to make the biggest financial contribution to the organization. A new terms and job title emerged – Strategic sourcing and Sourcing Managers. These professionals not only focused on the bidding process and negotiating with suppliers, but the entire supply function. In these roles they were able to add value and maximize savings for organizations. This value was manifested in lower inventories, less personnel, and getting the end product to the organization's consumer quicker. Purchasing manager's success in these roles resulted in new assignments outside to the traditional purchasing function – logistics, materials management, distribution, and warehousing. More and more purchasing managers were becoming Supply Chain Managers handling additional functions of their organizations operation. Purchasing managers were not the only ones to become Supply Chain Managers. Logistic managers, material managers, distribution managers, etc all rose the broader function and some had responsibility for the purchasing functions now.

In accounting, purchases is the amount of goods a company bought throughout this year. They are added to inventory. Purchases are offset by Purchase Discounts and Purchase Returns and Allowances. When it should be added depends on the Free On Board policy of the trade. For the purchaser, this new inventory is added on shipment if the policy was FOB shipping point, and the seller remove this item from its inventory. On the other hand, the purchaser added this inventory on receipt if the policy was FOB destination, and the seller remove this item from its inventory when it was delivered.

Goods bought for the purpose other than direct selling, such as for Research and Development, are added to inventory and allocated to Research and Development expense as they are used. On a side note, equipments bought for Research and Development are not added to inventory, but are capitalized as assets...

ACQUISITION PROCESS

The revised acquisition process for major systems in industry and defence is shown in figure. The process is defined by a series of phases during which technology is defined and matured into viable concepts, which are subsequently developed and readied for production, after which the systems produced are supported in the field.

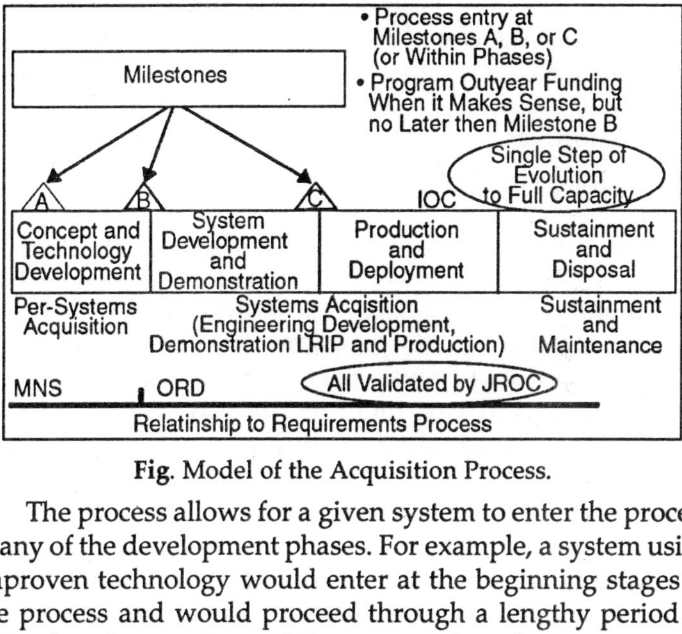

Fig. Model of the Acquisition Process.

The process allows for a given system to enter the process at any of the development phases. For example, a system using unproven technology would enter at the beginning stages of the process and would proceed through a lengthy period of technology maturation, while a system based on mature and proven technologies might enter directly into engineering development or, conceivably, even production.

The process itself includes four phases of development:

1. Concept and Technology Development: is intended to explore alternative concepts based on assessments of operational needs, technology readiness, risk, and affordability.
2. Concept and Technology Development phase begins with concept exploration. During this stage, concept studies are undertaken to define alternative concepts and to provide information about capability and risk that would permit an objective comparison of competing concepts.
3. System Development and Demonstration phase. This phase could be entered directly as a result of a techno-

logical opportunity and urgent user need, as well as having come through concept and technology development.

4. The last, and longest, phase is the Sustainment and Disposal phase of the programme. During this phase all necessary activities are accomplished to maintain and sustain the system in the field in the most cost-effective manner possible.

SELECTION OF BIDDERS

This is the process where the organization identifies potential suppliers for specified supplies, services or equipment. These suppliers' credentials and history are analysed, together with the products or services they offer. The bidder selection process varies from organization to organization, but can include running credit reports, interviewing management, testing products, and touring facilities. This process is not always done in order of importance, but rather in order of expense. Often purchasing managers research potential bidders obtaining information on the organizations and products from media sources and their own industry contacts. Additionally, purchasing might send Request for Information to potential suppliers to help gather information.

Engineering would also inspect sample products to determine if the company can produce products they need. If the bidder passes both of these stages engineering may decide to do some testing on the materials to further verify quality standards. These tests can be expensive and involve significant time of multiple technicians and engineers. Engineering management must make this decision based on the cost of the products they are likely to procure, the importance of the bidders' product to production, and other factors. Credit checks, interviewing management, touring plants as well as other steps could all be utilized if engineering, manufacturing, and supply chain managers decide they could help their decision and the cost is justifiable. Other organizations might have minority procurement goals to consider in selection of bidders. Organizations identify goals in the use of companies owned and operated by certain ethnicities or women owned business enterprises. Significant utilizing of minority suppliers may qualify the firm as a potential bidder for a contract with a company or governmental entity looking to increase their minority supplier programmes.

This selection process can include or exclude international suppliers depending on organizational goals and criteria. Companies looking to increase their pacific rim supplier base may exclude suppliers from the Americas, Europe, and Australia. Other organizations may be looking to purchase domestically to ensure a quicker response to orders as well as easier collaboration on design and production.

Organizational goals will dictate the criteria for the selection process of bidders. It is also possible that the product or service being procured is so specialized that the number of bidders are limited and the criteria must be very wide to permit competition. If only one firm can meet the specifications for the product then the purchasing managers must consider utilizing a "Sole Source" option or work with engineering to broaden the specifications if the project will permit alteration in the specifications. The sole source option is the part of the selection of bidders that acknowledges there is sometimes only one reasonable supplier for some services or products. This can be because of the limited applications for the product cannot support more than one manufacturer, proximity of the service provided, or the products are newly designed or invented and competition is not yet available.

BIDDING PROCESS

This is the process an organization utilizes to procure goods, services or equipment. Processes vary significantly from the stringent to the very informal. Large corporations and governmental entities are most likely to have stringent and formal processes. These processes can utilize specialized bid forms that require specific procedures and detail. The very stringent procedures require bids to be open by several staff from various departments to ensure fairness and impartiality.

Responses are usually very detailed. Bidders not responding exactly as specified and following the published procedures can be disqualified. Smaller private businesses are more likely to have less formal procedures. Bids can be in the form of an email to all of the bidders specifying products or services. Responses by bidders can be detailed or just the proposed dollar amount.

Most bid processes are multi-tiered. Acquisitions under a specified dollar amount can be "user discretion" permitting the requestor to choose who ever they want. This level can be as low as $100 or as high as $10,000 depending on the organization. The rationale is the savings realised by processing these request the same as expensive items is minimal and does not justify the time and expense. Purchasing departments watch for abuses of the user discretion privilege. Acquisitions in a mid range can be processed with a slightly more formal process. This process may involve the user providing quotes from three separate suppliers.

Purchasing may be asked or required to obtain the quotes. The formal bid process starts as low as $10,000 or as high as $100,000 depending on the organization. The bid usually involves a specific form the bidder fills out and must be returned by a specified deadline. Depending of the commodity being purchased and the organization the bid may specify a weighted evaluation criterion. Other bids would be evaluated at the discretion of purchasing or the end users. Some bids could be evaluated by a cross-functional committee. Other bids may be evaluated by the end user or the buyer in Purchasing. Especially in small, private firms the bidders could be evaluated on criteria or factors that have little if anything to do with the actual bid. Examples of these factors are history of the bidder with the company, history of the bidder with the company's senior management at other firms, and bidder's breadth of products.

TECHNICAL EVALUATION

Technical evaluations, evaluations of the technical suitability of the quoted goods or services, if required, are normally performed prior to the commercial evaluation. During this phase of the procurement process, a technical representative of the company will review the proposal and designate each bidder as either technically acceptable or technically unacceptable.

COMMERCIAL EVALUATION

Cost of Money is calculated by multiplying the applicable currency interest rate multiplied by the amount of money paid prior to the receipt of GOODS. If the money were to have remained in the buyer's account, interest would be drawn. That interest is essentially an additional cost associated with such Progress or Milestone payments.

The manufacturing location is taken into consideration during the evaluation stage primarily to calculate freight costs and regional issues which may be considered. For instance, in Europe it is common for factories to close during the month of August for Summer holiday. Labour agreements may also be taken into consideration and may be drawn into the evaluation if the particular region is known to frequent labour unions.The manufacturing lead-time is the time from the placement of the order until the goods are manufactured and prepared for delivery. Lead-times vary by commodity and can range from several days to years. Transportation time is evaluated while comparing the delivery of goods to the Buyer's required use-date. If Goods are shipped from a remote port, with infrequent vessel transportation, the transportation time could exceed the schedule and adjustments would need to be made.Delivery Charges - the charge for the Goods to be delivered to a stated point. Bid Validity Packing Bid Adjustments Terms and Conditions Seller's Services Standards Organizations Financial Review Payment Currency Risk Analysis - market volatility, financial stress within the bidders Testing

NEGOTIATING

Negotiating is a key skillset in the Purchasing field. One of the goals of Purchasing Agents is to acquire goods per the most advantageous terms of the buying entity. Purchasing Agents typically attempt to decrease costs while meeting the Buyer's other requirements such as an on-time delivery, compliance to the commercial terms and conditions.

Good negotiators, those with high levels of documented "cost savings", receive a premium within the industry relative to their compensation. Depending on the employment agreement between the Purchasing Agent and the employer, Buyer's cost savings can result in the creation of value to the business, and may result in a flat-rate bonus, or a percentage payout to the Purchasing Agent of the documented cost savings.

Purchasing Departments, while they can be considered as a support function of the key business, are actually revenue generating departments. For example, if the company needs to buy $30 million USD of widgets and the Purchasing Department secures the widgets for $25M USD, the Purchasing Department would have saved the company $5M USD. That savings could exceed the annual budget of the department, which in effect would pay the department's overhead - the employee's salaries, computers, office space, etc.

POST-AWARD ADMINISTRATION

Post-award administration typically consists of making minor changes, additions or subtractions, that in some way change the terms of the agreement or the Seller's Scope of Supply. Such changes are often minor, but for auditing purposes must be documented into the existing agreement. Examples include increasing the quantity of a Line Item or changing the metallurgy of a particular component.

PURCHASING MANAGEMENT

Purchasing management directs the flow of goods and services in a company and handles all data relating to contact with suppliers. Effective purchasing management requires knowledge of the supply chain, business and tax laws, invoice and inventory procedures, and transportation and logistics issues. Although a strong knowledge of the products and services to be purchased is essential, purchasing management professionals must also be able to plan, execute, and oversee purchasing strategies that are conducive to company profitability. Sourcing reliable suppliers is a crucial part of purchasing management. Purchasing managers, agents, and buyers usually learn about new products and services from Internet searches, trade shows, and conferences. They meet with potential suppliers in their plants whenever possible. Skills in foreign languages may be helpful for sourcing suppliers in other countries. Purchasing management professionals must always assess potential suppliers in terms of the supplier's ability to deliver quality merchandise at a suitable price on time.

Purchasing management professionals must be good negotiators, understand technical product information, have good mathematical ability, understand spreadsheet software, understand marketing methodology, and be outstanding decision makers. Increased responsibilities in purchasing management require good leadership skills, and higher positions often require a master's degree in a business related subject. Entry level purchasing management positions such as junior buyers, assistant buyers, and purchasing clerks, often require a college degree and some product knowledge.

Larger distributors may require a bachelor's degree for entry level purchasing management positions. Training and learning typically start in sales, then supervision, and invoice and stock monitoring. Professional purchasing management designations include Certified Purchasing Professional in the United States, and Certified Professional Purchaser in Canada. Purchasing managers, buyers, and materials managers control budgets, manage staff, and may analyse procurement methods as well as negotiate supplier contracts.

Purchasing management professionals must understand tax laws, purchasing trends, ethics, and global outsourcing issues. Buyers and purchasing agents usually deal specifically with purchasing tasks, while purchasing managers usually supervise others, including purchasing agents. However, titles and duties vary greatly between industries and employers.

Buyers often have assistants to place orders and keep track of delivery details.Buyers need the ability to select products that consumers will want to buy, so they need to understand trends as well as economic conditions that affect consumer buying decisions. Buyers employed in small stores may be responsible for purchasing the store's entire inventory, while buyers working for larger operations may focus on a few product lines. Merchandise managers may work with an advertising team to create a campaign for the goods they purchase. Follow up is an important part of purchasing management as responsibility does not end in purchasing goods. For example, merchandise managers need to check to be sure the products they buy are being displayed well to attract consumers. Buyers must keep track of customer demands for new products as well as determine how well goods are selling.

OBJECTIVES

To maintain uninterrupted flow of materials to support the development schedules:

- To procure materials economically at a cost consistent with the quality and service required. However, generally all purchases may be attempted at the lowest cost.
- To provide the necessary expertise, advice, information to the Curators and Education Officers with regard to the best quality of material available in the market, supplier's capability and performance etc.
- To develop and maintain good buyer-seller relationship.
- To promote source development.
- To maintain NCSM's reputation and credibility in the market by fair dealings and prompt payments.

FUNCTIONS

The main functions of the Purchase Department are defined as follows:

- Procurement of stores through indigenous and foreign sources as required in accordance with the rules in force.

- Checking of requisitions/purchase indents.
- Selection of suppliers for issue of enquiries.
- Issuing enquiries/tenders and obtaining quotations.
- Analysing quotations and bids etc., and preparation of comparative statement.
- Consultation with the Indentor for selection and approval of quotations and with Accounts Officer for pre-audit.
- Negotiating contracts.
- Checking legal conditions of contracts. Consulting Administrative Officer or Secretary, NCSM – where necessary.
- Issue of Purchase Orders.
- Follow-up of purchase orders for delivery in due time
- Verification and passing of suppliers' bills to see that payments are made promptly.
- Correspondence and dealing with suppliers, carriers etc., regarding shortages, rejections etc., reported by the Stores Department.
- Maintenance of purchase records.
- Maintenance of progressive expenditure statement, sub-head wise.
- Maintenance of vendor performance records/data.
- Arrangement for Insurance Surveys, as and when necessary.
- Clearance of foreign consignments.
- Keeping various Departments/Divisions informed of the progress of their indents in case of delay in obtaining supplies.
- Serving as an information centre on the materials' knowledge i.e. their prices, source of supply, specification and other allied matters.
- Development of reliable and alternate sources of supply.
  - It shall be particularly ensured:
  - That all purchase are made against properly authorized requisitions, and valid sanctions, showing the correct and detailed end-use.

- That all the materials requisitioned are duly ordered from the right source after full enquiries on most competitive price taking into account the trade discounts and tax benefits etc.
- That the right quantity of the goods consistent with the quality and the specification required is bought.
- That the deliveries of all goods are received within the stipulated period.
- That claims due to shortages or any other discrepancies are settled promptly.
- That cordial and harmonious relations with all parts/divisions are maintained for becoming an efficient service unit in the museum/centre.

- While receiving the planned requirement of the indentors, it should be prevailed upon the Indentors to certify clearly that the quantities indicated are definitely required for the project and specify the period within which the quantities indented will be consumed. It is the duty of the purchase part to check purchase indents against needs and suggest modification of quantities wherever necessary.

METHODS OF PURCHASE

The purchase method of accounting in current standards is similar to the "acquisition accounting" method used in previous accounting standards. Its use provides some useful safeguards.

Previous accounting standards allowed two methods of accounting for mergers and acquisitions; merger accounting and acquisition accounting. The former was generally a more favourable treatment in its impact on the P and L. The purchase method of accounting is now compulsory in the US, the EU and wherever IFRSs have been adopted.

The purchase method of accounting must identify the acquirer. Under IFRSs the acquisition must be valued at fair value. The difference between the purchase price and the fair value should be recognised as goodwill.

A company cannot create a restructuring provision to provide for future losses or restructuring costs as a result of an acquisition. Such costs must be treated as post acquisition costs. This makes the impact of restructuring costs on profits more visible, and prevents the abuse of provisions to take an exaggerated hit to profits on acquisition and thereafter boost reported profits in subsequent years.

The use of the purchase method improves accounts, but investors are likely to disregard the impact of goodwill, which is the largest change.

The elimination of provisions is more useful because of the extra visibility and the prevention of abuses:

- *Full*: The purchase of a receivable in its entirety.
- *Partial*: The purchase of immediate installments, with the seller retaining remaining installments and/or the balloon payment.
- *Reverse Partial*: The purchase of future installments, allowing the seller to continue receiving immediate installments for a specified period of time.
- *Split Disbursement Partial*: The purchase of a portion of each installment for a specified time and amount. Seller receives the remainder of each installment.
- *Multiple Stage Payout*: The full purchase of a receivable by means of a guaranteed staged payout of proceeds equaling or exceeding the principal balance. Seller receives stated payout regardless of the purchased receivable's performance.
- *Multiple Cash Flow*: The purchase of up to 50% of the cash flow created by multiple receivables held by a single seller.
- *Short Life Yield*: A method of calculating a higher buy price on a long term, Grade A receivable, by calculating the purchase price of the receivable as if there were a 10 year balloon payment.

We realise that you may desire an option other than the quote we provide. Please contact us with any questions you may have for an explanation of how these purchase options can be tailored to meet your needs, now or in the future. We look forward to working with you and providing the best service possible!

PURCHASING PROCEDURE

PURCHASE REQUEST

The specifications and number/quantity and delivery of equipment, devices and materials are determined by the department(s) that will be using the product(s) or materials. The Purchasing Department conducts purchase activities based on purchase requests submitted by the/these department(s).

SELECTION OF COMPANIES FOR ESTIMATE SUBMISSION

The Purchasing Department, at its sole discretion, selects companies from which estimates will be sought. Suppliers are selected from the files of "Companies with Previously Established Business Relationships", "Companies from Which Estimates Can Be Requested" and "Products and Suppliers". Selection is made by comprehensivly evaluating such factors as the quality and performance of the equipment, device(s) or materials to be purchased, compatibility with existing facilities, degree of reliability, product requirements including safety, delivery time, the scale of the order, after-sale service and the company's previous business record.

As a rule, Osaka Gas asks several companies to submit estimates. However, only one company may be specified for estimate submission in such special cases as those concerned with industrial property rights, those requiring maximum levels of safety that only one specific supplier can ensure, cases where only one specific supplier can assure compatibility with existing facilities, or in case of urgency.

ESTIMATE REQUEST

As a rule, when requesting an estimate from a company that it has selected, Osaka Gas will set out a specification from listing Osaka Gas's requirements in respects of quality, performance standard, size, inspection and method of inspection. The selected companies will be asked to submit cost estimates and specifications to Osaka Gas prior to a specified date.

SUBMISSION ESTIMATE

Specification sheets submitted by potential suppliers at their own expense are checked by the Purchasing Department and the department(s) that will be using the product(s), in order to determine whether the required standards are met by the product(s). All products must pass this examination. During this process, Osaka Gas may request additions or changes to the specifications.

NEGOTIATION

After valid cost estimates and specifications have been comprehensively evaluated in respect of price, technical requirements, etc. Osaka Gas will commence negotiation with the company with the most attractive proposal to discuss the amount of the contract and other terms and conditions. The selection of such a company shall be made by Osaka Gas at its sole discretion. Contract terms and conditions will be decided upon mutual agreement.

CONTRACT CONCLUSION

The business will be established upon conclusion of a contract, in the form of a written document if necessary. The obligations and liabilities of Osaka Gas arise only when such contract is concluded.

DELIVERY AND INSPECTION

Delivery dates specified in the contract must be strictly observed. Precise details of the delivery schedule will be agreed between the supplier and the relevant department(s) of Osaka Gas. Delivered equipment, device(s) or materials must pass inspections conducted by the relevant department(s) of Osaka Gas. When deemed significant, an interim inspection may be conducted during the manufacturing process.

PAYMENT

Payment will be made according to the payment terms specified in the contract.

VALUE ANALYSIS

CONCEPT OF VALUE

The value of a product will be interpreted in different ways by different customers. Its common characteristic is a high level of performance, capability, emotional appeal, style, etc. relative to its cost. This can also be expressed as maximizing the function of a product relative to its cost:

Value = (Performance + Capability)/Cost = Function/Cost

Value is not a matter of minimizing cost. In some cases the value of a product can be increased by increasing its function and cost as long as the added function increases more than its added cost. The concept of functional worth can be important. Functional worth is the lowest cost to provide a given function. However, there are less tangible "selling" functions involved in a product to make it of value to a customer.

INTRODUCTION TO VALUE ANALYSIS

Lawrence Miles conceived of Value Analysis (VA) in the 1945 based on the application of function analysis to the component parts of a product. Component cost reduction was an effective and popular way to improve "value" when direct labour and material cost determined the success of a product. The value analysis technique supported cost reduction activities by relating the cost of components to their function contributions.

Value analysis defines a "basic function" as anything that makes the product work or sell. A function that is defined as "basic" cannot change. Secondary functions, also called "supporting functions", described the manner in which the basic function(s) were implemented. Secondary functions could be modified or eliminated to reduce product cost. As VA progressed to larger and more complex products and systems, emphasis shifted to "upstream" product development activities where VA can be more effectively applied to a product before it reaches the production phase. However, as products have become more complex and sophisticated, the technique needed to be adapted to the "systems" approach that is involved in many products today. As a result, value analysis evolved into the "Function Analysis System Technique" (FAST) which is discussed later.

VALUE ANALYSIS METHOD

In all problem solving techniques, we are trying to change a condition by means of a solution that is unique and relevant. If we describe in detail what we are trying to accomplish, we tend to describe a solution and miss the opportunity to engage in divergent thinking about other alternatives. When trying to describe problems that affect us, we become locked in to a course of action without realizing it, because of our own bias. Conversely, the more abstractly we can define the function of what we are trying to accomplish, the more opportunities as suggested, have for divergent thinking.

This high level of abstraction can be achieved by describing what is to be accomplished with a verb and a noun. In this discipline, the verb answers the question, "What is to be done?" or, "What is it to do?" The verb defines the required action. The noun answers the question, "What is it being done to?" The noun tells what is acted upon. Identifying the function by a verb-noun is not as simple a matter as it appears. Identifying the function in the broadest possible terms provides the greatest potential for divergent thinking because it gives the greatest freedom for creatively developing alternatives. A function should be identified as to what is to be accomplished by a solution and not how it is to be accomplished. How the function is identified determines the scope, or range of solutions that can be considered.

That functions designated as "basic" represent the operative function of the item or product and must be maintained and protected. Determining the basic function of single components can be relatively simple. By definition then, functions designated as "basic" will not change, but the way those functions are implemented is open to innovative speculation. As important as the basic function is to the success of any product, the cost to perform that function is inversely proportional to its importance. This is not an absolute rule, but rather an observation of the consumer products market. Few people purchase consumer products based on performance or the lowest cost of basic functions alone.

When purchasing a product it is assumed that the basic function is operative. The customer's attention is then directed to those visible secondary support functions, or product features, which determine the worth of the product. From a product design point of view, products that are perceived to have high value first address the basic function's performance and stress the achievement of all of the performance attributes. Once the basic functions are satisfied, the designer's then address the secondary functions necessary to attract customers. Secondary functions are incorporated in the product as features to support and enhance the basic function and help sell the product. The elimination of secondary functions that are not very important to the customer will reduce product cost and increase value without detracting from the worth of the product.

The cost contribution of the basic function does not, by itself, establish the value of the product. Few products are sold on the basis of their basic function alone. If this were so, the market for "no name" brands would be more popular than it is today. Although the cost contribution of the basic function is relatively small, its loss will cause the loss of the market value of the product. One objective of value analysis or function analysis, to improve value by reducing the cost-function relationship of a product, is achieved by eliminating or combining as many secondary functions as possible.

VALUE ANALYSIS PROCESS

The first step in the value analysis process is to define the problem and its scope. Once this is done, the functions of the product and its items are derived. These functions are classified into "basic" and "secondary" functions. A Cost Function Matrix or Value Analysis Matrix is prepared to identify the cost of providing each function by associating the function with a mechanism or component part of a product. Product functions with a high cost-function ratio are identified as opportunities for further investigation and improvement. Improvement opportunities are then brainstormed, analysed, and selected.

The objective of the Function Cost Matrix approach is to draw the attention of the analysts away from the cost of components and focus their attention on the cost contribution of the functions. The Function Cost Matrix displays the components of the product, and the cost of those components, along the left vertical side of the graph. The top horizontal legend contains the functions performed by those components. Each component is then examined to determine how many functions that component performs, and the cost contributions of those functions.

Detailed cost estimates become more important following function analysis, when evaluating value improvement proposals. The total cost and per cent contribution of the functions of the item under study will guide the team, or analyst, in selecting which functions to select for value improvement analysis. A variation of the Function-Cost Matrix is the Value Analysis Matrix. This matrix was derived from the Quality Function Deployment (QFD) methodology.

It is more powerful in two ways. First, it associates functions back to customer needs or requirements. In doing this, it carries forward an importance rating to associate with these functions based on the original customer needs or requirements. Functions are then related to mechanisms, the same as with the Function-Cost Matrix. Mechanisms are related to functions as either strongly, moderately or weakly supporting the given function. This relationship is noted with the standard QFD relationship symbols. The associated weighting factor is multiplied by customer or function importance and each columns value is added. These totals are normalized to calculate each mechanism's relative weight in satisfying the designated functions. This is where the second difference with the Function-Cost Matrix arises. This mechanism weight can then be used as the basis to allocate the overall item or product cost. The mechanism target costs can be compared with the actual or estimated costs to see where costs are out of line with the value of that mechanism as derived from customer requirements and function analysis.

FUNCTION ANALYSIS SYSTEM TECHNIQUE

Function Analysis System Technique is an evolution of the value analysis process created by Charles Bytheway. FAST permits people with different technical backgrounds to effectively communicate and resolve issues that require multi-disciplined considerations. FAST builds upon VA by linking the simply expressed, verb-noun functions to describe complex systems.

FAST is not an end product or result, but rather a beginning. It describes the item or system under study and causes the team to think through the functions that the item or system performs, forming the basis for a wide variety of subsequent approaches and analysis techniques. FAST contributes significantly to perhaps the most important phase of value engineering: function analysis. FAST is a creative stimulus to explore innovative avenues for performing functions.

The FAST diagram or model is an excellent communications vehicle. Using the verb-noun rules in function analysis creates a common language, crossing all disciplines and technologies. It allows multi-disciplined team members to contribute equally and communicate with one another while addressing the problem objectively without bias or preconceived conclusions. With FAST, there are no right or wrong model or result.

The problem should be structured until the product development team members are satisfied that the real problem is identified. After agreeing on the problem statement, the single most important output of the multi-disciplined team engaged in developing a FAST model is consensus. Since the team has been charged with the responsibility of resolving the assigned problem, it is their interpretation of the FAST model that reflects the problem statement that's important. The team members must discuss and reconfigure the FAST model until consensus is reached and all participating team members are satisfied that their concerns are expressed in the model. Once consensus has been achieved, the FAST model is complete and the team can move on to the next creative phase.

FAST differs from value analysis in the use of intuitive logic to determine and test function dependencies and the graphical display of the system in a function dependency diagram or model. Another major difference is in analyzing a system as a complete unit, rather than analyzing the components of a system. When studying systems it becomes apparent that functions do not operate in a random or independent fashion. A system exists because functions form dependency links with other functions, just as components form a dependency link with other components to make the system work. The importance of the FAST approach is that it graphically displays function dependencies and creates a process to study function links while exploring options to develop improved systems.

There are normally two types of FAST diagrams, the technical FAST diagram and the customer FAST diagram. A technical FAST diagram is used to understand the technical aspects of a specific portion of a total product. A customer FAST diagram focuses on the aspects of a product that the customer cares about and does not delve into the technicalities, mechanics or physics of the product. A customer FAST diagram is usually applied to a total product.

CREATING A FAST MODEL

The FAST model has a horizontal directional orientation described as the HOW-WHY dimension. This dimension is described in this manner because HOW and WHY questions are asked to structure the logic of the system's functions. Starting with a function, we ask HOW that function is performed to develop a more specific approach. This line of questioning and thinking is read from left to right. To abstract the problem to a higher level, we ask WHY is that function performed. This line of logic is read from right to left.

There is essential logic associated with the FAST HOW-WHY directional orientation. First, when undertaking any task it is best to start with the goals of the task, then explore methods to achieve the goals. When addressing any function on the FAST model with the question WHY, the function to its left expresses the goal of that function. The question HOW, is answered by the function on the right, and is a method to perform that function being addressed. A systems diagram starts at the beginning of the system and ends with its goal. A FAST model, reading from left to right, starts with the goal, and ends at the beginning of the "system" that will achieve that goal.

Second, changing a function on the HOW-WHY path affects all of the functions to the right of that function. This is a domino effect that only goes one way, from left to right. Starting with any place on the FAST model, if a function is changed the goals are still valid but the method to accomplish that function, and all other functions on the right, are affected.

Finally, building the model in the HOW direction, or function justification, will focus the team's attention on each function element of the model. Whereas, reversing the FAST model and building it in its system orientation will cause the team to leap over individual functions and focus on the system, leaving function "gaps" in the system. A good rule to remember in constructing a FAST Model is to build in the HOW direction and test the logic in the WHY direction. The vertical orientation of the FAST model is described as the WHEN direction. This is not part of the intuitive logic process, but it supplements intuitive thinking. WHEN is not a time orientation, but indicates cause and effect.

Scope lines represent the boundaries of the study and are shown as two vertical lines on the FAST model. The scope lines bound the "scope of the study", or that aspect of the problem with which the study team is concerned. The left scope line determines the basic function(s) of the study. The basic functions will always be the first function(s) to the immediate right of the left scope line. The right scope line identifies the beginning of the study and separates the input function(s) from the scope of the study.

The objective or goal of the study is called the "Highest Order Function", located to the left of the basic functions and outside of the left scope line. Any function to the left of another function is a "higher order function".

Functions to the right and outside of the right scope line represent the input side that "turn on" or initiate the subject under study and are known as lowest order functions. Any function to the right of another function is a "lower order" function and represents a method selected to carry out the function being addressed.

Those functions to the immediate right of the left scope line represent the purpose or mission of the product or process under study and are called Basic Function(s). Once determined, the basic function will not change. If the basic function fails, the product or process will lose its market value. All functions to the right of the basic function(s) portray the conceptual approach selected to satisfy the basic function. The concept describes the method being considered, or elected, to achieve the basic functions. The concept can represent either the current conditions (as is) or proposed approach (to be). As a general rule, it is best to create a "to be" rather than an "as is" FAST Model, even if the assignment is to improve an existing product.

This approach will give the product development team members an opportunity to compare the "ideal" to the "current" and help resolve how to implement the differences. Working from an "as is" model will restrict the team's attention to incremental improvement opportunities.

An "as is" model is useful for tracing the symptoms of a problem to its root cause, and exploring ways to resolve the problem, because of the dependent relationship of functions that form the FAST model. Any function on the HOW-WHY logic path is a logic path function. If the functions along the

WHY direction lead into the basic function(s), than they are located on the major logic path. If the WHY path does not lead directly to the basic function, it is a minor logic path. Changing a function on the major logic path will alter or destroy the way the basic function is performed.

Changing a function on a minor logic path will disturb an independent function that enhances the basic function. Supporting functions are usually secondary and exist to achieve the performance levels specified in the objectives or specifications of the basic functions or because a particular approach was chosen to implement the basic function(s).

Independent functions describe an enhancement or control of a function located on the logic path. They do not depend on another function or method selected to perform that function. Independent functions are located above the logic path functions, and are considered secondary, with respect to the scope, nature, level of the problem, and its logic path. An example of a FAST Diagram for a pencil is.

The next step in the process is to dimension the FAST model or to associate information to its functions. FAST dimensions include, but are not limited to: responsibility, budgets, allocated target costs, estimated costs, actual costs, subsystem groupings, placing inspection and test points, manufacturing processes, positioning design reviews, and others. There are many ways to dimension a FAST model. The two popular ways are called Clustering Functions and the Sensitivity Matrix.

Clustering functions involves drawing boundaries with dotted lines around groups of functions to configure subsystems. Clustering functions is a good way to illustrate cost reduction targets and assign design-to-cost targets to new design concepts. For cost reduction, a team would develop an "as is" product FAST model, cluster the functions into subsystems, allocate product cost by clustered functions, and assign target costs. During the process of creating the model, customer sensitivity functions can be identified as well as opportunities for significant cost improvements in design and production.

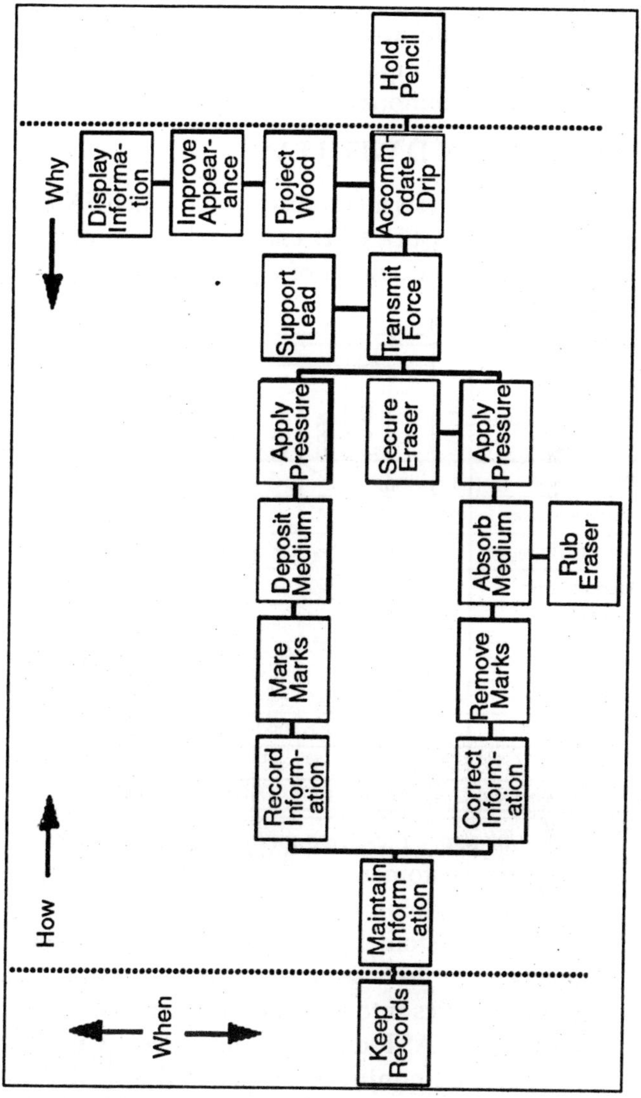

Fig. FAST Diagram- Pencil

Following the completion of the model, the subsystems can be divided among product development teams assigned to achieve the target cost reductions. The teams can then select cost sensitive sub-systems and expand them by moving that segment of the model to a lower level of abstraction. This exposes the detail components of that assembly and their function/cost contributions.

INTEGRATING QFD WITH FAST

A powerful analysis method is created when FAST is used in conjunction with QFD. QFD enables the uses of the Value Analysis Matrix. An example of a value analysis matrix for the pencil example.

Customer Requirements/ Functions	Importance	Mechanisms: Lead	Eraser	Body	Paint	Band
Make Marks	30	◎ 150				
Remove Marks	20		◎ 100			
Prevent Smudges	15	○ 45		○ 45		
Support Lead	5			◎ 25		
Impprove Appearance	10			○ 30	○ 30	△ 10
Accomodate Grip	20			◎ 100	△ 20	
Column Weight	555	195	100	200	50	10
Mech. Weight	1.0	.351	.180	.360	.090	.018
Mech. Target Cost	2.80	.98	.51	1.01	.25	.05
Mech. Actual Cost	2.92	1.20	.43	.94	.10	.25

- ◎ Strong Correlation Weight Factor = 5
- ○ Moderate Correlation Weight Factor = 3
- △ Weak Correlation Weight Factor = 1

The steps for using these two methodologies are as follows:

1. Capture customer requirements and perform QFD product planning with the product planning matrix. Translate customer needs into directly into verb-noun functions or use a second matrix to translate technical characteristics into verb-noun functions.
2. Prepare a FAST diagram and develop the product concept in conjunction with the QFD concept selection matrix. Review the verb-noun functions in the QFD matrix and assure that they are included in the FAST diagram. Revise verb-noun function descriptions if necessary to assure consistency between the QFD matrix and the FAST diagram.
3. Dimension the system in the FAST diagram into

subsystems/assemblies/parts. These are generically referred to as mechanisms.

4. Develop value analysis matrix at system level. The "what's" or system requirements/function in the value analysis matrix are derived from either a customer FAST diagram or by selecting those function statements that correspond to the customer needs or technical characteristics in the product planning matrix. The importance rating is derived from the product planning matrix as well.
5. Complete the value analysis matrix by relating the mechanisms to the customer requirements/functions and calculate the associated weight. Summarize the column weights and normalize to create mechanism weights. Allocate the target cost based on the mechanism weights. This represents the value to the customer based on the customer importance. Compare with either estimated costs based on the product concept or actual costs if available.
6. Identify high cost to value mechanisms/subsystems by comparing the mechanism target costs to the mechanism estimated/actual costs

A product or system such as an automobile contains a great many components and would result in an extremely complex FAST model. The complexity of the process is not governed by the number of components in a product, but the level of abstraction selected to perform the analysis.

With an automobile, a high level of abstraction could contain the major subsystems as the components under study, such as: the power train, chassis, electrical system, passenger compartment, etc. The result of the FAST model and supporting cost analysis might then focus the team's attention on the power train for further analysis.

Moving to a lower level of abstraction, the power train could then be divided into its components for a more detailed analysis. In other words, the concept of decomposition is applied to a FAST model. The initial FAST model will stay at a high level of abstraction. Starting at a higher level of abstraction allows for uncluttered macro analysis of the overall problem until those key functions can be found, isolated, and the key issues identified. If a function is identified for further study. A supporting FAST diagram is then created for that subsystem function. This process of decomposition or moving to lower levels of abstraction could be carried down several levels if appropriate. Once high cost to value mechanisms are identified in the initial system value analysis matrix, the next step is to focus more attention on those mechanisms and associated functions. Dimensioning groups the functions together into those associated with a particular subsystem, assembly or part. The FAST diagram can be expanded into a lower level of abstraction in the area under investigation.

The steps involved are as follows:

- Use QFD to translate higher-level customer needs to subsystem technical characteristics.
- Create FAST diagram at lower level of abstraction for targeted mechanism/subsystem.
- Prepare a FAST diagram and develop the product concept in conjunction with the QFD concept selection matrix
- Dimension the 'system in the FAST diagram into assemblies/parts or identify the assemblies/parts needed to perform the given function.
- Develop value analysis matrix at a lower level of abstraction for the targeted subsystem. The "what's" or system requirements/function in the value analysis matrix are derived from either a customer FAST diagram or by selecting those function statements that correspond to the customer needs or technical characteristics in the subsystem planning matrix.
- Complete the value analysis matrix and identify high cost to value mechanisms by comparing the mechanism target costs to the mechanism estimated/actual costs

VALUE IMPROVEMENT PROCESS

Performing value analysis or producing the FAST model and analyzing functions with the value analysis matrix are only the first steps in the process. The real work begins with brainstorming, developing and analyzing potential improvements in the product.

These subsequent steps are supported by:

- The QFD Concept Selection Matrix is a powerful tool to evaluate various concept and design alternatives based on a set of weighted criteria that ultimately tie back to customer needs.
- Benchmarking competitors and other similar products helps to see new ways functions can be performed and breaks down some of the not-invented-here paradigms.
- Product cost and life cycle cost models support the estimating of cost for the Function-Cost and Value Analysis Matrices and aid in the evaluation of various product concepts.
- Technology evaluation is leads us to new ways that basic functions can be performed in a better or less costly way. Concept development should involve people with a knowledge of new technology development and an open mind to identify how this technology might relate to product functions that need to be performed. Methods such as the theory of inventive problem solving or TRIZ are useful in this regard.
- Design for Manufacturability/Assembly principles provide guidance on how to better design components and assemblies that are more manufacturable and, as a result, are lower in cost.

Value Analysis or Function Analysis provide the methods to identify the problem and to begin to define the functions that need to be performed. As we proceed in developing a FAST model, implicit in this process is developing a concept of operation for the product which is represented by all of the lower order functions in a FAST diagram. Concept alternatives will be developed through brainstorming, benchmarking other products performing similar functions, and surveying and applying new technology. Since multiple concepts need to be evaluated, we want to use a higher level of abstraction for the FAST model to provide us with the greatest flexibility and a minimum level of effort. Trade studies and technical analysis will be performed to evaluate various product concepts. A concept selection matrix is a good tool to summarize a variety of different data and support making a decision about the preferred concept.

All of these steps may be iterative as a preferred concept evolves and gets more fully developed. In addition, there should be a thorough evaluation of whether all functions are needed or if there is a different way of accomplishing a function as the concept is developed to a lower level of abstraction. When a Function Cost or Value Analysis Matrix is prepared, functions that are out of balance with their worth are identified, further challenging the team to explore different approaches.

STOCK CONTROL SYSTEMS

FIXED RE-ORDER STOCK LEVEL

This method of stock control is where a business decides the minimum level of stocks it can tolerate, and then re-orders before the stocks reach this level. The exact timing will depend how long the stocks take to arrive. This can be illustrated as follows:

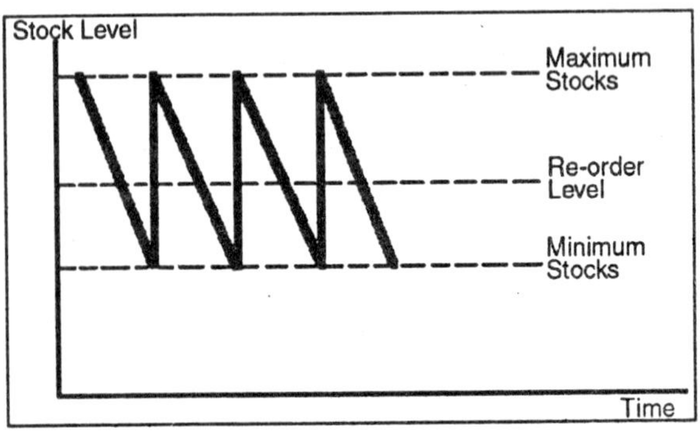

The distance between the re-order line and the minimum stocks level depends how long it may take for the order to arrive - this time is known as the lead time.

FIXED TIME REORDERING

This method is exactly as its title suggests. The firm reorders stocks at a fixed time each month or week. It can offer a good solution as it represents a routine for the firm and ensures that stocks are regularly supplemented. However, it may well mean the level of stocks fluctuating quite a bit depending on the rate they are used up. It is a little inflexible as a system as well unless used very carefully.

ECONOMIC ORDER QUANTITY

For any company there is an optimum level of stocks. The precise level of this will vary in different firms and industries. They have to balance the costs of holding stocks with the costs of ordering stock. The more firms order at once, the better the deal they will usually get.

The level of stocks that strikes the balance between these two things is known as the economic order quantity. If this is taken to be the optimum level of stocks it should help to minimise the firm's costs - an important pre-requisite to maximising profit.

JUST-IN-TIME PRODUCTION

Because stocks cost so much to keep, another method of stock-control was developed in Japan and has now become much more common in the UK. The just-in-time method involves keeping stocks to an absolute minimum, and the raw materials are ordered only when they are needed. In other words just-in-time.

This time period in some cases has been reduced to minutes or hours, and the raw materials arrive on site moments before they are needed. This can be wonderful for helping to reduce the need for working capital, but requires a very high level of organisational skill and a very close relationship with suppliers.

8

Inventory Management

CONCEPT

Inventory management is primarily about specifying the size and placement of stocked goods. Inventory management is required at different locations within a facility or within multiple locations of a supply network to protect the regular and planned course of production against the random disturbance of running out of materials or goods.

The scope of inventory management also concerns the fine lines between replenishment lead time, carrying costs of inventory, asset management, inventory forecasting, inventory valuation, inventory visibility, future inventory price forecasting, physical inventory, available physical space for inventory, quality management, replenishment, returns and defective goods and demand forecasting. Balancing these competing requirements leads to optimal inventory levels, which is an on-going process as the business needs shift and react to the wider environment.

Other definitions of inventory management from across the web:

- Involves a retailer seeking to acquire and maintain a proper merchandise assortment while ordering, shipping, handling, and related costs are kept in check.
- Systems and processes that identify inventory requirements, set targets, provide replenishment techniques and report actual and projected inventory status.
- Handles all functions related to the tracking and management of material. This would include the

monitoring of material moved into and out of stockroom locations and the reconciling of the inventory balances. Also may include ABC analysis, lot tracking, cycle counting support etc.

- Management of the inventories, with the primary objective of determining/controlling stock levels within the physical distribution function to balance the need for product availability against the need for minimizing stock holding and handling costs.

BUSINESS INVENTORY

REASONS FOR KEEPING STOCK

There are three basic reasons for keeping an inventory:

1. *Time*: The time lags present in the supply chain, from supplier to user at every stage, requires that you maintain certain amount of inventory to use in this "lead time".
2. *Uncertainty*: Inventories are maintained as buffers to meet uncertainties in demand, supply and movements of goods.
3. *Economies of scale*: Ideal condition of "one unit at a time at a place where user needs it, when he needs it" principle tends to incur lots of costs in terms of logistics. So bulk buying, movement and storing brings in economies of scale, thus inventory.

All these stock reasons can apply to any owner or product stage:

- Buffer stock is held in individual workstations against the possibility that the upstream workstation may be a little delayed in long setup or change-over time. This stock is then used while that change-over is happening. This stock can be eliminated by tools like SMED.

These classifications apply along the whole Supply chain not just within a facility or plant. Where these stocks contain the same or similar items it is often the work practice to hold all these stocks mixed together before or after the sub-process to which they relate. This 'reduces' costs. Because they are mixed-up together there is no visual reminder to operators of the adjacent sub-processes or line management of the stock which is due to a particular cause and should be a particular individual's responsibility with inevitable consequences. Some plants have centralized stock holding across sub-processes which makes the situation even more acute.

SPECIAL TERMS USED IN DEALING WITH INVENTORY

- Stock Keeping Unit (SKU) is a unique combination of all the components that are assembled into the purchasable item. Therefore any change in the packaging or product is a new SKU. This level of detailed specification assists in managing inventory.
- Stockout means running out of the inventory of an SKU.
- "New old stock" (sometimes abbreviated NOS) is a term used in business to refer to merchandise being offered for sale which was manufactured long ago but that has never been used. Such merchandise may not be produced any more, and the new old stock may represent the only market source of a particular item at the present time.

TYPOLOGY

- Buffer/safety stock
- Cycle stock (Used in batch processes, it is the available inventory excluding buffer stock)
- De-coupling (Buffer stock that is held by both the supplier and the user)
- Anticipation stock (building up extra stock for periods of increased demand - e.g. ice cream for summer)
- Pipeline stock (goods still in transit or in the process of distribution - have left the factory but not arrived at the customer yet)

INVENTORY EXAMPLES

While accountants often discuss inventory in terms of goods for sale, organizations - manufacturers, service-providers and not-for-profits - also have inventories (fixtures, furniture, supplies,...) that they do not intend to sell. Manufacturers', distributors', and wholesalers' inventory tends to cluster in warehouses. Retailers' inventory may exist in a warehouse or in a shop or store accessible to customers. Inventories not intended for sale to customers or to clients may be held in any premises an organization uses. Stock ties up cash and if uncontrolled it will be impossible to know the actual level of stocks and therefore impossible to control them.

While the reasons for holding stock are covered earlier, most manufacturing organizations usually divide their "goods for sale" inventory into:

- *Raw materials*: Materials and components scheduled for use in making a product.
- *Work in process, WIP*: Materials and components that have begun their transformation to finished goods.
- *Finished goods*: Goods ready for sale to customers.
- *Goods for resale*: Returned goods that are salable.

PRINCIPLE OF INVENTORY PROPORTIONALITY

PURPOSE

Inventory proportionality is the goal of demand driven inventory management. The primary optimal outcome is to have the same number of days (or hours, etc.) worth of inventory on hand across all products so that the time of runout of all products would be simultaneous. In such a case, there is no "excess inventory", that is, inventory that would be left over of another product when the first product runs out. Excess inventory is sub-optimal because the money spent to obtain it could have been deployed better elsewhere, i.e. to the product that just ran out.

The secondary goal of inventory proportionality is inventory minimization. By integrating accurate demand forecasting with inventory management, replenishment inventories can be scheduled to arrive just in time to replenish the product destined to run out first, while at the same time balancing out the inventory supply of all products to make their inventories more proportional, and thereby closer to achieving the primary goal. Accurate demand forecasting also allows the desired inventory proportions to be dynamic by determining expected sales out into the future; this allows for inventory to be in proportion to expected short term sales or consumption rather than to past averages, a much more accurate and optimal outcome. Integrating demand forecasting with inventory management in this way also allows for the prediction of the "can fit" point when inventory storage is limited on a per product basis.

APPLICATIONS

The technique of inventory proportionality is most appropriate for inventories that remain unseen by the consumer. As opposed to "keep full" systems where a retail consumer would like to see full shelves of the product they are buying so as not to think they are buying something old, unwanted, or stale; and differentiated from the "trigger point" systems where product is reordered when it hits a certain level; inventory proportionality is used effectively by just-in-time manufacturing processes and retail applications where the product is hidden from view.

One early example of inventory proportionality used in a retail application in the United States is for motor fuel. Motor fuel (e.g. gasoline) is generally stored in underground storage tanks. The motorists do not know whether they are buying gasoline off the top or bottom of the tank, nor need they care. Additionally, these storage tanks have a maximum capacity and cannot be overfilled. Finally, the product is expensive. Inventory proportionality is used to balance the inventories of the different grades of motor fuel, each stored in dedicated tanks, in proportion to the sales of each grade. Excess inventory is not seen or valued by the consumer, so it is simply cash sunk (literally) into the ground. Inventory proportionality minimizes the amount of excess inventory carried in underground storage tanks. This application for motor fuel was first developed and implemented by Petrolsoft

Corporation in 1990 for Chevron Products Company. Most major oil companies use such systems today.

ROOTS

The use of Inventory Proportionality in the United States is thought to have been inspired by Japanese just-in-time (business) parts inventory management made famous by Toyota Motors in the 1980s.

HIGH LEVEL INVENTORY MANAGEMENT

It seems that around about 1880 there was a change in manufacturing practice from companies with relatively homogeneous lines of products to vertically integrated companies with unprecedented diversity in processes and products. Those companies (especially in metalworking) attempted to achieve success through economies of scope - the gains of jointly producing two or more products in one facility. The managers now needed information on the effect of product mix decisions on overall profits and therefore needed accurate product cost information.

A variety of attempts to achieve this were unsuccessful due to the huge overhead of the information processing of the time. However, the burgeoning need for financial reporting after 1900 created unavoidable pressure for financial accounting of stock and the management need to cost manage products became overshadowed. In particular it was the need for audited accounts that sealed the fate of managerial cost accounting. The dominance of financial reporting accounting over management accounting remains to this day with few exceptions and the financial reporting definitions of 'cost' have distorted effective management 'cost' accounting since that time. This is particularly true of inventory.

Hence high level financial inventory has these two basic formulas which relate to the accounting period:

1. Cost of Beginning Inventory at the start of the period + inventory purchases within the period + cost of production within the period = cost of goods

2. Cost of goods " cost of ending inventory at the end of the period = cost of goods sold

The benefit of these formulae is that the first absorbs all overheads of production and raw material costs in to a value of inventory for reporting. The second formula then creates the new start point for the next period and gives a figure to be subtracted from sales price to determine some form of sales margin figure. Manufacturing management is more interested in inventory turnover ratio or average days to sell inventory since it tells them something about relative inventory levels.

Inventory turn over ratio (also known as inventory turns) = cost of goods sold/Average Inventory = Cost of Goods Sold/((Beginning Inventory + Ending Inventory)/2) and its inverse Average Days to Sell Inventory = Number of Days a Year/Inventory Turn Over Ratio = 365 days a year/Inventory Turn Over Ratio This ratio estimates how many times the inventory turns over a year.

This number tells us how much cash/goods are tied up waiting for the process and is a critical measure of process reliability and effectiveness. So a factory with two inventory turns has six months stock on hand which generally not a good figure (depending upon industry) whereas a factory that moves from six turns to twelve turns has probably improved effectiveness by 100%. This improvement will have some negative results in the financial reporting since the 'value' now stored in the factory as inventory is reduced.

Whilst the simplicity of these accounting measures of inventory are very useful they are in the end fraught with the danger of their own assumptions. There are in fact so many things which can vary hidden under this appearance of simplicity that a variety of 'adjusting' assumptions may be used.

These include:

- Specific Identification
- Weighted Average Cost
- Moving-Average Cost
- FIFO and LIFO.

Inventory Turn is a financial accounting tool for evaluating inventory and it is not necessarily a management tool. Inventory management should be forward looking. The methodology applied is based on historical cost of goods sold. The ratio may not be able to reflect the usability of future production demand as well as customer demand.

Business models including Just in Time (JIT) Inventory, Vendor Managed Inventory (VMI) and Customer Managed Inventory (CMI) attempt to minimize on-hand inventory and increase inventory turns. VMI and CMI have gained considerable attention due to the success of third party vendors who offer added expertise and knowledge that organizations may not possess.

ACCOUNTING FOR INVENTORY

Each country has its own rules about accounting for inventory that fit with their financial reporting rules. So for example, organizations in the U.S. define inventory to suit their needs within US Generally Accepted Accounting Practices (GAAP), the rules defined by the Financial Accounting Standards Board (FASB) (and others) and enforced by the U.S. Securities and Exchange Commission (SEC) and other federal and state agencies. Other countries often have similar arrangements but with their own GAAP and national agencies instead.

It is intentional that financial accounting uses standards that allow the public to compare firms' performance, cost accounting functions internally to an organization and potentially with much greater flexibility. A discussion of inventory from standard and Theory of Constraints-based (throughput) cost accounting perspective follows some examples and a discussion of inventory from a financial accounting perspective.

The internal costing/valuation of inventory can be complex. Whereas in the past most enterprises ran simple one process factories, this is quite probably in the minority in the 21st century. Where 'one process' factories exist then there is a market for the goods created which establishes an independent market value for the good. Today with multi-stage process companies there is much inventory that would once have been finished goods which is now held as 'work-in-process' (WIP). This needs to be valued in the accounts but the valuation is a management decision since there is no market for the partially finished product. This somewhat arbitrary 'valuation' of WIP combined with the allocation of overheads to it has led to some unintended and undesirable results.

FINANCIAL ACCOUNTING

An organization's inventory can appear a mixed blessing, since it counts as an asset on the balance sheet, but it also ties up money that could serve for other purposes and requires additional expense for its protection. Inventory may also cause significant tax expenses, depending on particular countries' laws regarding depreciation of inventory, as in Thor Power Tool Company v. Commissioner.

Inventory appears as a current asset on an organization's balance sheet because the organization can, in principle, turn it into cash by selling it. Some organizations hold larger inventories than their operations require in order to inflate their apparent asset value and their perceived profitability.

In addition to the money tied up by acquiring inventory, inventory also brings associated costs for warehouse space, for utilities, and for insurance to cover staff to handle and protect it, fire and other disasters, obsolescence, shrinkage (theft and errors), and others. Such holding costs can mount up: between a third and a half of its acquisition value per year.

Businesses that stock too little inventory cannot take advantage of large orders from customers if they cannot deliver. The conflicting objectives of cost control and customer service often pit an organization's financial and operating managers against its sales and marketing departments. Sales people, in particular, often receive sales commission payments, so unavailable goods may reduce their potential personal income.

This conflict can be minimised by reducing production time to being near or less than customer expected delivery time. This effort, known as "Lean production" will significantly reduce working capital tied up in inventory and reduce manufacturing costs.

ROLE OF INVENTORY ACCOUNTING

By helping the organization to make better decisions, the accountants can help the public sector to change in a very positive way that delivers increased value for the taxpayer's investment. It can also help to incentivise progress and to ensure that reforms are sustainable and effective in the long term, by ensuring that success is appropriately recognized in both the formal and informal reward systems of the organization.

To say that they have a key role to play is an understatement. Finance is connected to most, if not all, of the key business processes within the organization. It should be steering the stewardship and accountability systems that ensure that the organization is conducting its business in an appropriate, ethical manner. It is critical that these foundations are firmly laid. So often they are the litmus test by which public confidence in the institution is either won or lost.

Finance should also be providing the information, analysis and advice to enable the organizations' service managers to operate effectively. This goes beyond the traditional preoccupation with budgets – how much have we spent so far, how much have we left to spend? It is about helping the organization to better understand its own performance. That means making the connections and understanding the relationships between given inputs – the resources brought to bear – and the outputs and outcomes that they achieve. It is also about understanding and actively managing risks within the organization and its activities.

FIFO VS. LIFO ACCOUNTING

When a merchant buys goods from inventory, the value of the inventory account is reduced by the cost of goods sold (CoG sold). This is simple where the CoG has not varied across those held in stock; but where it has, then an agreed method must be derived to evaluate it. For commodity items that one cannot track individually, accountants must choose a method that fits the nature of the sale. Two popular methods which normally exist are: FIFO and LIFO accounting (first in - first out, last in - first out). FIFO regards the first unit that arrived in inventory as the first one sold. LIFO considers the last unit arriving in inventory as the first one sold. Which method an accountant selects can have a significant effect on net income and book value and, in turn, on taxation. Using LIFO accounting for inventory, a company generally reports lower net income and lower book value, due to the effects of inflation. This generally results in lower taxation. Due to LIFO's potential to skew inventory value, UK GAAP and IAS have effectively banned LIFO inventory accounting.

STANDARD COST ACCOUNTING

Standard cost accounting uses ratios called efficiencies that compare the labour and materials actually used to produce a good with those that the same goods would have required under "standard" conditions. As long as similar actual and standard conditions obtain, few problems arise. Unfortunately, standard cost accounting methods developed about 100 years ago, when labour comprised the most important cost in manufactured goods. Standard methods continue to emphasize labour efficiency even though that resource now constitutes a (very) small part of cost in most cases.

Standard cost accounting can hurt managers, workers, and firms in several ways. For example, a policy decision to increase inventory can harm a manufacturing managers' performance evaluation. Increasing inventory requires increased production, which means that processes must operate at higher rates. When (not if) something goes wrong, the process takes longer and uses more than the standard labour time. The manager appears responsible for the excess, even thoughs/he has no control over the production requirement or the problem.

In adverse economic times, firms use the same efficiencies to downsize, rightsize, or otherwise reduce their labour force. Workers laid off under those circumstances have even less control over excess inventory and cost efficiencies than their managers.Many financial and cost accountants have agreed for many years on the desirability of replacing standard cost accounting. They have not, however, found a successor.

THEORY OF CONSTRAINTS COST ACCOUNTING

Eliyahu M. Goldratt developed the Theory of Constraints in part to address the cost-accounting problems in what he calls the "cost world". He offers a substitute, called throughput accounting, that uses throughput (money for goods sold to customers) in place of output (goods produced that may sell or may boost inventory) and considers labour as a fixed rather than as a variable cost. He defines inventory simply as everything the organization owns that it plans to sell, including buildings, machinery, and many other things in addition to the categories listed here. Throughput accounting recognizes only one class of variable costs: the trully variable costs like materials and components that vary directly with the quantity produced.

Finished goods inventories remain balance-sheet assets, but labour efficiency ratios no longer evaluate managers and workers. Instead of an incentive to reduce labour cost, throughput accounting focuses attention on the relationships between throughput (revenue or income) on one hand and controllable operating expenses and changes in inventory on the other. Those relationships direct attention to the constraints or bottlenecks that prevent the system from producing more throughput, rather than to people - who have little or no control over their situations.

FACTORS AFFECTING INVENTORY

In inventories of businesses around the world there are a number of conflicting influences that are affecting the way that companies work. Company managers have experienced inventory- related conflicts, which have been used for some companies own gain and others it has just been a headache that they have been trying to fix. Well- in substance by Sidney

Bacendale, Lynn Boyd and Mahesh Gupta they offer a solution to this growing problem that companies are dealing with in their inventory. The substance starts out with a summery from a novel that is surprising fitting for the substance's topic. The passage is taken from a novel titled "The Goal, by Eliyahi Goldratt.

In the passage it discusses a plant manager having a conversation with his controller, and the controller asks the manager a question it is the following: "what manager could be surprised that inventory is recorded as an asset on his balance sheet? (Baxendale, Boyd and Gupta)". That is a very good question, because as a manager that gives your area of management a good reputation, however, as individuals the authors are trying to explain that as a business you must know what an "asset" really is to fully understand whether the assets your company has are good or not.

This is not the only focus of the substance however, there is much more. Another key point that the authors are trying to get across in this substance is the fact that if a company reduces their inventory in the long term the company will get benefits. In doing this the company will have more completed products, this in return will give the company more assets as opposed to having unfinished supplies on hand. In addition the company's overhead will bring more fixed manufacturing overhead which will increase profits, increased manufacturing flexibility, higher product quality, lower manufacturing lead time, and improved return on assets.

ECONOMIC ORDER QUANTITY

Economic order quantity is the level of inventory that minimizes the total inventory holding costs and ordering costs. It is one of the oldest classical production scheduling models. The framework used to determine this order quantity is also known as Wilson EOQ Model or Wilson Formula.

The model was developed by F. W. Harris in 1913, but R. H. Wilson, a consultant who applied it extensively, is given credit for his early in-depth analysis it. Assume that the demand for a product is constant over the year and that each new order is delivered in full when the inventory reaches zero. There is a fixed cost charged for each order placed, regardless of the number of units ordered. There is also a holding or storage cost for each unit held in storage (sometimes expressed as a percentage of the purchase cost of the item). We want to determine the optimal number of units of the product to order so that we minimize the total cost associated with the purchase, delivery and storage of the product.

The required parameters to the solution are the total demand for the year, the purchase cost for each item, the fixed cost to place the order and the storage cost for each item per year. Note that the number of times an order is placed will also affect the total cost, however, this number can be determined from the other parameters

UNDERLYING ASSUMPTIONS

- The ordering cost is constant.
- The rate of demand is constant
- The lead time is fixed
- The purchase price of the item is constant i.e no discount is available
- The replenishment is made instantaneously, the whole batch is delivered at once.

EOQ is the quantity to order, so that ordering cost + carrying cost finds its minimum. (A common misunderstanding is that the formula tries to find when these are equal.)

VARIABLES

- Q = order quantity
- Q^* = optimal order quantity
- D = annual demand quantity of the product
- P = purchase cost per unit
- S = fixed cost per order (not per unit, in addition to unit cost)
- H = annual holding cost per unit (also known as carrying cost or storage cost) (warehouse space, refrigeration, insurance, etc. usually not related to the unit cost)

THE TOTAL COST FUNCTION

The single-item EOQ formula finds the minimum point of the following cost function:

Total Cost = purchase cost + ordering cost + holding cost

- Purchase cost: This is the variable cost of goods: purchase unit price × annual demand quantity. This is P×D
- Ordering cost: This is the cost of placing orders: each order has a fixed cost S, and we need to order D/Q times per year. This is S × D/Q
- Holding cost: the average quantity in stock (between fully replenished and empty) is Q/2, so this cost is H × Q/2

$$TC = PD + \frac{DS}{Q} + \frac{HQ}{2}$$

To determine the minimum point of the total cost curve, set the ordering cost equal to the holding cost:

$$\frac{DS}{Q} = \frac{HQ}{2}$$

Solving for Q gives Q* (the optimal order quantity):

$$\frac{H}{2} = \frac{DS}{Q^2}$$

$$Q^2 = \frac{2DS}{H}$$

$$\text{Therefore: } Q^* = \sqrt{\frac{2DS}{H}}$$

Note that interestingly, Q* is independent of P; it is a function of only S, D, H.

EXTENSIONS

Several extensions can be made to the EOQ model, including backordering costs and multiple items. Additionally, the economic order interval can be determined from the EOQ and the economic production quantity model (which determines the optimal production quantity) can be determined in a similar fashion. A version of the model, the Baumol-Tobin model, has also been used to determine the money demand function, where a person's holdings of money balances can be seen in a way parallel to a firm's holdings of inventory.

ORDERING LEVEL OR RE-ORDER LEVEL

Ordering level is that level of material in the store where store keeper initiates fresh requisition to the purchasing departments for purchase of materials. This level is fixed some where between minimum level and maximum level.

This level depends upon the following factors:

- Lead time or delivery time.
- Rate of consumption of the materials.
- Economic order quantity.
- Minimum level.

Basing upon the factors, the following formula has been derived:

Order level or (Reordering level) = Minimum level + consumption during the time required to get fresh delivery.

ABC ANALYSIS

ABC analysis, Pareto's law or "80/20 rule" are all-synonymous of the same tool which basically states that 20% of a given population represents 80% of a specific characteristic. In purchasing, the basic ABC analysis is used to identify which segments represent most of the spend in a given category or portfolio. Most of the time, few segments in a portfolio constitute the largest part of the total spend.

Usually:

- The A segments represent approximately 80% of the total spend within a category
- The B segments represent the following 15% of the total spend within a category
- The C segments are the remaining (most of the time several segments) which represents the final 5% of the total spend

The ABC approach can also be used in other analyses such as:

- *Spend per supplier in a portfolio*: Few suppliers will represent most of the spend
- *Number of orders per supplier*: Few suppliers will have most of the orders in a portfolio

- *Number of items bought per supplier*: Few suppliers will deliver most of the substances in a portfolio

WHEN AND WHY TO USE IT?

The ABC analysis can be also be useful in several steps of the Sourcing Value Chan:

- Demand Identification, to gather the annual spend of a site
- Demand Aggregation, to gather the annual spend of several sites
- Opportunity Assessment, to identify leveraging opportunities

The ABC tool is used to identify the "vital few" from the "trivial many", according to a defined set of criteria (e.g. annual expenditure, number of orders, number of claims, occupied space in the inventory, etc.). Different decisions may be taken from the result of the ABC analysis. The basic utilization of the ABC analysis for a buyer is to use it with the spend as a criterion. It helps the buyer to identify the few A segments which will require special attention due to the "large amount of money" they represent.

A small "mistake" in managing the few A segments may cost a lot to your company. The C segments will require a different approach to simplify the administrative burden to handle them. Special attention must be given to some C segments which may represent high risk for the business! This is one of the limits of the ABC analysis on spend!

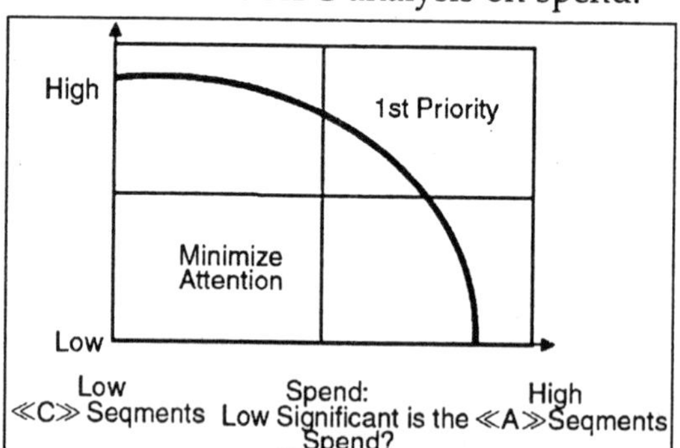

ABC Analysis

Risk must be discussed with the stakeholders. They will define with the buyer which of the C segments may be "risky" for the business and will require special attention from the buyer. Different categories will have different "risk" criteria. For examples: production items may be classified by "lead time". The longer the lead-time the "riskier" the segment is. Other criteria for risk may be customer sensitivity to the segment, safety issues, etc...

TOOL DESCRIPTION

The following 6-step's are used to perform an ABC analysis:

1. *1st step*: Identify the objective and the analysis criterion
2. *2nd step*: Collect data about the analysed population
3. *3rd step*: Sort out the list by decreasing impact
4. *4th step*: Calculate the accumulated impact and the percentage
5. *5th step*: Identify the classes
6. *6th step*: Analyse the classes and take appropriate decisions

1st Step – Identify the Objective and the Analysis Criterion

In this step, the objective is clearly understood. In the proposed example, we are responsible for buying security material for a plant. Our objective is to generate savings on the price of the different equipments, by renegotiating existing contracts. We would like to know which equipment segment should be considered for renegotiation efforts and resources, so that the maximum savings are generated. Therefore, we choose to undertake an ABC analysis of the purchasing category, classified by annual spend.

2nd Step – Collect Data about the Analysed Population

In this step, collect the data necessary to carry out the analysis: The list of the different safety equipments, and the corresponding annual spend.

Table. Cetegory: Safety Equipment

	Description	Annual Spend
1	Hard aats	27 900.00 €
2	Safety boots	122 500.00 €
3	Safety glasses	49 200.00 €
4	Ear plugs	4 600.00 €
5	Mashs, respirators	19 700.00 €
6	Safety gloves	35 400.00 €
7	Eye wash stations	19 300.00 €
8	First aid kits	9 150.00 €
9	Fire extinguishers	16 100.00 €
10	Thermal underware	300.00 €
11	Safety beacons	11 180.00 €
12	Monitoring systems	367 000.00 €
13	Safety signs	7 750.00 €
14	Welding protection clothes	2 700.00 €
15	Coveralls	650 000.00 €
16	Apparel shirts, jackets	120 600.00 €
17	Safety reflective taps	2 600.00 €
18	Floor marking paint	1 090.00 €
19	Fall arrest equipment	6 600.00 €
	Total	1 473 670.00 €

3rd Step – Sort Out the List by Decreasing Impact

In this step, sort out the list of equipment, in decreasing order, according to our criterion of analysis, i.e., annual spend.

Table. Cetegory: Safety Equipment

	Description	Annual Spend
15	Coveralls	650 000.00 €
12	Monitoring systems	367 000.00 €
2	Safety boots	122 500.00 €
16	Apparel shirts, jackets	120 600.00 €
3	Safety glasses	49 200.00 €
6	Safety gloves	35 400.00 €
1	Hard aats	27 900.00 €

5	Mashs, respirators	19 700.00 €	
7	Eye wash stations	19 300.00 €	
9	Fire extinguishers	16 100.00 €	
11	Safety beacons	11 180.00 €	
8	First aid kits	9 150.00 €	13
	Safety signs	7 750.00 €	19
	Fall arrest equipment	6 600.00 €	
4	Ear plugs	4 600.00 €	
14	Welding protection clothes	2 700.00 €	17
	Safety reflective taps	2 600.00 €	18
	Floor marking paint	1 090.00 €	
10	Thermal underware	300.00 €	
	Total	1 473 670.00 €	

4th Step – Calculate the Accumulated Impact and the Percentage

In this step, accumulate the annual expense and calculate the percentage of the accumulated spend compared to the total. *Example*: the coverall category alone makes 650 k€, which is 44.11% of the total spend; the coverall and monitoring systems make together 1017 k€, which is 69.01% of the total expense. Coverall + monitoring systems + safety boots make 1139 k€, which is 77.32% of the total spend. Etc.

Table. Cetegory: Safety Equipment

	Description	Annual spend	Cumulative	Percentage
15	Coveralls	650 000.00 €	650 000.00 €	44.11%
12	Monitoring systems	367 000.00 €	1 017 000.00 €	69.01%
2	Safety boots	122 500.00 €	1 139 500.00 €	77.32%
16	Apparel shirts, jackets	120 600.00 €	1 260 100.00 €	85.51%
3	Safety glasses	49 200.00 €	1 309 300.00 €	88.85%
6	Safety gloves	35 400.00 €	1 344 700.00 €	91.25%
1	Hard hats	27 900.00 €	1 372 600.00 €	93.14%
5	Masks, respirators	19 700.00 €	1 392 300.00 €	94.48%
7	Eye wash stations	19 300.00 €	1 411 600.00 €	95.79%
9	Fire extinguishers	16 100.00 €	1 427 700.00 €	96.88%
11	Safety beacons	11 180.00 €	1 438 880.00 €	97.64%
8	First aid kits	9 150.00 €	1 448 030.00 €	98.26%
13	Safety signs	7 750.00 €	1 455 780.00 €	98.79%
19	Fall arrest equipment	6 600.00 €	1 462 380.00 €	99.23%
4	Ear plugs	4 600.00 €	1 466 980.00 €	99.55%
14	Welding protection clothes	2 700.00 €	1 469 680.00 €	99.73%
17	Safety reflective tape	2 600.00 €	1 472 280.00 €	99.91%
18	Floor marking paint	1 090.00 €	1 473 370.00 €	99.98%
10	Thermal underwear	300.00 €	1 473 670.00 €	100.00%
	Total	**1 473 670.00 €**		

5th Step – Identify the Buy Classes

In this step, separate the categories into three different classes. Keep in mind that the aim of the game is not to go for precise 20%-80%, but rather to understand which segments to focus efforts to get the results that are expected in the example by renegotiating prices.

Table. Cetegory: Safety Equipment

	Description	Annual spend	Cumulative	Percentage	
15	Coveralls	650 000.00 €	650 000.00 €	44.11%	
12	Monitoring systems	367 000.00 €	1 017 000.00 €	69.01%	A segments
2	Safety boots	122 500.00 €	1 139 500.00 €	77.32%	
16	Apparel shirts, jackets	120 600.00 €	1 260 100.00 €	85.51%	
3	Safety glasses	49 200.00 €	1 309 300.00 €	88.85%	
6	Safety gloves	35 400.00 €	1 344 700.00 €	91.25%	
1	Hard hats	27 900.00 €	1 372 600.00 €	93.14%	
5	Masks, respirators	19 700.00 €	1 392 300.00 €	94.48%	B segments
7	Eye wash stations	19 300.00 €	1 411 600.00 €	95.79%	
9	Fire extinguishers	16 100.00 €	1 427 700.00 €	96.88%	
11	Safety beacons	11 180.00 €	1 438 880.00 €	97.64%	
8	First aid kits	9 150.00 €	1 448 030.00 €	98.26%	
13	Safety signs	7 750.00 €	1 455 780.00 €	98.79%	
19	Fall arrest equipment	6 600.00 €	1 462 380.00 €	99.23%	
4	Ear plugs	4 600.00 €	1 466 980.00 €	99.55%	C segments
14	Welding protection clothes	2 700.00 €	1 469 680.00 €	99.73%	
17	Safety reflective tape	2 600.00 €	1 472 280.00 €	99.91%	
18	Floor marking paint	1 090.00 €	1 473 370.00 €	99.98%	
10	Thermal underwear	300.00 €	1 473 670.00 €	100.00%	
	Total	**1 473 670.00 €**			

6th Step – Analyse the Classes and Make Appropriate Decisions

In this final step, do a final analysis to determine next steps. *The decisions out of this analysis could be:*

- To investigate how many suppliers offer coveralls (and monitoring systems and safety boots). If there are several, what do we gain by consolidating the volume on one supplier?
- Should an on-line negotiation be considered?

Note: the ABC analysis does not provide a direct solution: it is used to point out the "few important areas" to explore for further leveraging opportunities. As it was already stated, it does not mean that the class C segments are not important: They are not important regarding negotiation levers, since the spend is very low, and the potential savings would probably not be worth the necessary efforts.

REQUIRED RESOURCES

An ABC analysis requires directionally correct data. It relies on the availability of systems allowing measurement of the criteria chosen for the analysis. This availability of data becomes critical whenever the population on target is spread over several sites, countries, etc., or worse, is not coded in a homogeneous way. Sometimes, a conversion of data using product standard codes is mandatory.

TOOL LIMITATIONS/COMMON PITFALLS

Most of the time only past annual spend is available to perform an ABC analysis. By definition it is what was "bought" but not what will be the next year's spend. The use of past annual spend is fine if the business needs will not change in the near future.

The buyer may consider that next year figures will be the same as the last year's one. In the case where the buyer considers that the future needs may vary from the past figures, it would be better, whenever available, to use "future annual spend" provided by the internal customers or "budgeted" figures.

9

Quality Management

CONCEPT

Quality Management is the assembly and management of all activities aimed at the production of quality by organizations of various kinds. In the present case this implies the introduction and proper running of a "Quality System" in laboratories. A statement of objectives and policy to produce quality should be made for the organization or department concerned. This statement also identifies the internal organization and responsibilities for the effective operation of the Quality System. Quality Management can be considered a somewhat wider interpretation of the concept of "Good Laboratory Practice" (GLP). Therefore, inevitably the basics of the present Guidelines largely coincide with those of GLP.

Note. An even wider concept of quality management is presently coming into vogue: "Total Quality Management" (TQM). This concept includes additional aspects such as leadership style, ethics of the work, social aspects, relation to society, etc. For an introduction to TQM the reader is referred to Parkany.

QUALITY ASSURANCE

Proper Quality Management implies consequent implementation of the next level: Quality Assurance. The ISO definition reads: "the assembly of all planned and systematic actions necessary to provide adequate confidence that a product, process, or service will satisfy given quality requirements." The result of these actions aimed at the production of quality, should ideally be checked by someone independent of the work: the Quality Assurance Officer. If no QA officer is available, then usually the Head of Laboratory performs this job as part of his quality management task. In case of special projects, customers may require special quality assurance measures or a Quality Plan.

QUALITY CONTROL

A major part of the quality assurance is the Quality Control defined by ISO as "the operational techniques and activities that are used to satisfy quality requirements. " An important part of the quality control is the Quality Assessment: the system of activities to verify if the quality control activities are effective, in other words: an evaluation of the products themselves. Quality control is primarily aimed at the prevention of errors. Yet, despite all efforts, it remains inevitable that errors are be made. Therefore, the control system should have checks to detect them.

When errors or mistakes are suspected or discovered it is essential that the "Five Ws" are trailed:

1. What error was made?
2. Where was it made?
3. When was it made?
4. Who made it?
5. Why was it made?

Only when all these questions are answered, proper action can be taken to correct the error and prevent the same mistake being repeated.

The techniques and activities involved in Quality Control can be divided into four levels of operation:

1. First-line control: Instrument performance check.
2. Second-line control: Check of calibration or standardization.
3. Third-line control: Batch control.
4. Fourth-line control: Overall check.

Because the first two control levels both apply to the correct functioning of the instruments they are often taken together and then only three levels are distinguished.

This designation is used throughout the present Guidelines:

- *First-line control*: Instrument check/calibration.
- *Second-line control*: Batch control
- *Third-line control*: External check

It will be clear that producing quality in the laboratory is a major enterprise requiring a continuous human effort and input of money. The rule-of-fist is that 10-20% of the total costs of analysis should be spent on quality control.

Therefore, for quality work at least four conditions should be fulfilled:

1. Means are available
2. Efficient use of time and means
3. Expertise is available
4. Upholding and improving level of output

In quality work, management aspects and technical aspects are inherently cobbled together and for a clear insight and proper functioning of the laboratory these aspects have to be broken down into their components.

GOOD LABORATORY PRACTICE

Quality Management in the present context can be considered a modem version of the hitherto much used concept "Good Laboratory Practice" with a somewhat wider interpretation. The OECD Document defines GLP as follows: "Good Laboratory Practice is concerned with the organizational process and the conditions under which laboratory studies are planned, performed, monitored, recorded, and reported."

Thus, GLP prescribes a laboratory to work according to a system of procedures and protocols. This implies the organization of the activities and the conditions under which these take place are controlled, reported and filed. GLP is a policy for all aspects of the laboratory which influence the quality of the analytical work.

When properly applied, GLP should then:

- Allow better laboratory management
- Improve efficiency
- Minimize errors

- Allow quality control
- Stimulate and motivate all personnel
- Improve safety
- Improve communication possibilities, both internally and externally.

The result of GLP is that the performance of a laboratory is improved and its working effectively controlled. An important aspect is also that the standards of quality are documented and can be demonstrated to authorities and clients. This results in an improved reputation for the laboratory.

In short, the message is:

- Say what you do
- Do what you say
- Do it better
- Be able to show what you have done

The basic rule is that all relevant plans, activities, conditions and situations are recorded and that these records are safely filed and can be produced or retrieved when necessary. These aspects differ strongly in character and need to be attended to individually.

As an assembly, the involved documents constitute a so-called Quality Manual.

This comprises then all relevant information on:

- Organization and Personnel
- Facilities
- Equipment and Working materials
- Analytical or testing systems
- Quality control
- Reporting and filing of results.

Since institutions having a laboratory are of divergent natures, there is no standard format and each has to make its own Quality Manual. The present Guidelines contain examples of forms, protocols, procedures and artificial situations. They need at least to be adapted and many new ones will have to be made according to the specific needs, but all have to fulfil the basic requirement of usefulness and verifiability. As already indicated, the guidelines for Quality Management given here are mainly based on the principles of Good Laboratory Practice as they are laid down in various relevant documents such as ISO and ISO/IEC guides, ISO 9000 series, OECD and CEN documents, national standards, as well as a number of text books. The consulted documents are listed in the Literature.

Use is also made of documents developed by institutes which have obtained accreditation or are working towards this. This concerns mainly so-called Standard Operating Procedures and Protocols. Sometimes these documents are hard to acquire as they are classified information for reasons of competitiveness. The institutes and persons which cooperated in the development of these Guidelines are listed in the Acknowledgements.

CONCEPT OF QUALITY

Quality in business, engineering and manufacturing has a pragmatic interpretation as the non-inferiority or superiority of something. Quality is a perceptual, conditional and somewhat subjective attribute and may be understood differently by different people. Consumers may focus on the specification quality of a product/service, or how it compares to competitors in the marketplace.

Producers might measure the conformance quality, or degree to which the product/service was produced correctly. Numerous definitions and methodologies have been created to assist in managing the quality-affecting aspects of business operations.

Many different techniques and concepts have evolved to improve product or service quality. There are two common quality-related functions within a business. One is quality assurance which is the prevention of defects, such as by the deployment of a quality management system and preventative activities like FMEA.

The other is quality control which is the detection of defects, most commonly associated with testing which takes place within a quality management system typically referred to as verification and validation.

DEFINITIONS

The common element of the business definitions is that the quality of a product or service refers to the perception of the degree to which the product or service meets the customer's expectations. Quality has no specific meaning unless related to a specific function and/or object. Quality is a perceptual, conditional and somewhat subjective attribute. The business meanings of quality have developed over time.

Various interpretations are:

- *ISO 9000*: "Degree to which a set of inherent characteristics fulfills requirements." The standard defines requirement as need or expectation.
- *Six Sigma*: "Number of defects per million opportunities."
- *Subir Chowdhury*: "Quality combines people power and process power."
- *Philip B. Crosby*: "Conformance to requirements." The requirements may not fully represent customer expectations; Crosby treats this as a separate problem.
- *Joseph M. Juran*: "Fitness for use." Fitness is defined by the customer.
- *Noriaki Kano and others, present a two-dimensional model of quality*: "must-be quality" and "attractive quality." The former is near to "fitness for use" and the latter is what the customer would love, but has not yet thought about. Supporters characterize this model more succinctly as: "Products and services that meet or exceed customers' expectations."
- *Robert Pirsig*: "The result of care."
- *Genichi Taguchi, with two definitions*:
  - "Uniformity around a target value." The idea is to lower the standard deviation in outcomes, and to keep the range of outcomes to a certain number of standard deviations, with rare exceptions.
  - "The loss a product imposes on society after it is shipped." This definition of quality is based on a more comprehensive view of the production system.

- American Society for Quality: "A subjective term for which each person has his or her own definition. In technical usage, quality can have two meanings:
  - The characteristics of a product or service that bear on its ability to satisfy stated or implied needs;
  - A product or service free of deficiencies."
- *Peter Drucker*: "Quality in a product or service is not what the supplier puts in. It is what the customer gets out and is willing to pay for."
- *W. Edwards Deming*: concentrating on "the efficient production of the quality that the market expects," and he linked quality and management: "Costs go down and productivity goes up as improvement of quality is accomplished by better management of design, engineering, testing and by improvement of processes."
- *Gerald M. Weinberg*: "Value to some person".

MARKET SECTOR PERSPECTIVES

Operations Management

The dimensions of quality refer to the attributes that quality achieves in Operations Management:

- Quality supports Dependability
- Dependability supports Speed
- Speed supports Flexibility
- Flexibility supports Cost

Quality <-> Dependability <-> Speed <-> Flexibility <-> Cost

Manufacturing

In the manufacturing industry it is commonly stated that "Quality drives productivity." Improved productivity is a source of greater revenues, employment opportunities and technological advances. However, this has not been the case historically, and in the early 19th century it was recognised that some markets,such as those in Asia, preferred cheaper products to those of quality Most discussions of quality refer to a finished part, wherever it is in the process. Inspection, which is what quality insurance usually means, is historical, since the work is done. The best way to think about quality is in process control. If the process is under control, inspection is not necessary.

However, there is one characteristic of modern quality that is universal. In the past, when we tried to improve quality, typically defined as producing fewer defective parts, we did so at the expense of increased cost, increased task time, longer cycle time, etc. We could not get fewer defective parts and lower cost and shorter cycle times, and so on.

However, when modern quality techniques are applied correctly to business, engineering, manufacturing or assembly processes, all aspects of quality - customer satisfaction and fewer defects/errors and cycle time and task time/productivity and total cost, etc.- must all improve or, if one of these aspects does not improve, it must at least stay stable and not decline. So modern quality has the characteristic that it creates AND-based benefits, not OR-based benefits.

Customers

The most progressive view of quality is that it is defined entirely by the customer or end user and is based upon that person's evaluation of his or her entire customer experience. The customer experience is the aggregate of all the touch points that customers have with the company's product and services, and is by definition a combination of these. For example, any time one buys a product one forms an impression based on how it was sold, how it was delivered, how it performed, how well it was supported etc.

QUALITY MANAGEMENT TECHNIQUES

- Quality Management Systems
- Total Quality Management
- Design of experiments
  - Fractional factorial design
  - Optimal design

   - Response surface methodology
- Continuous improvement
- Six Sigma
- Statistical Process Control
- Quality circles
- Requirements analysis
- Verification and Validation
- Zero Defects
- Theory of Constraints
- Business Process Management
- Business process re-engineering
- Capability Maturity Models

INSPECTION

An inspection is a formal examination or evaluation exercise. It normally involves measurements, gauges and tests to determine whether the characteristics of the object or activity being inspected confirm to pre-decided standards.

Inspections are usually not destructive; rather, inspection is required at all levels in society to ensure that most ordinances are enforced as fairly and efficiently as possible, thus ensuring safety and security for everyone. Automobiles, buildings and homes may be inspected for this purpose. One could also have inspections at various stages of purchase, like pre-purchase and post-purchase of products or when refurnishing one's home. For instance, when a person visits an auto dealer to buy a new car, various aspects like interiors, components and quality are inspected by the buyer. Software inspection refers to the review of the work by peers following standardized testing and inspection procedures.

Normally government officials or private inspectors are employed for assessing the commercial and personal properties. These inspectors are highly trained personnel who are entrusted with the job of assessing and generating reports. These reports in turn help people to abide by the rules and regulations set by the authorities. Thus, a lot of unnecessary expenses are reduced by timely inspection. Nowadays with the use of the Internet, inspections can be performed online, thereby saving time and money. The main purpose of inspection is to ensure that safety standards are adhered to, both at the public and personal level. During the investigation, if the inspector notices low standards, corrective measures are taken immediately.

Inspections such as home inspections and building inspections are highly beneficial to owners as well as to buyers who plan to make huge investments. In all inspections, standards of compliance in accordance with the state are ensured. Therefore a good inspection guarantees public safety by enforcing municipal and state regulations typically for construction activities.

QUALITY CONTROL

Quality control is a process employed to ensure a certain level of quality in a product or service. It may include whatever actions a business deems necessary to provide for the control and verification of certain characteristics of a product or service. The basic goal of quality control is to ensure that the products, services, or processes provided meet specific requirements and are dependable, satisfactory, and fiscally sound. Essentially, quality control involves the examination of a product, service, or process for certain minimum levels of quality. The goal of a quality control team is to identify products or services that do not meet a company's specified standards of quality.

If a problem is identified, the job of a quality control team or professional may involve stopping production temporarily. Depending on the particular service or product, as well as the type of problem identified, production or implementation may not cease entirely. Usually, it is not the job of a quality control team or professional to correct quality issues. Typically, other individuals are involved in the process of discovering the cause of quality issues and fixing them.

Once such problems are overcome, the product, service, or process continues production or implementation as usual. Quality control can cover not just products, services, and processes, but also people. Employees are an important part of any company. If a company has employees that don't have adequate skills or training, have trouble understanding directions, or are misinformed, quality may be severely diminished. When quality control is considered in terms of human beings, it concerns correctable issues. However, it should not be confused with human resource issues.

Often, quality control is confused with quality assurance. Though the two are very similar, there are some basic differences. Quality control is concerned with the product, while quality assurance is process–oriented. Even with such a clear-cut difference defined, identifying the differences between the two can be hard. Basically, quality control involves evaluating a product, activity, process, or service. By contrast, quality assurance is designed to make sure processes are sufficient to meet objectives. Simply put, quality assurance ensures a product or service is manufactured, implemented, created, or produced in the right way; while quality control evaluates whether or not the end result is satisfactory.

QUALITY ASSURANCE

Quality assurance is the process of verifying or determining whether products or services meet or exceed customer expectations. Quality assurance is a process-driven approach with specific steps to help define and attain goals. This process considers design, development, production, and service. The most popular tool used to determine quality assurance is the Shewhart Cycle, developed by Dr. W. Edwards Deming. This cycle for quality assurance consists of four steps: *Plan, Do, Check,* and *Act*. These steps are commonly abbreviated as PDCA.

The four quality assurance steps within the PDCA model stand for:

1. *Plan*: Establish objectives and processes required to deliver the desired results.
2. *Do*: Implement the process developed.
3. *Check*: Monitor and evaluate the implemented process by testing the results against the predetermined objectives

4. *Act*: Apply actions necessary for improvement if the results require changes.

PDCA is an effective method for monitoring quality assurance because it analyses existing conditions and methods used to provide the product or service customers. The goal is to ensure that excellence is inherent in every component of the process. Quality assurance also helps determine whether the steps used to provide the product or service are appropriate for the time and conditions. In addition, if the PDCA cycle is repeated throughout the lifetime of the product or service, it helps improve internal company efficiency.

Quality assurance demands a degree of detail in order to be fully implemented at every step. *Planning*, for example, could include investigation into the quality of the raw materials used in manufacturing, the actual assembly, or the inspection processes used. The *Checking* step could include customer feedback, surveys, or other marketing vehicles to determine if customer needs are being exceeded and why they are or are not. *Acting* could mean a total revision in the manufacturing process in order to correct a technical or cosmetic flaw.

Competition to provide specialized products and services results in breakthroughs as well as long-term growth and change. Quality assurance verifies that any customer offering, regardless if it is new or evolved, is produced and offered with the best possible materials, in the most comprehensive way, with the highest standards. The goal to exceed customer expectations in a measurable and accountable process is provided by quality assurance.

EARLY EFFORTS TO CONTROL THE QUALITY OF PRODUCTION

Early civil engineering projects needed to be built from specifications, for example the four sides of the base of the Great Pyramid of Giza were required to be perpendicular to within 3.5 arcseconds. During the Middle Ages, guilds adopted responsibility for quality control of their members, setting and maintaining certain standards for guild membership.

Royal governments purchasing material were interested in quality control as customers. For this reason, King John of England appointed William Wrotham to report about the construction and repair of ships. Centuries later, Samuel Pepys, Secretary to the British Admiralty, appointed multiple such overseers. Prior to the extensive division of labour and mechanization resulting from the Industrial Revolution, it was possible for workers to control the quality of their own products. Working conditions then were arguably more conducive to professional pride.

The Industrial Revolution led to a system in which large groups of people performing a similar type of work were grouped together under the supervision of a foreman who was appointed to control the quality of work manufactured.

WARTIME PRODUCTION

Around the time of World War I, manufacturing processes typically became more complex with larger numbers of workers being supervised. This period saw the widespread introduction of mass production and piecework, which created problems as workmen could now earn more money by the production of extra products, which in turn led to bad workmanship being passed on to the assembly lines.

To counter bad workmanship, full time inspectors were introduced into the factory to identify, quarantine and ideally correct product quality failures. Quality control by inspection in the 1920s and 1930s led to the growth of quality inspection functions, separately organised from production and big enough to be headed by superintendents.

The systematic approach to quality started in industrial manufacture during the 1930s, mostly in the USA, when some attention was given to the cost of scrap and rework. With the impact of mass production, which was required during the Second World War, it became necessary to introduce a more appropriate form of quality control which can be identified as Statistical Quality Control, or SQC. Some of the initial work for SQC is credited to Walter A. Shewhart of Bell Labs, starting with his famous one-page memorandum of 1924.

SQC came about with the realization that quality cannot be fully inspected into an important batch of items. By extending the inspection phase and making inspection organizations more efficient, it provides inspectors with control tools such as sampling and control charts, even where 100 per cent inspection is not practicable. Standard statistical techniques allow the producer to sample and test a certain proportion of the products for quality to achieve the desired level of confidence in the quality of the entire batch or production run.

POSTWAR

In the period following World War II, many countries' manufacturing capabilities that had been destroyed during the war were rebuilt. The U.S. sent General Douglas MacArthur to oversee the re-building of Japan. During this time, General MacArthur involved two key individuals in the development of modern quality concepts: W. Edwards Deming and Joseph Juran. Both individuals promoted the collaborative concepts of quality to Japanese business and technical groups, and these groups utilized these concepts in the redevelopment of the Japanese economy. Although there were many individuals trying to lead United States industries towards a more comprehensive approach to quality, the U.S. continued to apply the Quality Control concepts of inspection and sampling to remove defective product from production lines, essentially ignoring advances in QA for decades.

ACCURACY OF QUALITY ASSURANCE

There is an extensive process of trial and error in order to ensure quality assurance. By the end of the trials you arrive at an acceptable process that helps you decide the reliability and efficiency of the sample. The process involves meeting specifications such as performance measures and depends on environment operation. The costs of resulting in failure is very high which result in the process of Quality Assurance to be extensive and it is acceptable to delay production until all tests are done and double-checked.

STEPS FOR QUALITY ASSURANCE PROCESS

- Plan to improve
- Design to include improvements and requirements
- Manufacture with improvements
- Review new item and improvements
- Test new item

The process for Quality Assurance is very rigorous and requires a lot of testing and planning. The team or firm has to comply with previous requirements, implement new requirements and improve the old item. Other than following requirements, the team or firm has to comply with consumers needs.

QUALITY ASSURANCE VERSUS QUALITY CONTROL

Quality control emphasizes testing of products to uncover defects, and reporting to management who make the decision to allow or deny the release, whereas quality assurance attempts to improve and stabilize production, and associated processes, to avoid, or at least minimize, issues that led to the defects in the first place.. On applying Quality Assurance in Education the gross purpose of applying quality assurance is served.

To prevent mistakes from arising, several QA methodologies are used. However, QA does not eliminate the need for QC: some product parameters are so critical that testing is still essential. QC activities are treated as one of the overall QA processes.

Failure Testing

A valuable process to perform on a whole consumer product is failure testing or stress testing. In mechanical terms this is the operation of a product until it fails, often under stresses such as increasing vibration, temperature, and humidity. This exposes many unanticipated weaknesses in a product, and the data are used to drive engineering and manufacturing process improvements. Often quite simple changes can dramatically improve product service, such as changing to mold-resistant paint or adding lock-washer placement to the training for new assembly personnel.

Statistical Control

Many organizations use statistical process control to bring the organization to Six Sigma levels of quality, in other words, so that the likelihood of an unexpected failure is confined to six standard deviations on the normal distribution. This probability is less than four one-millionths. Items controlled often include clerical tasks such as order-entry as well as conventional manufacturing tasks.

Traditional statistical process controls in manufacturing operations usually proceed by randomly sampling and testing a fraction of the output. Variances in critical tolerances are continuously tracked and where necessary corrected before bad parts are produced.

Total Quality Management

Invariably, the Quality of output is directly dependent upon that of the participating constituents, some of which are sustainably and effectively controlled while others are [not]. The fluid state spells lack of Quality control, and the processes which are properly managed for Quality such that Quality is assured, pertain to Total Quality Management. The major problem which leads to a decrease in sales was that the specifications did not include the most important factor, "What the specifications have to state in order to satisfy the customer requirements?".

The major characteristics, ignored during the search to improve manufacture and overall business performance were:

- Reliability
- Maintainability
- Safety
- Strength

As the most important factor had been ignored, a few refinements had to be introduced:

- Marketing had to carry out their work properly and define the customer's specifications.

- Specifications had to be defined to conform to these requirements.
- Conformance to specifications i.e. drawings, standards and other relevant documents, were introduced during manufacturing, planning and control.
- Management had to confirm all operators are equal to the work imposed on them and holidays, celebrations and disputes did not affect any of the quality levels.
- Inspections and tests were carried out, and all components and materials, bought in or otherwise, conformed to the specifications, and the measuring equipment was accurate, this is the responsibility of the QA/QC department.
- Any complaints received from the customers were satisfactorily dealt with in a timely manner.
- Feedback from the user/customer is used to review designs.
- Consistent data recording and assessment and documentation integrity.
- Product and/or process change management and notification.

If the specification does not reflect the true quality requirements, the product's quality cannot be guaranteed. For instance, the parameters for a pressure vessel should cover not only the material and dimensions but operating, environmental, safety, reliability and maintainability requirements.

TOTAL QUALITY MANAGEMENT (TQM)

TQM is the way of managing for the future, and is far wider in its application than just assuring product or service quality – it is a way of managing people and business processes to ensure complete customer satisfaction at every stage, internally and externally. TQM, combined with effective leadership, results in an organisation doing the right things right, first time.

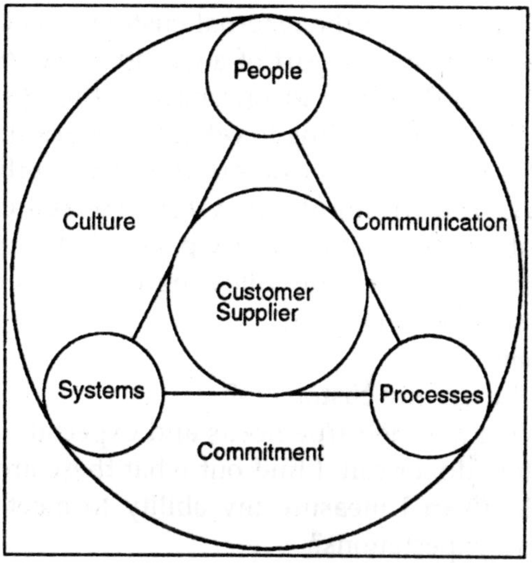

The core of TQM is the customer-supplier interfaces, both externally and internally, and at each interface lie a number of processes. This core must be surrounded by commitment to quality, communication of the quality message, and recognition of the need to change the culture of the organisation to create total quality.

These are the foundations of TQM, and they are supported by the key management functions of people, processes and systems in the organisation. This part discusses each of these elements that, together, can make a total quality organisation. Other parts explain people, processes and systems in greater detail, all having the essential themes of commitment, culture and communication running through them.

CUSTOMERS AND SUPPLIERS

There exists in each department, each office, each home, a series of customers, suppliers and customersupplier interfaces. These are "the quality chains", and they can be broken at any point by one person or one piece of equipment not meeting the requirements of the customer, internal or external. The failure usually finds its way to the interface between the organisation and its external customer, or in the worst case, actually to the external customer. Failure to meet the requirements in any part of a quality chain has a way of multiplying, and failure in one part of the system creates problems elsewhere, leading to yet more failure and problems, and so the situation is exacerbated.The ability to meet customers' requirements is vital. To achieve quality throughout an organisation, every person in the quality chain must be trained to ask the following questions about every customer-supplier interface.

Customers:

- Who are my customers?
- What are their true needs and expectations?
- How do, or can, I find out what these are?
- How can I measure my ability to meet their needs and expectations?
- Do I have the capability to meet their needs and expectations?
- Do I continually meet their needs and expectations?
- How do I monitor changes in their needs and expectations?

Suppliers:

- Who are my internal suppliers?
- What are my true needs and expectations?
- How do I communicate my needs and expectations to my suppliers?
- Do my suppliers have the capability to measure and meet these needs and expectations?
- How do I inform them of changes in my needs and expectations?

As well as being fully aware of customers' needs and expectations, each person must respect the needs and expectations of their suppliers. The ideal situation is an open partnership style relationship, where both parties share and benefit.

POOR PRACTICES

To be able to become a total quality organisation, some of the bad practices must be recognised and corrected..

These may include:

- Leaders not giving clear direction
- Not understanding, or ignoring competitive positioning
- Each department working only for itself
- Trying to control people through systems
- Confusing quality with grade
- Accepting that a level of defects or errors is inevitable
- Firefighting, reactive behaviour
- The "It's not my problem" attitude

THE ESSENTIAL COMPONENTS OF TQM – COMMITMENT AND LEADERSHIP

TQM is an approach to improving the competitiveness, effectiveness and flexibility of an organisation for the benefit of all stakeholders. It is a way of planning, organising and understanding each activity, and of removing all the wasted effort and energy that is routinely spent in organisations. It ensures the leaders adopt a strategic overview of quality and focus on prevention not detection of problems. Whilst it must involve everyone, to be successful, it must start at the top with the leaders of the organisation. All senior managers must demonstrate their seriousness and commitment to quality, and middle managers must, as well as demonstrating their commitment, ensure they communicate the principles, strategies and benefits to the people for whom they have responsibility. Only then will the right attitudes spread throughout the organisation.

A fundamental requirement is a sound quality policy, supported by plans and facilities to implement it. Leaders must take responsibility for preparing, reviewing and monitoring the policy, plus take part in regular improvements of it and ensure it is understood at all levels of the organisation. Effective leadership starts with the development of a mission statement, followed by a strategy, which is translated into action plans down through the organisation. These, combined with a TQM approach, should result in a quality organisation, with satisfied customers and good business results.

The 5 requirements for effective leadership are:

1. Developing and publishing corporate beliefs, values and objectives, often as a mission statement
2. Personal involvement and acting as role models for a culture of total quality
3. Developing clear and effective strategies and supporting plans for achieving the mission and objectives
4. Reviewing and improving the management system
5. Communicating, motivating and supporting people and encouraging effective employee participation

The task of implementing TQM can be daunting. The following is a list of points that leaders should consider; they are a distillation of the various beliefs of some of the quality gurus

- The organisation needs a long-term commitment to continuous improvement.
- Adopt the philosophy of zero errors/defects to change the culture to right first time
- Train people to understand the customer/supplier relationships
- Do not buy products or services on price alone – look at the total cost
- Recognise that improvement of the systems must be managed
- Adopt modern methods of supervising and training – eliminate fear
- Eliminate barriers between departments by managing the process – improve communications and teamwork
- Eliminate goals without methods, standards based only on numbers, barriers to pride of workmanship and fiction – get facts by studying processes
- Constantly educate and retrain – develop experts in the organisation
- Develop a systematic approach to manage the implementation of TQM

CULTURE CHANGE

The failure to address the culture of an organisation is frequently the reason for many management initiatives either having limited success or failing altogether.

Understanding the culture of an organisation, and using that knowledge to successfully map the steps needed to accomplish a successful change, is an important part of the quality journey. The culture in any organisation is formed by the beliefs, behaviours, norms, dominant values, rules and the "climate".

A culture change, e.g, from one of acceptance of a certain level of errors or defects to one of right first time, every time, needs two key elements:

1. Commitment from the leaders
2. Involvement of all of the organisation's people

There is widespread recognition that major change initiatives will not be successful without a culture of good teamwork and cooperation at all levels in an organisation, as discussed in the part on People.

PROCESSES, PEOPLE, MANAGEMENT SYSTEMS AND PERFORMANCE MEASUREMENT

Everything we do is a Process, which is the transformation of a set of inputs, which can include action, methods and operations, into the desired outputs, which satisfy the customers' needs and expectations.

In each area or function within an organisation there will be many processes taking place, and each can be analysed by an examination of the inputs and outputs to determine the action necessary to improve quality.

In every organisation there are some very large processes, which are groups of smaller processes, called key or core business processes. These must be carried out well if an organisation is to achieve its mission and objectives. The part on Processes discusses processes and how to improve them, and Implementation covers how to prioritise and select the right process for improvement.

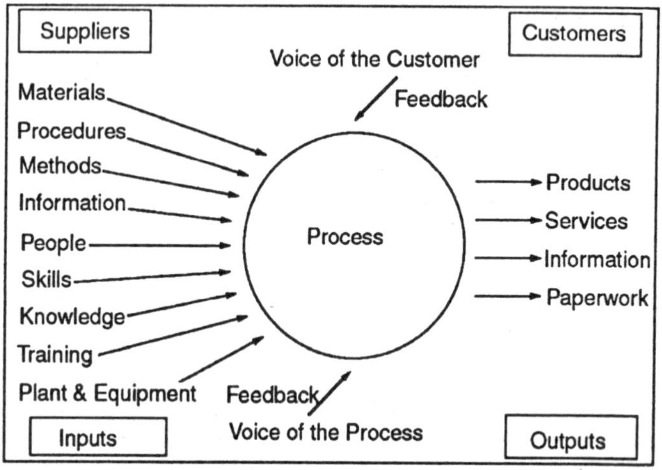

The only point at which true responsibility for performance and quality can lie is with the People who actually do the job or carry out the process, each of which has one or several suppliers and customers. An efficient and effective way to tackle process or quality improvement is through teamwork. However, people will not engage in improvement activities without commitment and recognition from the organisation's leaders, a climate for improvement and a strategy that is implemented thoughtfully and effectively.

The part on People expands on these issues, covering roles within teams, team selection and development and models for successful teamwork. An appropriate documented Quality Management System will help an organisation not only achieve the objectives set out in its policy and strategy, but also, and equally importantly, sustain and build upon them. It is imperative that the leaders take responsibility for the adoption and documentation of an appropriate management system in their organisation if they are serious about the quality journey. The Systems part discusses the benefits of having such a system, how to set one up and successfully implement it.

Once the strategic direction for the organisation's quality journey has been set, it needs Performance Measures to monitor and control the journey, and to ensure the desired level of performance is being achieved and sustained. They can, and should be, established at all levels in the organisation, ideally being cascaded down and most effectively undertaken as team activities and this is discussed in the part on Performance.

CONTROL CHART

A control chart is a statistical tool used to distinguish between variation in a process resulting from common causes and variation resulting from special causes. It presents a graphic display of process stability or instability over time. Every process has variation. Some variation may be the result of causes which are not normally present in the process. This could be special cause variation. Some variation is simply the result of numerous, ever-present differences in the process. This is common cause variation. Control Charts differentiate between these two types of variation. One goal of using a Control Chart is to achieve and maintain process stability. Process stability is defined as a state in which a process has displayed a certain degree of consistency in the past and is expected to continue to do so in the future. This consistency is characterized by a stream of data falling within control limits based on plus or minus 3 standard deviations of the centreline. As suggested, discuss methods for calculating 3 sigma limits later in this module.

Note: Control limits represent the limits of variation that should be expected from a process in a state of statistical control. When a process is in statistical control, any variation is the result of common causes that effect the entire production in a similar way. Control limits should not be confused with specification limits, which represent the desired process performance.

CHART DETAILS

A control chart consists of:

- Points representing a statistic of measurements of a quality characteristic in samples taken from the process at different times [the data]
- The mean of this statistic using all the samples is calculated

- A centre line is drawn at the value of the mean of the statistic
- The standard error of the statistic is also calculated using all the samples
- Upper and lower control limits that indicate the threshold at which the process output is considered statistically 'unlikely' are drawn typically at 3 standard errors from the centre line

The chart may have other optional features, including:

- Upper and lower warning limits, drawn as separate lines, typically two standard errors above and below the centre line
- Division into zones, with the addition of rules governing frequencies of observations in each zone
- Annotation with events of interest, as determined by the Quality Engineer in charge of the process's quality

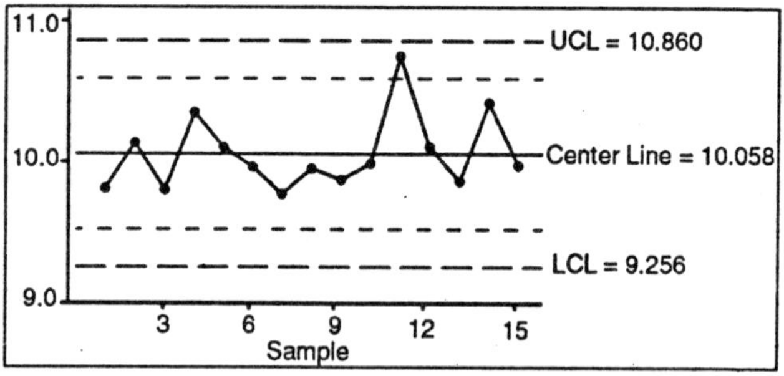

Fig. Quality Characteristic

Chart Usage

If the process is in control, all points will plot within the control limits. Any observations outside the limits, or systematic patterns within, suggest the introduction of a new source of variation, known as a special-cause variation. Since increased variation means increased quality costs, a control chart "signaling" the presence of a special-cause requires immediate investigation. This makes the control limits very important decision aids. The control limits tell you about process behaviour and have no intrinsic relationship to any specification targets or engineering tolerance. In practice, the process mean may not coincide with the specified value of the quality characteristic because the process' design simply can't deliver the process characteristic at the desired level.

Control charts limit specification limits or targets because of the tendency of those involved with the process to focus on performing to specification when in fact the least-cost course of action is to keep process variation as low as possible. Attempting to make a process whose natural centre is not the same as the target perform to target specification increases process variability and increases costs significantly and is the cause of much inefficiency in operations. Process capability studies do examine the relationship between the natural process limits and specifications, however.

The purpose of control charts is to allow simple detection of events that are indicative of actual process change. This simple decision can be difficult where the process characteristic is continuously varying; the control chart provides statistically objective criteria of change. When change is detected and considered good its cause should be identified and possibly become the new way of working, where the change is bad then its cause should be identified and eliminated. The purpose in adding warning limits or subdividing the control chart into zones is to provide early notification if something is amiss. Instead of immediately launching a process improvement effort to determine whether special causes are present, the Quality Engineer may temporarily increase the rate at which samples are taken from the process output until it's clear that the process is truly in control. Note that with three sigma limits, one expects to be signaled approximately once out of every 370 points on average, just due to common-causes.

Choice of Limits

Shewhart set 3-sigma limits on the following basis:

1. The coarse result of Chebyshev's inequality that, for any probability distribution, the probability of an outcome greater than k standard deviations from the mean is at most $1/k^2$.

2. The finer result of the Vysochanskii-Petunin inequality, that for any unimodal probability distribution, the probability of an outcome greater than k standard deviations from the mean is at most $4/(9k^2)$.
3. The empirical investigation of sundry probability distributions reveals that at least 99% of observations occurred within three standard deviations of the mean.

Shewhart summarized the conclusions by saying:

"... the fact that the criterion which we happen to use has a fine ancestry in highbrow statistical theorems does not justify its use. Such justification must come from empirical evidence that it works. As the practical engineer might say, the proof of the pudding is in the eating".

Though he initially experimented with limits based on probability distributions, Shewhart ultimately wrote:

Some of the earliest attempts to characterize a state of statistical control were inspired by the belief that there existed a special form of frequency function f and it was early argued that the normal law characterized such a state. When the normal law was found to be inadequate, then generalized functional forms were tried. Today, however, all hopes of finding a unique functional form f are blasted.

The control chart is intended as a heuristic. Deming insisted that it is not a hypothesis test and is not motivated by the Neyman-Pearson lemma. He contended that the disjoint nature of population and sampling frame in most industrial situations compromised the use of conventional statistical techniques. Deming's intention was to seek insights into the cause system of a process...under a wide range of unknowable circumstances, future and past.... He claimed that, under such conditions, 3-sigma limits provided... a rational and economic guide to minimum economic loss... from the two errors:

1. Ascribe a variation or a mistake to a special cause when in fact the cause belongs to the system
2. Ascribe a variation or a mistake to the system when in fact the cause was special.

Calculation of Standard Deviation

As for the calculation of control limits, the standard deviation required is that of the common-cause variation in the process. Hence, the usual estimator, in terms of sample variance, is not used as this estimates the total squared-error loss from both common- and special-causes of variation. An alternative method is to use the relationship between the range of a sample and its standard deviation derived by Leonard H. C. Tippett, an estimator which tends to be less influenced by the extreme observations which typify special-causes.

RULES FOR DETECTING SIGNALS

The most common sets are:

- The Western Electric rules
- The Wheeler rules
- The Nelson rules

There has been particular controversy as to how long a run of observations, all on the same side of the centre line, should count as a signal, with 6, 7, 8 and 9 all being advocated by various writers.The most important principle for choosing a set of rules is that the choice be made before the data is inspected. Choosing rules once the data have been seen tends to increase the Type I error rate owing to testing effects suggested by the data.

ALTERNATIVE BASES

In 1935, the British Standards Institution, under the influence of Egon Pearson and against Shewhart's spirit, adopted control charts, replacing 3-sigma limits with limits based on percentiles of the normal distribution. This move continues to be represented by John Oakland and others but has been widely deprecated by writers in the Shewhart-Deming tradition.

PERFORMANCE OF CONTROL CHARTS

When a point falls outside of the limits established for a given control chart, those responsible for the underlying process are expected to determine whether a special cause has occurred. If one has, then that cause should be eliminated if possible. It is known that even when a process is in control, there is approximately a 0.27% probability of a point exceeding 3-sigma control limits. Since the control limits are evaluated each time a point is added to the chart, it readily follows that every control chart will eventually signal the possible presence of a special cause, even though one may not have actually occurred. For a Shewhart control chart using 3-sigma limits, this false alarm occurs on average once every 1/0.0027 or 370.4 observations. Therefore, the in-control average run length of a Shewhart chart is 370.4.

Meanwhile, if a special cause does occur, it may not be of sufficient magnitude for the chart to produce an immediate alarm condition. If a special cause occurs, one can describe that cause by measuring the change in the mean and/or variance of the process in question. When those changes are quantified, it is possible to determine the out-of-control ARL for the chart.

It turns out that Shewhart charts are quite good at detecting large changes in the process mean or variance, as their out-of-control ARLs are fairly short in these cases. However, for smaller changes, the Shewhart chart does not detect these changes efficiently. Other types of control charts have been developed, such as the EWMA chart and the CUSUM chart, which detect smaller changes more efficiently by making use of information from observations collected prior to the most recent data point.

CRITICISMS

Several authors have criticised the control chart on the grounds that it violates the likelihood principle. However, the principle is itself controversial and supporters of control charts further argue that, in general, it is impossible to specify a likelihood function for a process not in statistical control, especially where knowledge about the cause system of the process is weak. Some authors have criticised the use of average run lengths for comparing control chart performance, because that average usually follows a geometric distribution, which has high variability and difficulties.

TYPES OF CHARTS

Chart	Process observation	Process observations relationships	Process observations type	Size of shift to detect
$\bar{x}$ and R chart	Quality characteristic measurement within one subgroup	Independent	Variables	Large (? 1.5σ)
$\bar{x}$ and s chart	Quality characteristic measurement within one subgroup	Independent	Variables	Large (? 1.5σ)
Shewhart individuals control chart (ImR chart or XmR chart)	Quality characteristic measurement for one observation	Independent	Variables[†]	Large (? 1.5σ)
Three-way chart	Quality characteristic measurement within one subgroup	Independent	Variables	Large (? 1.5σ)
p-chart	Fraction nonconforming within one subgroup	Independent	Attributes[†]	Large (? 1.5σ)
np-chart	Number nonconforming within one subgroup	Independent	Attributes[†]	Large (? 1.5σ)
c-chart	Number of nonconformances within one subgroup	Independent	Attributes[†]	Large (? 1.5σ)
u-chart	Nonconformances per unit within one subgroup	Independent	Attributes[†]	Large (? 1.5σ)
EWMA chart	Exponentially weighted moving average of quality characteristic measurement within one subgroup	Independent	Attributes or variables	Small ($< 1.5\sigma$)
CUSUM chart	Cumulative sum of quality characteristic measurement within one subgroup	Independent	Attributes or variables	Small ($< 1.5\sigma$)
Time series model	Quality characteristic measurement within one subgroup	Autocorrelated	Attributes or variables	N/A
Regression Control Chart	Quality characteristic measurement within one subgroup	Dependent of process control variables	Variables	Large (? 1.5σ)

Some practitioners also recommend the use of Individuals charts for attribute data, particularly when the assumptions of either binomially-distributed data or Poisson-distributed data are violated. Two primary justifications are given for this practice. First, normality is not necessary for statistical control, so the Individuals chart may be used with non-normal data. Second, attribute charts derive the measure of dispersion directly from the mean proportion while Individuals charts derive the measure of dispersion from the data, independent of the mean, making Individuals charts more robust than attributes charts to violations of the assumptions about the distribution of the underlying population.

It is sometimes noted that the substitution of the Individuals chart works best for large counts, when the binomial and Poisson distributions approximate a normal distribution. i.e. when the number of trials $n > 1000$ for p- and np-charts or $\ddot{e} > 500$ for u- and c-charts. Critics of this approach argue that control charts should not be used then their underlying assumptions are violated, such as when process data is neither normally distributed nor binomially distributed. Such processes are not in control and should be improved before the application of control charts.

Additionally, application of the charts in the presence of such deviations increases the type I and type II error rates of the control charts, and may make the chart of little practical use.

ACCEPTANCE SAMPLING

Acceptance Sampling is used to make dispositions on accepting or rejecting a lot of product that has already been produced. A sample of product is used to determine acceptability. It is most often used to evaluate products that are received from outside sources and where it is not possible to implement Statistical Process Control.

Acceptance Sampling should be considered when the testing required is destructive, 100% inspection isn't feasible due to the cost or time involved, there is a high probability of errors from 100% inspection, or if the supplier has a strong history of supplying acceptable products. An Acceptance Sampling Plan is created to define how many samples must be taken to verify the lot. Acceptance Sampling isn't to be considered a replacement or alternative to Statistical Process Control. Statistical Process Control focuses on improving the process in order to improve future product, while Acceptance Sampling focuses on evaluation of products that have already been produced to ensure their quality. Acceptance Sampling includes Attribute Sampling, which makes accept/reject decisions based on the number of defectives within a lot and Variable Sampling, with makes accept/reject decisions based on measurement values.

There are many methods available for acceptance testing, but Acceptance Sampling plans which take into account the Acceptable Quality Level and Lot Tolerance Per cent Defective are considered to be the most statistically valid.

HOW DO SAMPLING PLANS WORK?

It would be great if we could always know that every bad lot would be rejected and that every good lot would be accepted, but since we are taking a sample of the lot there is always a risk of making the wrong decision. Sampling plans are used to control that risk.

A statistically valid sampling plan tells us the probability of accepting bad lots and the probability of rejecting good lots. A sampling plan is best understood through the Operating Characteristic Curve. The Operating Characteristic Curve or OC curve is a graph that shows the probability of acceptance of a lot through all possible levels of per cent defective. The OC Curve is created by plotting the per cent defective versus the matching probabilities of acceptance.

The probability of acceptance is based on the number of samples to be evaluated and the quantity of rejects that are to be allowed. The curve becomes more "sensitive", having a lower per cent defective for the same probability of acceptance as the sample quantity increases.

In the following OC Curve we can see that with this plan, a lot with 2% defective has around a 95% probability of acceptance while a lot with 6% defective has only a 15% probability of acceptance.

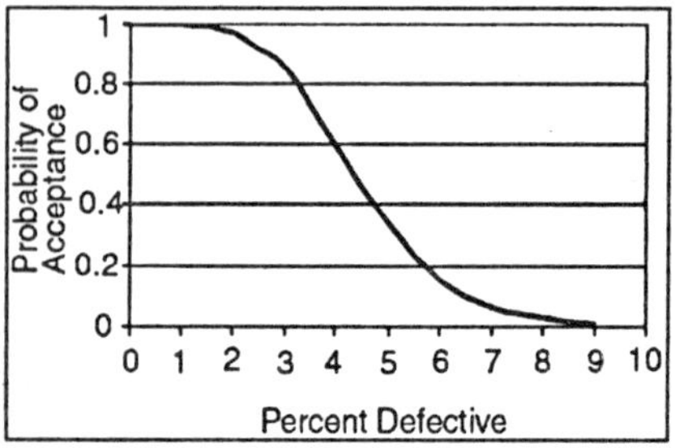

Fig. Operating Characteristic Curve

The OC Curve is usually summarized by two points on the curve: the Acceptable Quality Level or AQL and the Lot Tolerance Per cent Defective or LTPD. The Acceptable Quality Level is generally defined as the per cent defectives that the plan will accept 95% of the time. Lots that are at or better than the AQL will be accepted 95% of the time.

If the lot fails, we can say with 95% confidence that the lot quality level is worse than the AQL. Likewise, we can say that a lot at the AQL that is acceptable has a 5% chance of being rejected. The AQL isn't necessarily the quality level that is being produced or the quality level that is being accepted. It may not even be the quality goal.

It is simply the per cent defective at the Producer's Risk or the probability of rejecting the acceptable. The Producer's Risk is typically 5%. On the OC Curve chart, the AQL would be the Per cent Defective at the Probability of Acceptance of 0.95, approximately 2%. The Lot Tolerance Per cent Defective is generally defined as per cent defective that the plan will reject 90% of the time.

We can say that a lot at or worse than the LTPD will be rejected 90% of the time. If the lot passes, we can say with 90% confidence that the lot quality is better than the LTPD. We could also say that a lot at the LTPD that is defective has a 10% chance of being accepted. The LTPD is the per cent defective at the Consumer's Risk or the probability of accepting a defective sample. The Consumer's Risk is typically 10%. On the OC Curve chart, the LTPD would be the Per cent Defective at the Probability of Acceptance of 0.10, approximately 6.5%.

HOW DOES INFINITYQS ACCEPTANCE SAMPLING WORK?

InfinityQS creates a statistically valid sampling plan based on the Acceptable Quality Level and the Lot Tolerance Per cent Defective at a user defined Producer's Risk and Consumer's Risk. The Sampling Plan is created based on these two points of the Operating Characteristics Curve, the AQL and the LTPD.

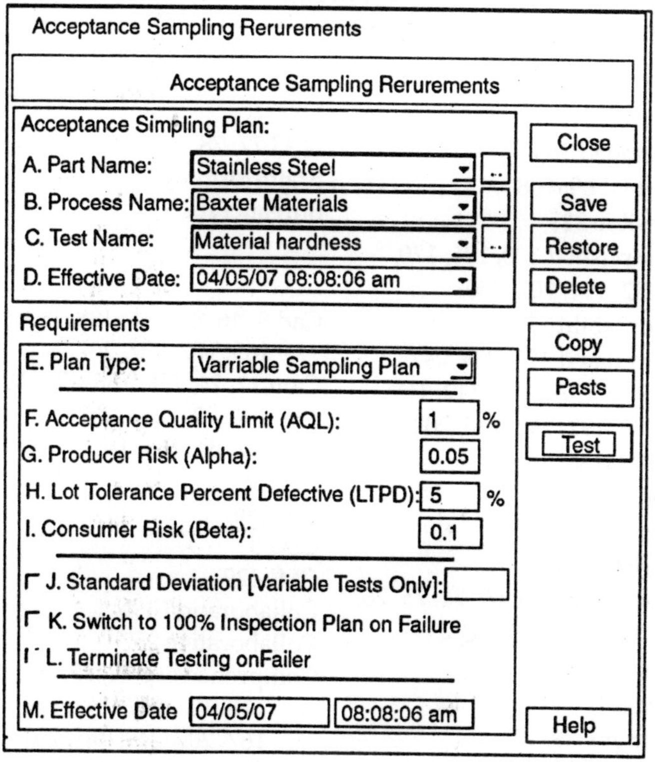

Index

A

Abandoned 165
Absorbed 69, 108
Accessible 225
Accomplished 100, 106, 120, 152, 194, 207, 250
Accountability 231
Accumulated 175, 239, 247
Acquisition 74, 110, 112, 169, 190, 192, 193, 196, 202, 207, 234
Acronyms 179
Affordability 193
Algorithm 105
Allocation 28, 34, 69, 71, 75, 76, 110, 112, 133, 183, 242
Alterations 21
Ambiguity 69
Ambitious 28, 30
ANOVA 180
Applicability 186
Architecture 189
Assembled 3, 224
Assimilated 129
Assumptions 45, 46, 47, 49, 50, 51, 52, 162, 182, 231, 239, 277

B

BCG 77, 78
Brainstorming 24, 219
Bureaucratic 152

C

Cad 9, 46, 81, 118, 128, 163, 165, 177, 257, 267
Cam 22, 24, 122, 130, 177, 185, 200, 227, 256, 257
CEO 62, 64, 164, 181
CFO 64
Cheapest 3
CIM 5
CMI 229
Collaboration 195
Collaborative 257
Comprehensive 32, 45, 112, 118, 126, 141, 142, 143, 167, 205, 249, 255, 257
CPA 38, 39, 43
CRAFT method 105
Criticism 184, 185, 272
CTQs 180

D

Demonstrate 25, 55, 146, 188, 247, 263

Demonstrated 146, 247
DFSS 180, 186, 187, 188, 189
DFSS Methods 189
Diligence 27
DMAIC 179, 180, 186, 187, 188
DPMO 183, 184

E

Emphasizes 77, 152, 258
Endeavor 28, 140
Engage 16, 60, 61, 207, 211, 266
EPISTEL 126, 139
ERD 189
Estimation 70
Eventually 79, 165, 272

F

FASB 229
Fluctuates 156
Foliage 166

G

GAAP 229, 232
GLP 244, 246, 247

H

Hierarchical 112, 152

I

Illustrated 174, 220
Influencers 61, 62, 63, 65
Insignificant 43
Instantaneous 151, 235
Interruptions 30
Irregularities 105, 169

J

JIT 159, 173, 174, 229

K

Kanbans 175, 176

L

Loophole 26

M

Mergers 202

N

NDA 137

O

OECD 246, 248

P

P.P.C. 13
Parallel 34, 35, 39, 44, 68, 93, 102, 126, 161, 169, 237
Permissible 41, 152
PERT 38, 44, 65, 66, 67, 68, 161
Pert 3, 9, 37, 52, 53, 80, 81, 140, 147, 150, 155, 177, 184, 185, 200, 204, 229, 246, 252, 259, 264
PEST 126, 139
Pest 3, 6
PIMS 124
PMBOK 51
Predetermined 123, 150, 151, 169, 171, 254
Preliminary 25, 167
Prince 2 51, 52

Prioritization 4, 60
Prioritize 30, 60, 64
Procurement 199

Q

QFD 209, 216, 218, 219
Quantifiable 120, 123, 151, 155, 178

R

Rigorous 45, 117, 125, 126, 258

S

Sequential 34, 35, 36, 39, 66, 69
Simultaneous 66, 69, 83, 113, 225
SIPOC 181
Six Sigma 177, 178, 179, 180, 181, 182, 183, 184, 185, 186, 187, 188, 189, 249, 252, 259
SKU 224
SMED 223
Sophisticated 124, 151, 173, 207
Statistical Methods 177
Steer 231
SWOT 126, 130, 139

T

Taguchi 181, 187
Tangible 3, 206
TQM 5, 138, 178, 244, 260, 261, 263, 264
TRIZ 181, 187, 219
Troublesome 153

U

Unequivocal 120, 125

V

VMI 229